MW01245713

SCHOOL REFORM CRITICS

The Struggle for
Democratic Schooling

EDITED BY
Joseph L. DeVitis
and Kenneth Teitelbaum

PETER LANG
New York • Washington, D.C./Baltimore • Bern
Frankfurt • Berlin • Brussels • Vienna • Oxford

Library of Congress Cataloging-in-Publication Data

School reform critics: the struggle for democratic schooling /
edited by Joseph L. DeVitis, Kenneth Teitelbaum.
pages cm
Includes bibliographical references and index.
1. Democracy and education. 2. Educational change.
3. Education and state. 4. Educational equalization. I. DeVitis, Joseph L.
LC71.S3236   379—dc23   2013028592
ISBN 978-1-4331-2040-4 (hardcover)
ISBN 978-1-4331-2039-8 (paperback)
ISBN 978-1-4539-1195-2 (e-book)

Bibliographic information published by **Die Deutsche Nationalbibliothek**.
Die Deutsche Nationalbibliothek lists this publication in the "Deutsche
Nationalbibliografie"; detailed bibliographic data is available
on the Internet at http://dnb.d-nb.de/.

The paper in this book meets the guidelines for permanence and durability
of the Committee on Production Guidelines for Book Longevity
of the Council of Library Resources.

Dedicated, with much love and appreciation, to:

Linda and Leigh
and
Nancy, and Rachael, Emily and Sarah

Contents

Introduction

KENNETH TEITELBAUM AND JOSEPH L. DeVITIS

Many of the authors in this volume have spent several decades contributing to educational scholarship, both theoretical and empirical. At times their intended audience has been primarily fellow academics; at other times it has been school practitioners; most often they have tried to write for both audiences, as is the case in this book.

Although clearly not in lock-step agreement, generally speaking these educators have advocated for progressive or critical school reform that fosters reflective and creative inquiry, equitable policies and practices, affirmation of diversity, democratic life, and caring and collaborative communities. This has been the case with regard to the 20,000-foot view of overarching federal and state school laws and policies as well as the 1,000-foot view, so to speak, of important school district policies and practices. Significantly, many of them have also focused their attention on the everyday life of schools and classrooms, attending to such related aspects as the beliefs and expectations of school participants; what is taught, including but going beyond academic content; curriculum materials; instructional and assessment strategies; academic grouping and labeling; classroom management; the roles of teachers and administrators; verbal and nonverbal communications; the involvement of parents and other family members; student groupings and identities; and the racial, socio-economic and cultural traits of school participants and communities.

In their efforts to expose and detail "the black box" of schooling, our colleagues have linked the practices and policies of schooling to educational ideas and purposes and, significantly, to the larger sociocultural, political, and economic contexts. This connection to larger social-structural issues is in fact crucial to much of their work. They have asked pointed questions, such as: To what extent have school and classroom policies and practices served to promote critical thinking, equity, diversity, democracy, and community? To what extent are professional educators as well as students and their families afforded the opportunity to participate in the decision-making process? Whose interests are actually being served by particular ideas, policies, and practices (Apple, 2004)? That is, they have examined what takes place in schools with reference to not just individual academic achievement levels or the economic needs of an industrialized, post-industrialized, or globalized society, but also to the oft-stated goals and current conditions of our so-called democratic society.

By now, it should be evident that school reform movements come and go and that "reform" does not necessarily result in "improvement." Perhaps the greatest weakness is when erstwhile reformers fail to consider hard questions of purpose, particularly when their private agendas mitigate against such questioning. For example, what ought public education really be about? What serves the public good? Moreover, without critical reflection on macro-structural issues surrounding education, reform is likely to be fraught with adverse outcomes. In a word, education, in and of itself, cannot be *the* panacea for all social, political, and economic ills. To think it so is to inhabit an Alice in Wonderland of illusions.

The authors and editors of this volume recognize that for educational reform to be substantial and lasting, it must be accompanied by deep changes in institutional and societal structures, involving employment, housing, health care, etc., that foster a real sense of hope, of possibility, among children and their families. At the same time, we must deal with schools and suggestions for reform that are current, that is, we cannot wait for these other structural transformations to occur.

Early in the process of putting together this volume, a colleague at another university questioned us about its title. In particular, would potential readers misunderstand what is meant by the term "school reform critics"? There are those, for example, as represented by many of the authors in this volume, who for years have critiqued traditional practices in K-12 and higher education settings and advocated reform strategies to provide a more rigorous and meaningful learning experience for young people. They have also sought a more inclusive education dedicated to enhancing critical and creative thinking skills, ethical behaviors, and a democratic and socially just character for our country and our communities. Would such critics be confused with other, more recent reformers who, in also critiquing traditional schooling, claim that the best education our nation can provide is characterized by more market-based privatization schemes and competition for public funding, more centralized control of school policies, more high-stakes standardized testing, more prescribed curriculum, more punitive measures to encourage good teaching and less respect for and trust of teachers, more direct instruction in the classroom, and more concern for discipline and conformity and less emphasis on students' personalized interests and needs? Clearly, the contributors to this volume are "school reform critics" of the first kind; and they have fundamental disagreements with many (though perhaps not all) of the changes being advocated by those in the second group. We wondered if the subtitle of our book might help avoid any confusion. But even then it seems to us that many of today's so-called "school reformers" have themselves incorporated the rhetoric of democracy when describing policies and practices that some critics believe will not actually serve (and arguably are not intended to serve) the lofty goals inherent in the ideals of democracy, equity, and inclusion.

Nevertheless, we have decided to keep our title because we proudly wear the mantle of school reform critics in the double meaning of the phrase; that is, espousing alternative, reformist ideas and strategies in opposition to traditional ways of schooling at the same time that we oppose what is purported in some circles to be "school reform" today. Moreover, we continue to advocate for more democratic schooling. With our contributors, we embrace rationales and strategies for integrating such a commitment as part of the varied and complex life of schooling, despite the barrage of verbiage and claims of evidence against related policies and practices by too many education leaders and entrepreneurs, politicians and think tankers, and business leaders and media pundits who have the deep pockets needed to gain considerable public access for their message. Of course we recognize that the debates represented by such conflicting views are nothing new in the history of American education (e.g., Kliebard, 2004).

We want readers to understand that we care deeply about what students are expected to learn, students staying in school to graduate, weeding out truly incompetent teachers who do not seek to improve their practice, preparing young people for successful future lives, enhancing the economic and physical security of our country (and world), and so forth. But it is in fact those reform efforts today that get the most attention that are taking us down a disastrous path, reinforcing the worst traits of neo-liberalism in the 21st century, with schooling, teaching and learning too often being narrowly conceived and primarily in the service of corporate interests. Indeed, as Kenneth Saltman (2008) suggests, the reliance on the language of market approaches (e.g., accountability, efficiency, choice, etc.) has in fact served to obscure "ongoing struggles over competing values, visions, and ideological perspectives" (p. 209).

We argue that principles of critical inquiry, equity, diversity, democracy, and community should be adopted as constituent elements of school life and not simply ignored, explained away, or otherwise minimized as at best future goals to pursue. We believe that administrators, teachers, staff members, students, and families need to establish collaborative and productive relationships, and they need to be provided with an appropriate level of tangible resources and other supports in order for educational settings to function among the next generations as incubators of the lofty principles we espouse. To not provide the conditions for such to happen, indeed, to undermine such efforts is to encourage very different kinds of interests and results. Real democratic reform should instead provide more than superficial slogans and trappings; it should mean addressing—and changing—those anti-democratic structural patterns that have come to permeate our schools and society.

Put simply, we fear for democracy—authentic, informed, everyday political and economic democracy and social justice—in which people feel and are empowered in their lives, in which people feel and are treated with fairness, and in which people (e.g., all children) are equipped as much as possible with meaningful content knowledge and critical thinking and problem-solving skills to participate in the improvement of their own lives and the lives of their fellow residents on this planet, even if in small ways. The chapters that follow attempt in different ways to problematize the current school reform movement, explaining why we need to call a halt to many current initiatives and rethink what is truly in the best interests of children and their teachers, families and the teaching profession, schools and communities, and our nation and the global community.

References

Apple, M. W. (2004). *Ideology and curriculum* (3rd ed.). New York: Routledge.

Kliebard, H. M. (2004). *The struggle for the American curriculum, 1893–1958* (3rd ed.). New York: Routledge.

Saltman, K. J. (2008). Schooling in disaster capitalism: How the political right is using disaster to privatize public schooling. In D. Boyles (Ed.), *The corporate assault on youth: commercialism, exploitation, and the end of innocence* (pp. 187–218). New York: Peter Lang.

Education in a Democracy

"While public education may be useful as an industrial policy, it is essential to healthy life in a democracy."
  —Deborah Meier

"Many of our elected officials have virtually handed the keys to our schools over to corporate interests. Presidential commissions on education are commonly chaired by the executives of large companies."
  —Alfie Kohn

"…the path of the Jeffersonian democrats is one of struggle, often defeat, but also rewards of a kind that can't even be imagined by those who succumb to the new [aristocratic] spirit of the age, gain wealth, forgetting all but self."
  —Noam Chomsky

CHAPTER ONE

Education in a Democracy

NEL NODDINGS

To describe education in a democracy, we first need to be clear on what we mean by *democracy*. Then we must also be clear on what we mean by *education*. Current schooling, I suggest, has gone wrong in its interpretation of these two great concepts. What might we do differently if we got the concepts right?

Democracy

It is almost a century since the publication of John Dewey's (1916) *Democracy and Education*, in which he wrote:

> A democracy is more than a form of government; it is primarily a mode of associated living, of conjoint communicated experience. The extension in space of the number of individuals who participate in an interest so that each has to refer his own action to that of others, and to consider the action of others to give point to his own, is equivalent to the breaking down of those barriers of class, race, and national territory which have kept men from perceiving the full import of their activity. (p. 87)

In his description of democracy, Dewey emphasized interaction, communication, and cooperation. Citizens in a democracy communicate widely and recognize their interdependence. It is not simply a matter of everyone's having an opportunity to climb the ladder of economic success by attaining a prescribed level of formal education. Rather, it is a matter of giving and receiving respect and appreciation for doing a necessary job well and for contributing to society as a person and a citizen. John Gardner (1984) put it well when he said:

> We must learn to honor excellence in every socially accepted human activity, however humble the activity, and to scorn shoddiness, however exalted the activity. An excellent plumber is infinitely more valuable than an incompetent philosopher. The society that scorns excellence in plumbing because plumbing is a

humble activity and tolerates shoddiness in philosophy because it is an exalted activity will have neither good plumbing nor good philosophy. Neither its pipes nor its theories will hold water. (p. 102)

Today, as we plan our programs of education, we are inclined to emphasize equality of opportunity, defined as the opportunity to go to college and secure a well-paying job. But if we listen to Dewey and Gardner, we would adopt a far different definition of equality of opportunity. All children should have an opportunity to find out what they are good at and to develop that talent, assured that their society will respect and appreciate their work if they do it well. This might mean going to college, but it might rather mean getting some other form of post-secondary education, or it might simply mean availing oneself of a strong secondary program.

With perhaps generous intentions, we have corrupted the meaning of equality. Too often, *equality* is defined as *sameness*. An "equal" education has come to mean the same education for everyone. Such a program denies inevitable differences among children on a host of aptitudes and interests. If these differences are properly respected, it is not anti-democratic to believe that many children are not cut out to flourish in traditional academic studies. Indeed, Charles Eliot, president of Harvard, argued in 1908 that failure to recognize this truth actually puts our democracy at risk:

> If democracy means to try to make all children equal or all men equal, it means to fight nature, and in that fight democracy is sure to be defeated. There is no such thing among men as equality of nature, of capacity for training, or of intellectual power. (Quoted in Kliebard, 1999, p. 43)

We must be careful here. Agreement with Eliot on the natural differences among human beings does not mean a ranking of those differences, nor does it imply that schools should sort and prepare students for their "probable destinies" as judged by school authorities. That interpretation is, as we know, the one that was acted upon in the early twentieth century, and the evils of tracking ensued. However, tracking—if it is interpreted democratically—need not be an evil. If students are well guided and allowed to *choose* their programs, if every program is rich in possibilities for critical thinking, if there are many opportunities for communication across programs (or tracks), offering a variety of programs to meet the needs and talents of a diverse population of students should be genuinely democratic. Notice the language used here. *Choice* is basic in a democracy. To guide students well requires open *communication*—listening as well as talking. And *critical thinking* is necessary if we are to develop a deliberative democracy.

Every form of education in a democracy should be intellectually rich; that is, it should encourage students to reflect continually on the connection between thinking and doing (Dewey, 1916). Such courses need not be defined and confined by the traditional, academic interpretation of "intellectual." Vocational courses can be (and often are) intellectually rich (Noddings, 2013; Rose, 2004); courses in algebra can be (and often are) intellectually impoverished.

When we insist that all students will now take the academic courses once required of a privileged few, it is likely that everyone will lose. Students who have little academic interest will lose doubly—cheated out of courses at which they might do well and doing poorly in the required classes. But those students who might be labeled "intellectual" in the traditional academic sense may also lose out:

By pretending that everyone will now participate in the same intellectual program, we are pushing young intellectuals to distinguish themselves only in terms of the highest GPA, not the richest level of understanding and creativity. The young intellectual should not be regarded as an example for all students to follow, nor is the life of an intellectual necessarily better than other ways of life. In our faulty attempts at intellectual equality through a common curriculum, we may be depriving everyone—even young intellectuals—of real opportunities to develop intellectually. (Noddings, 2013, p. 36)

Democratic Education

Education, especially democratic education, should not be construed merely as preparation for successful economic life. Education is an enterprise with multiple aims. Even when schooling was intended for a small number of males whose "probable destinies" were determined at birth, attention was given to the moral, aesthetic, spiritual, and civic growth of students. In our age of universal education, it is important to consider not only how to pursue these aims but, more broadly, how to prepare students in all three domains: personal/family, occupational, and civic. Today we may be putting our democracy at risk by giving almost exclusive attention to the occupational-financial domain.

Consider the neglect of home and family life in the school curriculum. Probably nothing is more important to children's school success than the quality of their parenting. Yet we stubbornly refuse to teach parenting in our schools. There are at least two related reasons for this neglect. The first is that schools were originally designed by males for males in public life. Most women were consigned to the home and a role as mothers and homemakers, and they learned—well or poorly—how to function in those roles from older women at home. When schools were at last open to females, their most prestigious programs were, of course, the ones designed for men. Some very fine female colleges did start out providing excellent courses aimed at home life, but they gave way rapidly to offering the more prestigious, traditional male curriculum, (Kerber, 1997). Thus, one reason that home life has been neglected is because it has been associated with women and private life. The feminist movement has helped somewhat to break down this separation, claiming the "the private is public" in an attack on the abuse of women in their homes by husbands who treated their wives like property.

It should be noted also that the feminist movement has made strides toward equality for women, but that equality has been defined and sought in a world defined by men. Little attention has been given to the possibility that men might learn from the experience of women. Perhaps it will take a new feminist movement to do this.

A second reason for the neglect of family life in our schools arises from the dominance of bureaucratic thinking. In this mode of thought, every problem or issue is assigned to a particular agency, bureau, or institution. The bureaucratic arrangement was supposed to make public life more efficient—carefully defining who was in charge of what and where people should go to acquire certain services. It has been common, for example, for people to claim a sharp separation between the function of schools and that of homes. Teachers often say, "If parents would do their job, I could do mine." And "strong" parents often object to the very idea of allowing schools to teach parenting, claiming that such teaching should be done by parents at home. Reaction to bureaucratic thinking and its unyielding separations is starting to develop as more and more people realize that important problems cannot often be solved by one agency acting alone. We are interdependent even at the level of highly developed expertise, and if we are serious about achieving meaning through education, we must work to break down the separation of disciplines from each other and from life in the three domains.

It follows that all teachers therefore have a responsibility to contribute to the growth of their students as future homemakers, workers, and citizens. Every teacher is a moral educator. Every teacher models and encourages the use of standard English. Every teacher engages in dialogue with students to promote critical thinking. Every teacher promotes an understanding and appreciation of human interdependence. Every teacher encourages aesthetic appreciation of the subjects studied. When a significant universal aim for life and well-being has been identified, every teacher must find a way to connect his or her subject to that aim.

Take the personal/family domain and the teaching of homemaking as an example. Its introduction into the curriculum is not best accomplished by adding a course, and we defeat our purpose when we press for this option—one that will predictably be opposed as "anti-intellectual." Rather integration should be the aim. What can mathematics teachers contribute to the topic of homemaking? Math courses might include material on budgets, financial planning, interest, savings, and wise shopping.

In the civic domain, lessons on probability could include an emphasis on gambling, with teachers encouraging a discussion on the ethics of gambling. Should government, for example, encourage gambling through lotteries?

But there is so much more. Virtually all students in algebra encounter the equation $x^2 - x - 2 = 0$ among their standard exercises, but few teachers take the time to discuss the wonders of its positive solution—the Golden Ratio, $\dot\phi$ (phi, ~1.618). To design an aesthetically pleasing rectangular room, for example, the length and width should conform to the Golden Ratio. Whole projects for students might be designed around the study and use of $\dot\phi$. It is also encountered in the Fibonacci sequence, philosophy, music, art, the growth of rose petals, poetry.Such a mathematics lesson therefore moves out to connect with history, literature, science, aesthetics, and architecture (Livio, 2002). Most students will not encounter quadratic equations in their adult lives, but they may remember the magical number called "phi" that appears in a host of interesting settings.

In social studies, some time might be given to the history of homes and homemaking. What would it be like to live, eat, work, and sleep in one large space with co-workers and their families? (See Rybczynski, 1986.) Where in Europe did the small family home originate? Was privacy always prized? By whom, and how was it attained? Students should be made aware of the work of women in designing homes and home workplaces. They surely have heard of Harriet Beecher Stowe and *Uncle Tom's Cabin*, but they should also learn about the work of Harriet and her sister, Catherine Beecher, in designing small, efficient homes with attention to heat, ventilation, and step-saving kitchen arrangements. They should hear, too, about the work of Lillian Gilbreth (made famous as the mother in *Cheaper by the Dozen*) and her career as an industrial engineer concerned with household management.

Science teachers might discuss the improvements in sanitation over the last two centuries and what those improvements have done to reduce illness and extend life. How much illness can be traced to contaminated water? Teachers of literature can join the dialogue here with a discussion of J.G. Farrell's *The Siege of Krishnapur* in which two doctors argue heatedly over the causes of cholera. (See Noddings, 2006.) Is cholera still a problem in parts of the world? And what about the widespread occurrence of childbed fever in the 19th century due to the germ-coated hands of physicians? Do such problems exist in 21st century medical facilities?

I am not trying to lay out a curriculum here—that is obviously a huge task—but only to suggest a way of thinking that should help to break down disciplinary boundaries and stretch each of the disciplines from within in order to make connections and attain meaning. E.O. Wilson (2006) has pointed out the vitality and usefulness of such an approach:

> What was once perceived as an epistemological divide between the great branches of learning is now emerging from the academic fog as something far different and much more interesting: a wide middle domain of mostly unexplored phenomena open to a cooperative approach from both sides of the former divide. (p. 136)

Imagination and well-informed thinking of this sort might effect real reform in curriculum It is highly unlikely that the general structure of curriculum will change; it is well stuck in a pattern centuries old. Students will continue to endure (and occasionally to enjoy) English, mathematics, science, social studies, and a foreign language. If they are fortunate, they will also be granted some art and music. To realize how difficult it is to make real changes in the school curriculum, one need only look at the failed struggle to change the middle school curriculum (Lounsbury, 2009; Lounsbury & Vars, 1978). After a valiant, thirty-year effort to humanize the middle school curriculum, Lounsbury tells us that "the valid middle school concept... has not been practiced and found wanting; rather, it has been found difficult to implement fully, and practiced then only partially" (2009, p. 3) and, worse, "since No Child Left Behind (NCLB) has been in force, mere arrested development has regretfully given way to regression" (p. 3).

The lesson here, I suggest, is to start with the structure we have and change it cooperatively from within. The one big exception to this might be to insist on the restoration of a strong vocational program to the secondary curriculum. Even this, however, is not new, and if done badly could itself be a regression. We turn to that topic next.

Reviving Vocational Education

If we believe that democracy is a form of associated living and conjoint communicated experience, one that requires respect for the wide array of human skills and talents, a recognition of interdependence, generous communication within and across groups, and a citizenry skilled in critical thinking, we will be committed to providing a variety of rich curricula from which students—with appropriate guidance—may make intelligent choices. This means that we must provide rich and relevant vocational programs as well as those in traditional college preparation.

A strong vocational education should not be defined as simply preparation for a particular job. Like every form of education in a genuine democracy, it should prepare students for life in all three great domains. Planning and implementing such a program requires the sort of cooperation characteristic of a democracy as Dewey described it. It requires that representatives of industry, higher education, secondary education, and government agencies work together to launch and maintain programs that will benefit both the students and the communities in which they will live and work. A host of important questions must be addressed: What jobs will be open in the community? How will students be prepared for them? At what level will the various objectives be addressed? How will students be introduced to the possibilities so that they can make intelligent choices? How will the programs be financed? How will we ensure that the programs will be intellectually rich as well as occupationally relevant?

A sound vocational education is an expensive enterprise. Recognition of this fact may arouse a cynical suspicion in thoughtful citizens. It is common today to claim that schools should provide the same, academically traditional program for all of our secondary school students. We now generously require—so we tell ourselves—all students to take the courses that will prepare them for college. But there may well be a less generous motive operating as well. Excellent vocational education is far more expensive than the routine academic education we now offer to all students. It often requires expensive machinery that must be kept up-to-date; it also requires specially trained teachers and smaller classes. The public must be persuaded that a considerable investment will produce a more competent, satisfied workforce and citizenry.

A really fine vocational program can be and should be intellectually rich; that is, it should encourage continual reflection on the connection between thinking and doing. As Mike Rose (2004) has reminded educators, the distinctions between the practical and theoretical, the physical and conceptual are distinctions of longstanding:

> These distinctions are not benign categories, are not neutral; in many contexts they carry significant differences in status and worth. As we get close to students doing their work, however, we see how complicated these distinctions are: the technical gives rise to reflection, the physical and conceptual blend, and aesthetics and ethics emerge continually from practical activity. (p. xxxii)

Matthew Crawford (2009) also extols the intellectual qualities of physical work, but he reminds us that educators and business experts in the early 20th century supported a sharp separation between the thinking of "scientific management" and the dull, repetitive work of the assembly line. We are unlikely, however, to repeat the errors of Taylorism today because the dullest, least challenging work is now done by machines. Using these machines and maintaining them provides a continual challenge to the connection between thinking and doing. Still, we must remain wary of the possible corruption of our well-intended vocational programs.

Connections should also be made across vocational and academic programs. Some attention in both programs should be given to the history and biographies of working-class intellectuals and their supporters. Students should hear something about the work of Scott Nearing, Myles Horton, Rosa Parks, Pete Seeger, Woody Guthrie, Paulo Freire, Eleanor Roosevelt, and Eugene Debs, among others. They should be informed on both the great contributions and the faults of trade unions. Citizens better informed on this history would, perhaps, be able to apply critical thinking to the current attacks on unions.

Again, both academic and vocational programs should include mention of utopian novels and philosophies. It is neither wise nor necessary to expect high school students to read difficult utopian tracts, but they should know that a variety of writers have grappled with the problems of poverty, hard labor, and persistent class differences. Should society's hardest, dirtiest tasks be distributed somehow over the whole population so that no individuals will have to spend entire working days on distasteful, ill-paid tasks? How could this be done? Should society provide special incentives to those who do such work? What visions have been put forth for the perfectly just society? Why are such works called "utopias"?

To accomplish the changes suggested here, teachers need to be better educated across the disciplines in matters concerning labor and vocations and in the history of their own profession. What events, for example, pushed Dewey toward socialism? Why did Scott Nearing choose a vocational school for his own secondary education, and how did that choice influence his political/social thought? How might we describe a non-violent revolution? Teachers today may defend or oppose unions, but they should at least be aware that the National Education Association (NEA) has given us some things to be proud of. For example: (1) It sponsored the Cardinal Principles Report (1918), which stated seven great aims for education: health, command of the fundamental processes, worthy home membership, vocation, citizenship, worthy use of leisure time, and ethical character. The Report was written by a mathematics teacher, Charles Kingsley. Have we made progress since 1918, or have we regressed in important ways? (2) It published "The Public School and the Immigrant Child," an essay by Jane Addams that should be read today. In it, Addams described an admirable balance between the preservation of original cultures and assimilation to the new one. Moving beyond this admirable balance, Addams recommended that the school introduce the child to "the beginnings of a culture so wide and deep and universal that he can interpret his own parents and countrymen by a standard which is world-wide and not provincial" (quoted in Lagemann, 1985, p. 138). (3) It sponsored the writing of the Pledge of Allegiance for the opening of the Chicago World's Fair in 1892. The writer, Francis Bellamy, was a Christian Socialist. (On this interesting story, see Jacoby, 2004.) This information should invite both appreciation and vigorous critical thinking. How are Christianity and socialism compatible? Why has "socialism" become a pejorative in today's political vocabulary?

Dewey, in his description of democracy as a mode of associated living, gave us a test for judging the strength of our democracy: the variety of shared interests within a group and the quantity and quality of interactions across groups. In our schools, we should support interaction across groups through both extracurricular activities and shared topics in curriculum. Similarly, the intellectual breadth attained by reaching beyond isolated, highly specialized subjects adds meaning to the depth treasured by specialists.

Conclusion

If we believe that democracy is more than a form of government, that it is indeed a mode of associated living, then we should think seriously about providing a variety of educational programs aimed at meeting the needs of students with widely different aptitudes and interests. At the same time, all of our programs should be intellectually rich—aimed at enhancing communication, cooperation, connection, and critical thinking. Such education recognizes that human beings seek participation and fulfillment in all three great domains of life: personal/family, occupation, and civic.

Schooling that recognizes democracy as a mode of associated living and education as an enterprise with multiple aims will work to break down disciplinary barriers that stand in the way of finding meaning, will redefine universal aims, and encourage appreciation for the huge variety of work that must be done well in a complex society.

References

Crawford, M. B. (2009). *Shop class as soulcraft.* New York: Penguin Press.

Dewey, J. (1916). *Democracy and education.* New York: Macmillan.

Gardner, J. (1984). Excellence. New York: W.W. Norton. (Original work published in 1961.)

Jacoby, S. (2004). *Freethinkers.* New York: Metropolitan Books.

Kerber, L. (1997). *Toward an intellectual history of Women.* Chapel Hill: University of North Carolina Press.

Kliebard, H. (1999). *Schooled to work: Vocationalism and the American curriculum 1876–1946.* New York: Teachers College Press.

Lagemann, E. C. (Ed.). (1985). *Jane Addams on education.* New York: Teachers College Press.

Livio, M. (2002). *The golden ratio: The story of phi, the world's most astonishing number.* New York: Broadway Books.

Lounsbury, J. H., & Vars, G. F. (1978). *A curriculum for the middle school years.* New York: Harper & Row.

Lounsbury, J.H. (2009). Deferred but determined: A middle school manifesto. Special article, *Middle School Journal*, Feb. 6.

Noddings, N. (2006). *Critical lessons: What our schools should teach.* New York: Cambridge University Press.

Noddings, N. (2013). *Education and democracy in the 21st century.* New York: Teachers College Press.

Rose, M. (2004). *The mind at work: Valuing the intelligence of the American worker.* New York: Penguin.

Rybczynski, W. (1986). *Home: A short history of an idea.* New York: Viking.

Wilson, E.O. (2006). *The creation: An appeal to save life on earth.* New York: W.W. Norton.

CHAPTER TWO

And They Call It Education Reform

SUSAN OHANIAN

A whale-ship was my Yale College and my Harvard.
   —Ishmael, Chapter XXIV *Moby Dick* by Herman Melville

You can get all A's and still flunk life.
   —Walker Percy, *The Second Coming*

Harvard University historian and *New Yorker* staff writer Jill Lepore (1998) points out that "Writing about war can be almost as difficult as waging it.... The words used to describe war have a great deal of work to do: they must communicate war's intensity, its traumas, fears, and glories; they must make clear who is right and who is wrong...they must document the pain of war, and in so doing, help to alleviate it." Make no mistake: we who care about the survival of public education are at war. The failure to step up and make clear who is right and who is wrong in the current education reform (deform) war is the horrific failure of our professional organizations, our teacher unions, academia, and teachers themselves. This silence puts education for the common good, the very fabric of democracy, at risk.

"Go West, young man!" advised Horace Greeley in 1851. As Samuel Bowles and Herbert Ginnis (1976) note, "A century later he probably would have said, 'Go to college!'" Just as Westward Expansion was hyped as a way out of poverty in the 19th century—with no mention of how many tombstones marked its path—now corporate politicos posit a college degree as the new promised land, cheerfully ignoring the reality of family legacy and the brass tacks of the 21st-century job market. Think of Mary Oliver's (2010) take on jobs in the Westward Expansion. She points out that when Pony Express needed riders, they looked for orphans: "that way, no one was likely to ask questions..."

Melinda Gates (2009) appeared on the "college for all" stump in 2009, announcing to the National Council of La Raza: "Everyone in this room knows that high school is not high enough. We have to create a society that expects all students to go on to college and complete a degree—whether it's a certificate, associate's degree, or bachelor's degree…." Gates features ugly stories about public schools, glorifies KIPP (Knowledge is Power Program) charter schools, and reiterates the cause into which the Gates Foundation has pumped hundreds of millions of dollars: "We need a common set of high standards so all teachers know exactly what their students need to learn. And we need to evaluate teachers based on how well their students are learning it."

Education as Exact Measurement of Exact Knowledge

In an interview with radio talk show host Marc Bernier (quoted in Weinstein, 2011), Florida governor Rick Scott offered his education-for-jobs scheme: "You know, we don't need a lot more anthropologists in the state. It's a great degree if people want to get it, but we don't need them here. I want to spend our dollars giving people science, technology, engineering, math (STEM) degrees. That's what our kids need to focus all their time and attention on. Those type of degrees. So when they get out of school, they can get a job." Note that Governor Scott has no hesitancy in declaring where kids need to focus "all their time and attention." Rick Scott, who made a couple hundred million dollars in a checkered career as a venture capitalist, has been labeled a Tea-Partier; but neoliberals embrace his education focus. Obama-Duncan education policy, which functions as an echo chamber for policies financed by the Bill and Melinda Gates Foundation, pushes STEM careers as the saviors of the U.S. economy. Mike Rose, a one-time vocational track student, has had long experience working with what he terms "the underprepared" (1989) and has offered stirring, detailed challenges to assumptions about these students—challenges to educators as well as the public. Rose (2011) points out that school reformers all whistle the same tune—because they talk to the same people: "When President Obama visited my home state of California, the person he met with to talk about education was Steve Jobs."

U.S. Secretary of Education Arne Duncan (2010) touts STEM over and over, "Everyone has a stake in improving STEM education. Inspiring all our students to be capable in math and science will help them contribute in an increasingly technology-based economy, and will also help America prepare the next generation of STEM professionals—scientists, engineers, architects and technology professionals—to ensure our competiveness." Duncan and Secretary of Health and Human Services Kathleen Sebelius (2013) joined hands in trumpeting the STEM theme for pre-school: "Strong early learning can translate into school success, which can lead to college and good jobs, and ultimately a robust economy." Make that STEM education—science, technology, engineering, and math degrees.

Education as Insurance

In 2012, at the 100Kin10 Partner Summit held at Google's DC offices, Duncan chanted his oft-repeated refrain: "I can't tell you how many CEOs I meet with who are trying to hire right now in a tough economy, thousands and thousands of good paying jobs…that they can't fill because we're not producing the workers with the skills they need to employ them. And so many of those skills lie in the STEM areas (Arkin, 2012)" Formed in 2011 by the Carnegie

Corporation of New York, Opportunity Equation, and NewSchools Venture Fund, 100Kin10 was announced at the Clinton Global Initiative (CGI) America Meeting in Chicago. Bill Clinton proved he hasn't lost the same touch for corporate affinity that he exhibited as Arkansan governor in the 1980s when he held hands with IBM chief Lou Gerstner to forge America 2000 for President Bush the Elder. That policy, which came directly from a Business Roundtable template, has morphed into Goals 2000, No Child Left Behind, and now Race to the Top and the Common Core Standards, appearing more oppressive with each iteration (Emery and Ohanian, 2004). As Bob Herbert (2009) began a *New York Times* column, "Policies that were wrong under George W. Bush are no less wrong because Barack Obama is in the White House."

Convening sponsor of the Chicago CGI Meeting was the J. B. & M. K. Pritzker Foundation (Penny Pritzker, listed by Forbes 2011 as the 263rd-richest person in the U.S and national chairwoman of Barack Obama's campaign finance team during his 2008 presidential run, was appointed to the Chicago School Board by mayor-in-charge-of-schools Rahm Emanuel). The Bill and Melinda Gates Foundation jumped in as a 2012 sponsor and speakers included Tennessee governor Bill Haslam, who changed teacher tenure laws in that state, tying the process of obtaining and maintaining tenure to student achievement.

Writing for *Mother Jones*, Rick Weinstein (2011) asks the fundamental question: *Is a degree's intrinsic value really reducible to its marketability?* The fact that the day after I received my master's degree in medieval literature I got on a plane for New York City and managed to get a job only because I was a very good typist (*Time* was typical: "We don't hire women in editorial.") didn't make me feel that studying Chaucer and Spenser had been foolhardy. Admittedly, one of my UC Berkeley professors asked me why I was in graduate school if I didn't plan to teach. My answer—"Because I like it"—may now seem a bit jejune, but better naïf than mercenary. It is beyond dishonest to look our students in the eye and tell them that they should "focus all their time and attention" learning to read and write according to Common Core scripts because such focus will deliver a future job, along with a two-car garage and a yearly trip to Disney World. Instead, I tell kids I'll help them find a book that will knock their socks off: immediate gratification with long-term possibilities. Every spring I attend concerts presented by the Middlebury College Department of Music, featuring young vocalists singing Rossini, Gluck, Bizet, Mozart, Strauss, Debussy, and so on. I'm grateful that some colleges still believe in the arts, but I worry that this will become a luxury offered only by private institutions while public institutions are ever-diminished by venture capitalists who think the world doesn't need lyric mezzos and baritones any more than it needs anthropologists.

We've had plenty of recent warnings that a college degree doesn't come with a security blanket. Iain Levison's *A Working Stiff's Manifesto: A Memoir of Thirty Jobs I Quit, Nine That Fired Me, and Three I Can't Remember* (2002) delivers a caution light to those who decide to major in the liberal arts. Using humor with a political bite, Levison describes the reality of working as an oil deliveryman, fish cutter, restaurant manager, and so on: "If you ask the rich why you're not capable of supporting yourself, they'll tell you it is your fault. The ones who make it to the lifeboats always think the ones in the water are to blame. . . ." I wonder what moral we might draw from the fact that, after publishing this book, Levison wrote satirical novels about people in menial jobs who take up a life of crime.

The so-called education reformers of all political stripes operate from the same neoliberal corporate playbook, insisting that economic solutions result from offering all children a so-called "equal opportunity." Handing out standards in the name of preparing everyone to meet the high skills that will be demanded for employment in the 21st century is as cynical as handing out menus to homeless people in the name of eradicating hunger. Does it matter how carefully the menu calibrates its offerings to the federal Food Pyramid—or Harvard's entrance requirements?

Let Them Eat Cake. Let Them Take Calculus

Reformers set up a system so that those who don't find success have only themselves to blame—themselves and their teachers. In reality, what NCLB and Race to the Top and the Common Core and its attendant tests offer is a technocratic approach to education, one in which teachers become increasingly expendable. Vicki Phillips (2010), Director of Education, College Ready at the Bill and Melinda Gates Foundation, told the PTA that teacher certification, master's degrees, and seniority don't matter. She was repeating Emperor Bill's proclamation at TED: "There are fairly effective teachers in a narrow set of places. So the top 20 percent of students have gotten a good education…. Once somebody has taught for three years their teaching quality does not change thereafter" (B. Gates, 2009). This was the same conference where Gates exhibited his sensitivity to human needs by launching a glass full of mosquitoes at the audience—to make a point about the deadly disease malaria. Gates reiterated this contempt for teachers in a 2011 interview with editors at the *Washington Post*, where his wife had served on the board for six years (Anderson, 2011). On tenure, Gates said he understood why it was needed for college professors. But he claimed to be perplexed by tenure rules that provide school teachers with significant due-process protections in personnel cases after they pass a probationary period. "The idea that this one shouldn't be about what goes on with the kids always seemed a little unusual," he said. "You know, maybe we should try tenure in other professions. Just, you know, mix it up a little bit. Pay newspaper editors by seniority. Have tenure for them and see how that works. Try it for hot-dog making or restaurants."

Teaching as Hot-Dog Making

Schott's Vocab, which ran as a blog in the *New York Times* for nearly three years, in 2011 offered this definition of Sheening: "To behave like Charlie Sheen—partying, questionable decision making and public humiliation." You can bet they'll never offer *Gatesing*: To behave like Bill Gates—voracious funding, questionable decision making and teacher humiliation. As scholar-activist and teacher Paul Thomas (2011) has noted, "If Bill Gates had no money, who would listen to him about education reform? No one—the same as who should listen to him now." But President Obama (2011) picked up on that "some good teachers" theme in a speech at TechBoston Academy:

> We are looking to make teaching one of the most honored professions in our society…. We've got to lift up teachers. We've got to reward good teachers. First, we also have to stop making excuses for bad teachers.

This is not accidental. Melinda Gates told Pulitzer reporter Daniel Golden (2010) that the relationship started when Arne Duncan was CEO of Chicago schools, and she toured the schools after the Foundation gave them $21.6 million. Golden noted, "Today, the Gates Foundation and Education Secretary Duncan move in apparent lockstep." Duncan's then-spokesman, Peter Cunningham, told Golden the foundation's agenda "is very much aligned with the Obama Administration agenda."

Education of the Foundation, by the Foundation, and for the Foundation

We hear a lot about bad teachers from both sides of the aisle. What goes unmentioned is poverty. In 2008–09, the U.S. Department of Education Date Express published figures indicating that 44.2% of students in U.S. public schools were identified as low income. They published the figures; they just didn't talk about them. Here are just a few of the statistics:

New Hampshire: 20.5%

California: 51.7%

New Mexico: 61.4%

Washington, D.C.: 67.1%

Mississippi: 68.3%

When poverty is mentioned, it's in the context of education being the cure. Arne Duncan's speech (2012) at the Harvard Graduate School of Education is typical, repeating the theme song for which Bill Gates wrote the lyrics: "I want to underline that great schools and great teachers are the most effective anti-poverty tool of all." Speaking the same year at the Loyola University in Chicago Commencement, Richard Rothstein (2012), research associate of the Economic Policy Institute and senior fellow of the Chief Justice Earl Warren Institute on Law and Social Policy at the University of California (Berkeley) School of Law, gave an evidence-based talk about the "conventional and widely shared diagnoses based on fantasy, with little relation to facts." Rothstein spelled out those facts, concluding: "Again, no matter how high your expectations, how accountable you are for results, if children are moving in and out of your classrooms, they cannot benefit from what schools have to offer. In short, underemployment of parents is not only an economic crisis—it is an educational crisis. You cannot ignore it and be good educators." At the same time corporate politicos are preaching the Common Core curriculum, Rothstein exhorted educators, "You simply cannot remain uninformed and silent about the social and economic context of your work."

Although we've all read heroic stories of students overcoming all odds, we must heed the reality. As past president of the American Educational Research Association David Berliner's research (2012) shows, "The general case is that poor people stay poor and teachers and schools serving impoverished youth do not often succeed in changing the chances for their students." Berliner points out that a huge part of this tragic reality lies in the fact that "we design social policies that are sure to fail since they are not based on reality." So, too, with education reform. There is no evidence that the Common Core State [sic] Standards will work. None. Actually, there is more evidence (Moss, 2013) that Kellogg's Frosted Mini-Wheats cereal improves student attentiveness ("Keeps 'em full. Keeps 'em focused.") than that the Common Core will improve public education.

But even if someone could wave a magic wand and produce "college for all," we must consider that more than thirty-five years ago, Samuel Bowles and Herbert Gintis (1976) pointed out that, by the late 1950s, the educational frontier was pressing its limits and college graduates were driving cabs and collecting unemployment. No matter how loudly Barack Obama and Bill Gates say that hiring remains so low in this economic recovery because employers can't find workers with the necessary education and skills, the data shows something different. From the Economic Policy Institute, Heidi Shierholz (2013) offers research evidence: "Workers don't lack skills; they lack work."

The gap between college degrees and jobs occasionally makes it into the business section of the *New York Times*. Louis Uchitelle (2005) was blunt: "Clearly there are more college graduates than unfilled jobs requiring their credentials." Noted researcher Gerald Bracey (2009) put it even stronger: "The impending shortage of scientists and engineers is one of the longest running hoaxes in the country." On EDDRA, the Internet discussion list he founded, Bracey warned, "Your 401(k)'s are not dying because not enough kids took calculus." At Salon.com, Michael Lind (2009), co-founder of the New America Project, observed that President Obama is a prisoner of the neoliberal cult and, "Like Bill Clinton before him, Barack Obama continues to tell American that to get higher wages they need to go to college and improve their skills, as though there weren't a surplus of underemployed college grads already." And Ian Gilbert (nd) founder of Independent Thinking, LTD, asks, "What if math is not as important as, say, art or music?"

What If?

For me, this is what democracy is about: Who chooses? Who gets choices? Chris Hedges (2009) warns, "As universities become glorified vocational schools for corporations, they adopt values and operating techniques of the corporations they serve." Hedges (2012) focuses on what this corporatization of the university does to students:

> Human imagination, the capacity to have vision, to build a life of meaning rather than utilitarianism, is as delicate as a flower. And if it is crushed, if a Shakespeare or a Sophocles is no longer deemed useful in the empirical world of business, careerism and corporate power, if universities think a Milton Friedman or a Friedrich Hayek is more important to their students than a Virginia Woolf or an Anton Chekhov, then we become barbarians. We assure our own extinction. Students who are denied the wisdom of the great oracles of human civilization—visionaries who urge us not to worship ourselves, not to kneel before the base human emotion of greed—cannot be educated. They cannot think.

Now the Common Core brings this corporatization to kindergarten. Marina Kravosky (2005) notes that a "preschool near the Stanford campus had the purposeful name 'Knowledge Beginnings,' whereas a preschool near a university in Switzerland was called 'Vanilla-Strawberry.'"

But this is about more than who gets the top jobs; it's about treating all workers fairly and with dignity. Nel Noddings (2008) has pointed out: "Occupations such as food preparation and service worker, retail salesperson, customer service representative, cashier, office clerk, and laborer and material mover will employ about five times more people than the computer/high-tech fields requiring a college education. No matter what we do in schools, most of our high school graduates will work at such jobs." The imperative, urges Noddings, is that rich and meaningful courses should be available for students who don't intend to go to college. "Students should not be forced into or excluded from academic courses, but they should be able to choose a nonacademic program with pride and confidence." What schools need to do is listen to Mike Rose (2004) instead of Bill Gates. We need to honor the highly skilled occupations of the waitress, hair stylist, plumber, mechanic, and carpenter that are so needed to hold our society together, and all students entering such occupations should have the benefit of a rich, meaningful, and provocative K-12 education.

John J. Viall (2013), a longtime teacher who writes the Teacher on Teaching blog, describes what happens when a busload of school reformers headed for a convention see three cars stranded by the side of the road. "None of the reformers knows a pile of shit from a spark plug when it comes to car repairs," relates Viall, but that doesn't stop them from offering solutions. Arne Duncan is the first with a reform plan: "We will call this plan 'Race to the Garage.' We will offer states $4.35 billion in federal aid if they agree to paint all their cars red." Likewise, none of the reformers knows a pile of shit from a book to knock a kid's socks off, from a teacher's joy when, ten years after leaving my class, a very difficult eighth grader drops me a note to say she checked *Flat Stanley* out of the library to read it to her stepchildren. Of course, reformers don't paint their own cars red nor send their kids to overcrowded urban schools passing out tablets loaded with Common Core curricula and assessments. In *Salt Sugar Fat: How the Food Giants Hooked Us*, Michael Moss (2013) points out that the grandchildren of Bob Drane, inventor of Kraft's Lunchables, have never eaten this food product. "We eat very healthfully," Drane's daughter said. Moss comments, "There is a class issue at work in processed foods, in which the inventors and company executives don't generally partake in their own creations." Small wonder. Geoffrey Bible (former owner of Kraft Foods) remarked he'd heard someone say, "If you take Lunchables apart, the most healthy item in it is the napkin." But as Moss observes, there's nothing accidental about this. Food is processed to scientific specifications; it's processed to be addictive.

The Feds give surplus chicken to schools (Morrison, Eisler & DeBarros, 2009), encouraging them to divert this chicken to processors like Tyson (2013), who turn it into products (Warner, 2010) that will appeal to children who qualify for free and reduced lunch. In matters of food, the Sidwell Friends School that President Obama's daughters attend, emphasizes "green," local, healthy menus, described on the web by Rebecca Cunningham, Executive Chef and Robin Menard, Director of Dining Services (2010). No bargain salt/sugar/fat-stuffed chicken products shipped in from Tyson. Similarly, Sidwell doesn't participate in the President's signature education reform plans, Race to the Top and the Common Core State [*sic*] Standards. The rich eat better than the poor, and they are offered richer education choices. But as Dave Barry (2005) observed, for public school kids, food and curriculum might meld: "If school officials believed that ingesting lizard meat improved FCAT performance, the cafeterias would be serving gecko nuggets."

Certainly, the Common Core Standards are not the only problem with public schools; but now these standards are a convenient diversion from key defects that have existed for decades, defects related to poverty and access to a meaningful curriculum. The Common Core will further divide the Haves from the Have-Nots. The corporate-politico Common Core plan is to hook teachers into an addiction to following directions, reading the script, doing what they're told—and training kids to do the same. Innovation may survive, but only in some suburban pockets where parents demand it. As publishers race to produce Common Core materials and technology companies produce tablets for every student that promise to "do everything" for the teacher, the Common Core becomes the sugar, salt, and fat of pedagogy. We are now a country of the rich, by the rich, and for the rich. Let the school cafeterias serving poor kids offer high-fat/high-salt/high-sugar items (what *New York Times* Pulitzer writer Timothy Egan refers to as "tasty gut bombs") and learn Common Core lessons from scripts sent in from Rupert

Murdoch's employees at Amplify. Snazzy brain bombs that deliver, analyze, and regurgitate data, the aphrodisiac of corporate America.

The Common Core is promoted as a state initiative; but this radical, untried, peculiar curriculum overhaul, which is an excuse for nonstop national testing, was paid for by the Bill and Melinda Gates Foundation without public—or teacher—advice and consent. Although there is a flurry of outrage in the blogosphere, there has been no institutional pushback: not from professional organizations, not from unions, not from colleges of education. And so teachers, whose profession's most common innate quality is that of people pleasing—people who are acculturated to get along and be helpful—figure they must obey. Bring on the lessons training eight-year-olds to write like bankers. The American Federation of Teachers, for one, offers enthusiastic support for the Common Core—a support that goes much deeper than the relatively paltry $1,000,000 they received from the Bill and Melinda Gates Foundation. The AFT website, "Share My Lesson," ostensibly offers lessons to help students accomplish Common Core bidding, but many of the lessons are written by the AFT's British website partners, who give no indication of ever having heard of the Common Core. An American contribution (a young WS, 2013) on informative/expository writing for third grade purports to deliver this standard: *Students will be able to: Core Standard W.3.2b: Develop the topic with facts, definitions, and details. Core Standard W.3.2c: Use linking words and phrases to connect ideas within categories of information.*

A handout is provided so kids can check off that they have used prescribed linking words (*Tell students that linking/transition words can be used to tie all their paragraphs together. This helps keep the flow for readers. Share with students that linking/transition words are a lot like using glue.*) Here are a few of the linking words third graders are asked to use:

To Indicate a Purpose or Reason
in hope that
in order to
so that
with this in mind
because

To Conclude:
all in all
as a result
finally
in conclusion
in summary
in brief
therefore
lastly
to sum up
overall

And so on. The handout has thirty-seven such phrases. I expect my insurance agent to write like this, not my third-grade student. Or me. These phrases don't turn up in the twenty-five books and several hundred articles that I've written; they don't appear in the books I read.

This may well be how bankers and hedge fund speculators write, but it's worse than misguided to foist such formulas on to third graders. My focal points of anger at the Common Core used to be their positioning of William Faulkner's *As I Lay Dying*, with its fifteen narrators, and *Pride and Prejudice* as exemplary text; but now the destructive power of *to sum up* and with *this in mind* prescriptions makes me weep. With a little encouragement, a lot of read-alouds, and heaps of free reading, third graders demonstrate a wonderful sense of voice. They love to imitate their favorite authors—from Beatrix Potter to Shel Silverstein, Dav Pilkey, and Jon Scieszka. Here's the kind of writing primary graders savor—and copy:

> And the little very very very very very very very old man smiled, and looking at the faerie he said: 'Why?'— e. e. cummings, *The Old Man Who Said Why*

I speak from first-hand, on-the-spot observation here. Children relish the good words that are given to them; and they give them back, taking great delight in pointing out, "Look! I write like Jack Prelutsky!" To deliberately set out to stifle this voice, to bury it in formalism, is worse than a crime: it's a mistake, definitely qualifying for Dante's eighth circle of hell. Of course, "Share My Lesson" is not unique. Once-respected publishers are churning out Common Core fellow traveler tomes; old-hand schlock merchants are putting new covers on old skills; upstart impresarios are spreading so-called Common Core skills faster than ragweed. Novelist Nicholas Sparks (2012) has jumped on the bandwagon. NCTE gave him a launch platform as featured speaker for its Conference on English Leadership (CEL) at the 2012 convention, where Sparks introduced his Novel Learning Series™, promising "ELA Common Core State Standards Alignment" with four of his most popular titles, brought out in study guide editions to help students prepare for the Common Core—and for college. The California State Department of Education offers a "Brokers for Expertise" website (http://www.myboe.org). The fun in writing about education policy is that one doesn't have to make anything up. Brokers of Expertise. How could anyone invent that? And all this is small potatoes compared to Student Achievement Partners, an outfit co-founded by David Coleman, that is now churning out Common Core curriculum. They're bankrolled by $6,533,350 from the Bill and Melinda Gates Foundation and $18,000,000 from the General Electric Foundation. Coleman has moved on to head the College Board ($31,178,497 in Gates funds).

Michael Crow (Blumenstyk, 2001), then-executive vice provost at Columbia, and currently president of Arizona State University, describes what's going on: "We use the word 'academic entrepreneurs.' We are expanding what it means to be a knowledge enterprise. We use knowledge as a form of venture capital.…" I find it mind-boggling that there's no secrecy here. Education as a venture capital enterprise, built on the backs of the human capital, aka children, while stealing their souls. It is no wonder that Chris Hedges (2011) advises, "The only gatherings worth attending from now on are acts that organize civil disobedience." Civil disobedience is needed to rescue democracy.

Organized Civil Disobedience

Teachers are supposed to sign in blood—or at the very least affirm very loudly—that we have universally high expectations and know that *all* children can learn at high levels. In a recent letter asking for funds (Bertin, 2013) the National Coalition Against Censorship shares a wonderful story about high expectations. Here's what Sherman Alexie, whose novel *The Absolutely*

True Diary of a Part-Time Indian is the subject of book challenges across the country, told the NCAC:

> The big moment for me was when I gave a reading in Spokane in 2009, and eight or nine Chicano boys drove up with their teacher from Ephrata, WA, which has a heavily migrant worker population. These Chicano boys were so into the book—and they told me that they had decided to put on ties to show respect to me and the book. Their excitement was amazing and all of them said it was the first book they'd ever finished.

The wonderful thing about good stories is they beget more stories, and the first book those Chicano boys had ever read all the way through reminds me of Keith's first book. It's a story I've told before (Ohanian, 1999) and by now it's a mantra as well as a story. Instinct kicked in with some pedagogy and frustration on the day Keith, who had studiously resisted free voluntary reading as well as teacher-imposed reading, came into class whining that he'd read every single book in the room—including two sets of encyclopedias. I grabbed *Hop on Pop* and shoved it at him. "Read this!" I commanded in a voice he recognized as She Who Must Be Obeyed. I walked away and Keith sat down and started turning the pages quickly—his approach to all books. But then something caught his eye and he stopped. He looked at a page, really looked. Then he went back to the preceding page and examined it closely. He stared at that page for a long time. Then he turned to the first page and started mouthing the words.

As he hunched over that book sounding out the words, Keith, a boy usually never still but always on the move, sat motionless for the entire period. Other kids picked up on the enfolding drama and, unusual for this group of seventh- and eighth-grade roughnecks, remained as silent witness to this miracle: Keith was reading a book. I am not exaggerating when I say the rest of us presented a frozen tableau rather like that old game of "Statues" while Keith, oblivious to the outside world, concentrated on his book. When he finally closed the last page, Keith's expression was puzzled. "I did it. I read this book." He looked at me. "Seriously, Miz O. I read it. For real. I read this book. You wanna see?" It wasn't fluent reading. Each word was pointed at, struggled over, sounded out. Then, Keith made the leap that had been missing for all those remedial reading years. After sounding out a word, he pronounced it, not as a sound, but as something that made sense. He even laughed at the fun of the text. He read it again.

Throughout the rest of the year, whenever things weren't going well for Keith, he'd say, "How would you like to hear that *Hop on Pop* book?" and he'd pull up a chair and calm himself by reading a few pages out loud. And he asked those magic words, "Did that Dr. Seuss write any more books?" ending the year having read more than one book. It's worth noting that a bunch of Seuss titles were in a seventh–eighth-grade classroom because I'd joined a beginning reader book club. Our school had budgets to order a $5,000 "complete reading program" and computer paraphernalia labeled "reading accountability system," and machines designed to control the speed at which students read, but the language arts coordinator looked at me like I was crazy when I asked for a subscription to a beginning reading club. Nor could I get even one subscription to the local newspaper (I'd asked for six) or six copies of Farley Mowat's account of his life with wolves—unless I paid for them myself.

Keith was fifteen years old and this is one of the easiest of the Seuss books—not near the level of sophistication of, say, *Cat in the Hat*. Lexile doesn't give it a number—just the code BR (Beginning Reading). The Common Core State [*sic*] Standards Lexile bands aren't yet committing themselves for K-1, but they start out Grade 2 at 450. Lexile for Grades 6–8 is 860—1185. So we can figure Keith at about 950 points or so below Common Core high expectation.

In a video produced by the Council of Great City Schools ($8,496,854 from Gates), self-proclaimed Common Core architect David Coleman offers an ultimatum to the student who, like Keith, reads "several grade levels below" the complex text assigned to his class: "You're going to practice it again and again and again and again…so there's a chance you can finally do that level of work" (Council of Great City Schools, n.d.). Reverence for fetishistic one-size-fits-all procedure and refusal to allow alternative resources reveal a lack of classroom experience as well as anal retentive personality traits. Offering a refried New Criticism, Coleman and his Common Core acolytes present reading as ritualistic analysis, absent of personal imagining. I think of Saul Bellow (2010), who wrote in a letter to Owen Barfield, "I confess…I am put off by critics who tell the world with full confidence exactly what you were up to in writing what you wrote, as though they kept a booth at the fair in the middle of your soul."

Of course, David Coleman and his band of marauders are set on embalming fiction and dumping it in a pauper's field of isolated skills, stripped bare of emotional response. This is so clearly wrong that it needs no rebuttal, but let's consider what professor of applied cognitive psychology at the University of Toronto Keith Oatley (2010) has noted:

> Fiction is about the content of what people do, and think, and feel…. Literature allows not just learning about emotions, but experiencing them, although in a form in which they may be clarified and better understood.

You'll never hear a word from the Common Core groupies on the importance of Dr. Seuss, but here's Pulitzer Prize book critic Michael Dirda (2005), who holds a Ph.D. in comparative literature:

> Dr. Seuss has written more immortal works than any other twentieth-century American author. Think about it. Virtually every child in this country has read, is reading, or will read *The Cat in the Hat*, *Horton Hears a Who*, *And to Think that I Saw It on Mulberry Street*, *The Butter Battle Book*, and perhaps a dozen others equally splendid. Consider too that each of Seuss's more than forty titles is read not once, not twice, but scores of times, usually to pieces…. And what do we learn from Seuss? The joy of words and pictures at play, of course, but also the best and most humane values any of us might wish to possess: pluck, determination, tolerance, reverence for the earth, suspicion of the martial spirit, the fundamental value of the imagination. This is why early reading matters. At any age, but especially in childhood, books can transform lives….(p. 69)

Especially in childhood. This is exactly why it's so tragic to rob young children of *Rotten Ralph*, *Ramona the Brave*, *The Just-So Stories*, *The Trumpet of the Swan*, *The Miraculous Journey of Edward Tulane*, *The Great Gilly Hopkins*, *Incident at Hawk's Hill*, and on and on and on. A child only gets one chance at childhood. In *The Power of Reading: Insights from the Research* and *Free Voluntary Reading*, Stephen Krashen (2004) makes the research-based case for free voluntary reading as "one of the most powerful tools we have in language education." Voluntary. Student choice. No book reports, no questions at the end of the chapter. Close contact with lots of books of their own choosing gives kids a chance at becoming readers. Good things happen when children—and adults—read for pleasure.

Paradoxically, while the AFT was busy pushing lessons to fulfill the instrumental purposes of the Common Core and NCTE was busy publishing a book series reassuring teachers they can live with the Common Core, Rotarians were getting a different message from Frank Bures (2013), who reported in the national magazine *Rotarian* on Keith Oatley's research, explaining that "reading more fiction enables you to understand other people better. Fiction is about exploring a range of circumstances and interactions and characters you're likely to meet."

Peter Meyer, Program Manager at the Institute for Public Policy at Roosevelt House at Hunter College and senior fellow at the Thomas B. Fordham Institute, moderated a Roosevelt House discussion between Hunter College Dean of Education David Steiner and Mark Bauerlein, Professor of English at Emory University and author of *The Dumbest Generation: How the Digital Age Stupefies Young Americans and Jeopardizes Our Future*. Noting Steiner's brief tenure as New York Commissioner of Education, Meyer asked him, "As commissioner you got everybody to sign on to the Common Core. Do you have any regrets about any part of that?" (Steiner, 2013).

Steiner replied emphatically, "No. I absolutely think it was the right thing to do...." Although he expressed some reservations about David Coleman's "reading like a detective, writing like an investigative reporter," calling it a forensic approach, Steiner offered no details of his doubts and added, "I was privileged to host one of David's early presentations [Coleman, 2011] in Albany." Privileged, indeed. That's where Coleman insisted that students must be trained to know that "people don't give a shit about what you feel or what you think." Watching this presentation on tape, I was appalled that not one educator in the audience objected.

For me, the eye-opener on school reform as fraud was Clinton Boutwell's *Shell Game: Corporate America's Agenda for Schools* (1997). Boutwell spells out in detail that the need for a greater supply of high-quality workers is a myth perpetuated by corporate vested interest. One case in point: Among the list of the fifteen highest-paid executives in America were those whose companies downsized and laid off workers to increase their profits—IBM, General Motors, Sears, Martin Marietta, General Dynamics, General Electric, RJR Nabisco, Time Warner, ITT, and Unisys. I lived in one of the lovely GE cities "Neutron Jack" Welch downsized into destitution. With lots of highly skilled workers competing for a limited number of jobs, corporate czars can make inordinate demands on workers while reducing salaries and benefits. Boutwell pointed out that educators must take their share of responsibility of the blame for the introduction of business goals into public schools policy—because they "succumbed to accusations that America's schools were not producing a world-class workforce." After all, then-Schools Chancellor Joel Klein hired Welch as chairman of a new academy to train principals. That's why outfits such as the Eli and Edythe Broad Foundation are so fond of getting people from business and the military into school leadership positions: they already know the corporate lingo and the procedures.

Arguing about the content of the Common Core State [*sic*] Standards is a dangerous diversion. The issue here is not which "informational text" (what a pompous, ignorant term, as though fiction and poetry didn't provide critical information) is assigned or which grade gets drilled on apostrophe use. The issue is, who decides? In a democracy, the decision should be local and never allowed to fossilize. The truth of the matter is that universal standards can't apply in a single classroom, never mind across the country. The issue is trusting teachers, trusting kids, and trusting them to find the books they need. The Common Core trusts nothing but computer-delivered and tested programs that train teachers and kids to do what they're told. Although I don't accept the premise of the very existence of these standards, I do have a question for the "leading scholars" of the Validation Committee of the Common Core State [*sic*] Standards. Looking at their very impressive credentials, I don't see any mention of teaching experience. I would ask when was the last time any of them was shut up in a room with twenty-five eight-year-olds—or twelve-year-olds—or seventeen-year-olds.

> In a widely quoted commencement speech at Stanford in 2005, college dropout Steve Jobs advised: You've got to find what you love. And that is as true for your work as it is for your lovers. Your work is going to fill a large part of your life, and the only way to be truly satisfied is to do what you believe is great work. And the only way to do great work is to love what you do. If you haven't found it yet, keep looking. Don't settle.

I've always regarded teaching as an act of love—love combined with skill, intuition, and stamina. Because I've run a website of resistance ever since No Child Left Behind was passed, I get a lot of mail from desperate teachers who say that the love, skill, and intuition no longer count; they're actually a detriment. As the data storm troopers take over, all teachers have left is stamina and desperation. It is with these teachers in mind that I listened to Chris Hedges end a talk at the University of Vermont in March, 2013:

> Living truth keeps the narrative alive. The Powers will keep ratcheting up the horror and our voice keeps the door open, keeps truth alive.

We must tell our stories to keep that door open. Hedges quoted Daniel Berrigan, who said, "We are called to do the good," adding, "Faith is the belief that this good goes somewhere. Buddhists call it karma."

We teachers need to keep the narrative alive, and to save ourselves and the very notion of public education, we need to do more: we must mobilize. Professor of Political Science Frances Fox Piven (2011) advises, "Before people can mobilize for collective action, they have to develop a proud and angry identity and a set of claims that go with that identity. They have to go from being hurt and ashamed to being angry and indignant." That's what my website is about. That's what this chapter is about. But to end on a positive note I'll tell one more story. In early 2013, teachers at Seattle's largest high school, Garfield High, joined together and refused to give a standardized test that served only as a time-waster and distraction from their curriculum. When a retired Florida kindergarten teacher heard about this act of resistance, she called a Seattle pizza shop and ordered five large pizzas with two toppings to be sent to the school.

Let's work to spread resistance and solidarity.

References

Anderson, N. (2011). "Bill Gates (briefly) talks school reform with The Post," *Washington Post: Class Struggle*. 2 Feb. http://voices.washingtonpost.com/class-struggle/2011/02/bill_gates_talks_school_reform.html

Arkin, J. (2012). "Ed Secretary Arne Duncan helps launch ambitious teacher training plan." Medill on the Hill. 21 Feb. http://medillonthehill.net/2012/02/ed-secretary-arne-duncan-helps-launch-ambitious-teacher-training-plan/

ayoungWS. (2013). "WriteSteps 3rd Grade Informative/Explanatory." AFT/TES Share My Lesson, 9 March. (free registration required) http://www.sharemylesson.com/teaching-resource/WriteSteps-3rd-Grade-Informative-Explanatory-50009761/s_cid/?s_cid=SMLNews2621249

Barry, D. (2005). "Are they insane?" *Miami Herald*. 4 Aug.

Bellow, S. (2010) *Letters* (Benjamin Taylor, Ed.). New York: Viking.

Berliner, D. (2012). "Effects of inequality and poverty vs. teachers and schooling on America's youth," Colloquium Series Educational Leadership Studies. 15 Nov. http://www.umassd.edu/media/umassdartmouth/seppce/edleadership/David_Berliner.pdf

Bertin, J. (2013). Letter from National Coalition Against Censorship. February. http://www.ncac.org/board-and-advisors

Blumenstyk, G. (2001). "Knowledge is 'a form of venture capital' for a top Columbia administrator," *Chronicle of Higher Education.* 9 Feb. http://chronicle.com/article/Knowledge-Is-a-Form-of/17565/

Boutwell, C. (1997). *Shell game: Corporate America's agenda for schools.* Bloomington, IN: Phi Delta Kappa Educational Foundation.

Bowles, S., and Ginnis, H. (1976). *Schooling in capitalist America: Educational reform and the contradictions of economic life.* New York: Basic Books.

Bracey, G. (2009). *Education hell: Rhetoric vs reality.* Alexandria, VA: Educational Research Service.

Bures, F. (2013). "The truth about fiction," *The Rotarian.* March. http://www.rotary.org/en/mediaandnews/therotarian/pages/business1303.aspx

Coleman, D. (2011). "Bringing the Common Core to life," speech, New York State Education Building 28 April, 2011. http://usny.nysed.gov/rttt/resources/bringing-the-common-core-to-life.htmltranscript: http://susanohanian.org/show_research.php?id=437

Council of Great City Schools. (n.d.). "From the page to the classroom: Implementing the Common Core State Standards: English Language Arts and Literacy." n.d. video. http://vimeo.com/44521437

Cunningham, R., and Menard, R. (2010). "The green cuisine at Sidwell Friends School." 1 Sept. http://www.sidwell.edu/feen/food/food/index.aspx?linkid=22739&moduleid=651

Dirda, M. (2005). *Book by book: Notes on reading and life.* New York: Henry Holt.

Duncan, A. (2010). "U.S. Education Secretary Arne Duncan issues statement on the release of the President's Council of Advisors on science and technology (Pcast) K-12 STEM Education Report." US Government Press Release. 3 Sept. http://www.ed.gov/news/press-releases/us-education-secretary-arne-duncan-issues-statement-release-presidents-council-a

Duncan, A. (2012). "Fighting the wrong education battle." Askwith Forum Harvard Graduate School of Education, 7 Feb. http://www.ed.gov/news/speeches/fighting-wrong-education-battles.

Duncan, A., and Sebelius, K.(2013). "America's middle class promise starts early," *Huffington Post.* 4 Mar. web. http://www.huffingtonpost.com/sec-kathleen-sebelius/americas-middle-class-pro_b_2805701.html http://www.ed.gov/blog/2013/03/americas-middle-class-promise-starts-early/

Emery, K., and Ohanian, S. (2004). *Why is corporate America bashing our public schools?* Portsmouth, NH: Heinemann.

Gates, B. (2009). "Mosquitos, malaria and education," TED. Feburary. http://www.ted.com/talks/bill_gates_unplugged.html

Gates, M. (2009). "At the National Council of La Raza, speaking on school reform." The Bill and Melinda Gates Foundation. 25 July, 2009. http://www.gatesfoundation.org/media-center/speeches/2009/07/melinda-french-gates-national-council-of-la-raza

Gilbert, I. (nd). "What If . . . ?" Independent Thinking, Ltd. http://www.independentthinking.co.uk/Cool+Stuff/Articles/108.aspx

Golden, D. (2010). "Bill Gates' school crusade," *Bloomberg Business Week.* 15 Jan.

Hedges, C. (2009). *Empire of illusion.* New York: Nation Books, Perseus Book Group.

Hedges, C. (2011). "Where liberals go to feel good," Truthdig. 24 Jan. http://www.truthdig.com/report/item/where_liberals_go_to_feel_good_20110124/

Hedges, C. (2012). "How to think," TruthDig. 9 Jul. http://www.truthdig.com/report/page2/how_to_think_20120709/

Hedges, C. (2013). "Cost of war," speech. University of Vermont. 20 Mar.

Herbert, B. (2009). "Who are we?"*New York Times,* 23 June. http://www.nytimes.com/2009/06/23/opinion/23herbert.html

Krashen, S. (2004). *The power of reading: Insights from the research.* Westport, CT. Libraries Unlimited; Portsmouth, NH: Heinemann.

Krashen, S. (2011). *Free voluntary reading.* Westport, CT. Libraries Unlimited.

Kravosky, M. (2005). "Dubious 'Mozart Effect' remains music to many Americans' ears," *The Stanford Report*. 2 Feb. http://news.stanford.edu/news/2005/february2/mozart-020205.html

Lepore, J. (1998). *The name of war: King Philip's war and the origins of American identity*. New York: Knopf.

Levison, I. (2002). *A working stiff's manifesto: A memoir of thirty jobs I quit, nine that fired me, and three I can't remember*. New York: Soho Press.

Lind, Michael. (2009). "Can Obama be deprogrammed?" Salon.com. 4 August. http://www.salon.com/2009/08/04/neoliberalism_2/

Morrison, B., Eisler, P., and DeBarros, A. (2009). "Old-hen meat fed to pets and schoolkids," *USA Today*. 16 Dec. http://usatoday30.usatoday.com/news/education/2009-12-08-hen-meat-school-lunch_N.htm

Moss, M. (2013). *Salt sugar fat: How the food giants hooked us*. New York: Random House.

Noddings, N. (2008). "All our students thinking," *Education Leadership*. February | Volume 65 | Number 5 http://www.ascd.org/publications/educational-leadership/feb08/vol65/num05/All-Our-Students-Thinking.aspx

Oatley, K. (2010). "Fiction as cognitive and emotional simulation," *New English Review*. http://www.newenglishreview.org/custpage.cfm/frm/67703/sec_id/67703

Obama, B. (2011). "President Obama on education at TechBoston," The White House. 8 March, 2011. http://www.whitehouse.gov/photos-and-video/video/2011/03/09/president-obama-education-techboston

Ohanian, S. (1999) *One size fits few: The folly of educational standards*. Portsmouth, NH: Heinemann.

Ohanian, S. (2001) *Caught in the middle: Nonstandard kids and a killing curriculum*. Portsmouth, NH: Heinemann.

Ohanian, S. (2002) *What happened to recess and why are our children struggling in kindergarten?* New York: McGraw-Hill.

Oliver, M. (2010). "The Riders" in *Swan: Poems and Prose Poems*. Boston: Beacon Press.

Phillips, V. (2010). Speech to the National PTA. 5 June. http://www.gatesfoundation.org/media-center/speeches/2010/06/vicki-phillips-speech-to-the-national-pta

Piven, F. P. (2011). "Mobilizing the jobless," *The Nation*. 11 January. http://www.thenation.com/article/157292/mobilizing-jobless#

Rose, M. (1989). *Lives on the boundary: A moving account of the struggles and achievements of America's educationally underprepared*. New York: Free Press.

Rose, M. (2004). *The mind at work: Valuing the intelligence of the American worker*. New York: Viking.

Rose, M. (2011). "Resolutions someone should make for 2011," blog. 7 Jan. http://mikerosebooks.blogspot.com/2011/01/resolutions-someone-should-make-for.htmlRose

Rothstein, R. (2012). "Prepared commencement address at the Loyola University Chicago School of Education." 10 May. http://www.epi.org/publication/richard-rothstein-commencement-address-loyola-university/.

Schott's Vocab. (2011). "Sheening," *New York Times*. 11 March. http://schott.blogs.nytimes.com/2011/03/11/sheening/

Shierholz, H. (2013). "Workers don't lack skills; they lack work," *Economic Policy Institute*. 6 Jan. http://www.epi.org/publication/workers-dont-lack-skills-lack-work/?utm_source=Economic+Policy+Institute&utm_campaign=9a05d04e26-1_18_2013&utm_medium=e

Sparks, N. (2012). *Novel learning series*®. New York: Grand Central Publishing. http://www.nicholassparks.com/nls

Steiner, D. (2013). "The ELA Common Core Standards: The path to a better educated America?" Institute for Public Policy at Roosevelt House. 28 Feb. video http://roosevelthouse.hunter.cuny.edu/ciep/event/the-ela-common-core-standards-path-to-a-better-educated-america/

Thomas, P. (2011). "Ironic lessons in ed reform from Bill Gates," OpEd News.com. 1 March. http://www.opednews.com/articles/Ironic-Lessons-in-Educatio-by-Paul-Thomas-110301-979.html

Tyson. (2013). Schools K-12. website. http://www.tysonfoodservice.com/Resources-and-Insights/Segments/Schools-K-12.aspxhttp://www.tysonfoodservice.com/Resources-and-Insights/Segments/Schools-K-12.aspx

Uchitelle, L. (2005). "College still counts, though not as much," *New York Times*. 5 Oct. http://www.nytimes.com/2005/10/02/jobs/02Uchitelle.html?ex=1128916800&en=30e132eb47d4298a&ei=5070&emc=eta1

Viall, J. J. (2013). "How many reformers does it take to really fix a school?" A Teacher on Teaching blog. 4 March. http://ateacheronteaching.blogspot.in/2013/03/how-many-reformers-does-it-take-to.html?%20showComment=1363058886667

Warner, M. (2010). "School lunch reform and why it may drive Tyson's dinosaur nuggets to extinction," *CBS Moneywatch*. May 14. http://www.cbsnews.com/8301-505123_162-44040797/school-lunch-reform-and-why-it-may-drive-tysons-dinosaur-nuggets-to-extinction/

Weinstein, A. (2011). "Rick Scott to liberal arts majors: Drop dead." *Mother Jones*. 11 Oct. web. http://www.motherjones.com/mojo/2011/10/rick-scott-liberal-arts-majors-drop-dead-anthropology

CHAPTER THREE

Picking Up the Pieces of Neoliberal Reform Machines in Urban Schools

DENNIS CARLSON

These are (and I cannot mince words here) catastrophic times for public schools—and particularly for urban public schools serving working class and poor youth. The very idea of democratic public education is being emptied of meaning when, in the name of equity and overcoming socioeconomic and racial achievement gaps, reforms are being implemented that actually have the opposite effect. The new privatized system of schooling that is emerging in urban America is organized around regimes of high-stakes testing that are leaving millions of children behind and pushing them out of school. These tests, in turn, are linked to a curriculum driven by an economic "human capital" rationale, designed to prepare young people for a new, more inequitable labor force and social order, with most urban youth positioned as future service industry workers.

We know by now that state reform movements in public education over the past several decades have not led us down a path of democratic progress toward overcoming persistent race- and class-based achievement gaps. Indeed, urban school reforms have played a decisive role in producing, legitimating, and exacerbating achievement gaps. They have, in effect, turned urban public schools into "mis-education" factories, places where cultural capital is "subtracted" from young people rather than added.[1] But high-stakes testing reforms are not just impacting urban youth in these direct ways. To make things worse, these reforms provide a mechanism for privatizing public education in urban districts when schools do not live up to annual yearly progress (AYP) expectations. The machines of urban school reform are quite quickly dismantling the system of public education as we have known it in urban communities and replacing it with a privatized, for-profit system for "skilling" young people for their expected roles in the new global labor market.

All of these interrelated reform discourses and movements that circulate in urban education—from high-stakes testing to privatization—are manifestations of a dominant, or hegemonic, "commonsense," which is to say, they all frame educational aims and responses in terms of a set of core beliefs and values that are typically unquestioned and hence taken for granted as the natural way things are when, in fact, they represent the interests and cultural politics of dominant social and economic groups.[2] This hegemonic commonsense is often referred to in cultural studies as "neoliberalism," the commonsense of global, free market capitalism in a postmodern information age.[3] "Liberalism" in this case is a reference to liberal economic theory in England in the 18th and 19th centuries that supported free market capitalism, regulated only by the "iron hand" of competition and supply and demand, and with only a minimalist role for government.

In some ways, the changes that are occurring now are as dramatic and irrevocable as those that were ushered in by the industrial revolution. They signal a return to the free market ideology as capitalism transforms itself again on a global scale with new digital technologies and information webs and networks, and with labor markets and production now globalized as well. But neo-liberalism is not just a commonsense that stays in the economy, so to speak. Instead, it has been re-territorialized, lifted out of its economic context and applied in only slightly modified form to public institutions such as public schools. As a hegemonic commonsense, it has effectively become "the only game in town," the only way to "think" about not only economic productivity, but also about "productivity" in public schools; and it presents itself as the savior of urban public schools in a time when change is needed.

How do we respond in the face of this commonsense reform discourse, and in the face of this collapse of the democratic promise of public education? That is the question I want to pose in what follows, although I must say at the outset that there is no easy answer, and that these are difficult issues that must continue to be the subject of a "complicated conversation" among progressives.[4] Furthermore, democratic progressive responses will have to be constructed "in progress," and in unique, specific sites and contexts. If the specifics of democratic progressive responses to neoliberal reformism in education must remain vague and unclear at this point, and be left open enough to allow for differences, I argue that they need to be grounded in a common set of ethico-political claims and a call to ethical responsibility. Derrida asks us to begin with these questions: "Whom do we represent? Are we responsible? For what and to whom?"[5] In the context of the current dismantling of public education as we have known it, I want to argue that democratic progressive responses involve responsibility for the yet unfulfilled "promise" of democratic public education and public life. It means keeping that promise alive now in a cynical age in which many have abandoned hope that a truly democratic alternative to current reform discourses is possible, given the elite economic and political forces behind the current reform initiative and given the continuing restructuring of the U.S. economy to produce greater inequality.

Keeping the promise of democratic public education alive does not, however, mean rushing to defend a romanticized image of public education as it has been. The old, centralized bureaucratic system of "schooling" never served most urban youth well. To borrow Joel Spring's term, urban public schools emerged in the progressive era as "sorting machines," sites for sorting and selecting young people in ways that reproduced rather than challenged class and race inequalities.[6] Standardized tests were developed early on in the Progressive era and used by school guidance counselors to begin sorting young people for different curriculum tracks—

vocational, general education, and college preparatory. Although there are very real differences between the sorting machines of urban schooling in the Progressive era and the new sorting machines of neoliberal reform, both have expressed and represented the interests of economic elites more than democratic publics. Those interests have overwhelmingly had to do with using urban public schools to prepare young people to be disciplined and docile workers for the entry-level labor force. To the extent that public education has been legitimated as a "great equalizer," some efforts have been undertaken to increase equality of opportunity through curriculum reforms, although these efforts must remain largely token in a system that still works to reproduce, more than challenge, socioeconomic and racial privilege. Given all this, progressives will need to do more than rally around the "old" system as it comes under attack.

In what follows, I want to explore the possibility of re-launching the idea of democratic public education in new and profoundly unsettling times. Here again, I think Derrida is useful. He argued that a democracy to come could only be imagined by re-working an inheritance of democratic speaking and writing in specific social movements and sites of cultural production. But he also cautioned that, because we are inheritors, "that should not mean we receive something solid, unified, and already formed as an inheritance."[7] The utility of an inheritance "can only consist in the injunction to reaffirm by choosing." To choose is to "filter, select, criticize…[and] sort out among several of the possibilities which inhabit the same injunction."[8] Through such a process, an inheritance becomes a living memory, open to being reworked and relaunched in new times on a new cultural terrain. That cultural terrain has now been thoroughly reworked by neoliberal reform discourses and machines. Thus, a democratic progressive response to neoliberalism will need to use the new technologies created by global capitalism. These include the global information grid, networking, and personal computer and cell phone technologies (first, to resist neoliberal reforms; and second, to begin creating a democratic counter-hegemonic movement organized around networks of not-for-profit, public charter schools) connected through new digital technologies to broader interpretive communities. They, in turn, should be engaged in practicing equity and diversity and mobilizing to advance democratic aims through the renewal of public education.

Finally, a democratic progressive discourse on the re-launching of public education must link educational renewal to economic renewal and to greater equity in income and wealth in America. Everything we know about the relationship between socioeconomic background and educational attainment suggests that we will not get very far in overcoming persistent achievement gaps in American education without policies that begin to counter the increasing income inequality in the economy and labor force. This makes good sense, and it is something we have known now for some time.[9] Yet it is not part of the commonsense of neoliberalism, and not part of the conversation as it has been framed by neoliberal reform discourses. It is a truth that is an invisible presence—one the neo-liberal reform discourse goes out of its way not to see in order not to make visible the elephant in the room.

The Tools of Neoliberalism and the Achievement Gap

To better appreciate how neoliberal reform discourse works, and with what effects, we have to recognize that every discourse is also a practice, not just "talk," and that every practice is mediated by technology. Foucault referred, for example, to the prison as organized by a discourse on criminality and delinquency that produces the criminal and the delinquent as an effect of power, with the prison (like the school, he argued) arranged as a technology of power, a "pan-optic" apparatus for producing bodies as criminal bodies subject to regimes of discipline and confinement.[10] Much the same can be said of the "machines" or technologies of urban school-ing in a neoliberal age. That is, they produce student bodies as underachieving bodies, needing close surveillance and an individualized regime of remediation to overcome their deficiencies.[11]

These machines include state and district mandates for high-stakes testing, test data re-porting and analysis, test-related curriculum materials and instructional planning systems, teacher accountability and "value-added" assessment programs, remediation plans for students identified as "at risk," and so on. These reform technologies, or machines, participate in a com-mon project; and they also are undermined by common contradictions that cannot totally be resolved within neoliberal reform discourse. These contradictions drive the system toward crisis and provide an opening for democratic progressives to provide a coherent alternative (although this must remain a potential at this point, since both Republican and Democratic educational policy remain neoliberal). The machines of neoliberalism may be classified according to their aims as labor power machines, quantification of quality machines, cultural deficit machines, and "vulture capital" or privatizing machines. All work together to advance the hegemonic project in urban education so that they cannot really be analyzed in isolation from one another, although I want to take them up separately here.

Labor power machines are state policy documents and curriculum materials and texts, along with tracking and ability grouping practices, designed to prepare young people to be workers in various strata of the labor force. In neoliberal discourse this means preparing young people to be workers in an age of transnational capitalism and globalizing labor markets. This is an overt human capital rationale for the role of public education in a globalizing, economically competitive age, which does away with the language of democracy and democratic citizenry almost entirely. No longer is "learning to labor" the hidden or covert curriculum of schooling.[12] It has become the overt and only purpose of schooling in a neoliberal age. As Hardt and Negri observe: "No one could accuse the current versions of the human capital rationale of subtlety or deception about the aims and processes of education that they presuppose."[13]

The grand, if always flawed, project of a democratic public education, i.e., to prepare criti-cal and informed citizens to participate in an active public life and public dialogue on issues both local and national—citizens who would make and keep democracy as a way of life—is abandoned for a project of education for economic functionalism, of preparing young people in this case with "21st-century skills" for a "21st-century workforce." This overt human capital logic has been around, of course, at least since *A Nation At Risk* (1983), the report of President Ronald Reagan's Commission on Excellence in Education, which argued that, in a globalizing labor market, the U.S. was at risk of losing economic supremacy if it could not keep up with Japan and other nations investing in a "high-tech" workforce.

The curriculum that emerged out of the reform movement that followed was actually not about preparing everyone to be a high-tech worker since, in the new "post-Fordist" economy, more service industry jobs were being created than high-skill, high-tech, or managerial/profes-sional jobs. Consequently, and following the human capital rationale, students expected to enter the new service industry as entry-level workers are now prepared with basic functional literacy and math skills—the so-called "basic skills" tested on state proficiency exams for high school graduation. Meanwhile, the college-bound track is being reorganized around the kind of skills the new high-tech computer-based companies like Microsoft and Apple seek to create new products, new software, and new ideas.

The new discourse on "knowledge workers" as the new generators of surplus value or in business discourse, value added) is pervasive in U.S. educational policy and finds expression in powerful collaborative partnerships between public education, business, and government leaders such as the Partnership for 21st Century Skills, a policy-making collaborative that includes representatives from the U.S. Department of Education, the NEA, AOL Time Warner Foundation, Apple Computer, Cable in the Classroom, Cisco Systems, Dell Computer Corporation, and Microsoft Corporation. According to the Partnership for 21st Century Skills, the overarching skills needed by 21st-century workers include the "4C's": critical thinking and problem solving, communication, collaboration, and creativity and innovation. The prototypical worker who is the focus of much of the "21st-century skills" discourse is a college graduate who is high-tech "savvy," and according to at least one text, his or her work emphasizes creativity and innovation as expressed through "work on unsolved problems"; the generation of "theories and models; a willingness to take risks; and to "pursue promising ideas and plans." While these are presented as skills all workers will need in the new labor force, and consequently as "core" skills for all students, they are also presented in conjunction with a developmental theory so that "creativity and innovation skills" at the entry level may be exhibited through a capacity to "internalize given information" based on the assumption that "someone else has the answer or knows the truth." Collaboration skills at the entry level might entail "dividing responsibility to create a finished product."[14] Both "entry-level" and "high-skill" students and workers are, in this schema, knowledge workers, engaged in what Hardt and Negri call "immaterial" labor. What is "immaterial" is not the labor itself, but rather the product (which is digitized and circulated within a virtual community).[15] In order to roughly prepare young people for these new conditions of work in the economy, schools are making learning a form of immateriality as students are plugged into computer-programming systems and digital technologies to produce output data, including test scores.

Most urban students, our policy makers have decided, are going to be entering the vastly expanding service industry, where basic math and English literacy skills are expected of workers and immaterial labor involves coding and entering data into given programs. From the perspective of economic and policy elites, urban public schools have not being doing a very good job at their assigned role of preparing young people for this new world of work. For example, many urban schools do not have enough computers and other digital media, so that students are not adequately computer literate when they graduate and have to be taught these skills on the job. Consequently, groups such as the Gates Foundation have been able to argue with some success that a system of for-profit "public" charter schools, outfitted with the latest computer technologies and with instruction much more computer-based and monitored, would do a better job of teaching basic skills than "failing" public schools have. That remains to be seen since the problems urban schools face run far deeper than a lack of the latest digital media and have to do with the alienation of urban youth being prepared for a very bleak future of underemployment, poverty, and social abandonment. There is no "good" system for preparing young people for such a future, no way of doing it without facing student resistance (even if it is self-defeating resistance). That remains the central contradiction of neoliberal labor power machines, along with the fact that as more White youth face the same, or almost the same, economic future as Black and Brown youth, they forge new, more socially and politically conscious alliances (as is happening, for example, through hip-hop).

A second major cluster of neoliberal machines might be called "quantification of quality" machines, a term I borrow from the cultural studies theorist Roland Barthes.[16] For Barthes, one of the ways that capitalism works to establish the playing field for institutional life is by reducing all discussions of quality to a quantifiable indicator, i.e., a number. This is a reflection of the reduction of all qualities to the "bottom line" in the business world, that is, profits measured in dollars-and-cents terms. Capitalism drives institutions to maximize profit (or what passes for profit, such as test score gains) while lowering costs (primarily labor costs). This basic framework is a driving force wherever cost-efficient systems of instruction are being devised to increase test scores while lowering expenditures per pupil. Within such a system, quantitative data on student progress in various skill areas is the new bottom line. In this "audit culture," as Michael Apple has written, "only that which is measurable is important," an attitude that "has caused some of the most creative and critical practices that have been developed [in schools]... to be threatened."[17] By treating standardized test scores as if they are the holy grail in education, quantification of quality machines encourage what sociologists call "goal displacement." Producing test scores according to expectations for annual yearly progress (AYP) becomes the real goal in urban schools, for both teachers and administrators and for political leaders, rather than actually engaging young people in culturally relevant, critical, and creative learning experiences.

A good example of such goal displacement is represented in the so-called "Houston Miracle" of the 1990s, and the "miracles" that have followed in urban school districts, each based on the claim to have dramatically raised achievement levels. While governor of Texas, George W. Bush worked closely with corporate leadership to overhaul the state's system of public instruction to bring urban school districts into alignment with the latest approaches to cost-effective basic skills instruction, tied to high-stakes testing. Houston was much touted by the governor and other political leaders as an exemplary model of school reform based on holding teachers, students, and administrators accountable for raising test scores. The district reported steadily rising passing rates on the new Texas Assessment of Academic Skills (TAAS) test and appeared to be making remarkable progress in eliminating the achievement gap between White and Black and Latina/o students. When Bush became president, he brought with him as new education secretary Houston's superintendent, Rod Paige.

The "No Child Left Behind" law signed by President Bush in January 2002 gave public schools twelve years (until 2014) to match the progress made in Houston's schools in narrowing socioeconomic and racial achievement gaps. Yet, when the *New York Times* investigated the "Houston miracle," it quickly became apparent that the district had engaged in a "rampant undercounting of school dropouts," along with an over-reporting of how many high school graduates were college-bound. Although 88 percent of Houston's student body was Black and Latina/o, few left high school "college ready," because while the school district claimed its curriculum was "college preparatory" for all students, the emphasis was on "minimum skills" rather than what colleges expected in a college preparatory education. It also turned out that gains made on the TAAS were not transferable to other standardized tests of academic achievement, which indicated that students were being narrowly prepared for one version of one test.[18]

Aside from the goal displacement that high-stakes testing machines promote, they actually have the effect of subtracting cultural capital from urban youth rather than adding to their cultural capital. Despite proclaimed intents, high-stakes testing has most often been used to hold back urban students rather than help them get ahead. Grade retention is a classic example of a "well-intentioned" reform that has had these effects. As the cult of high-stakes testing has taken hold in urban school reform, testing has begun as early as kindergarten; and many states now have laws that require young people be held back if they do not pass a high-stakes test at the end of the third grade. State officials are quick to point out that these laws are not meant to hold anyone back. Instead, they are presumably meant to promote intervention and remediation at an early age so that, by the time students finish the third grade, they will be at "grade level" in reading and math. Furthermore, these same officials will tell you (as they have told me) that research indicates that, if students are not reading and doing math at grade level by the end of the third grade, they will fall further behind their classmates in subsequent years. If this is true, it is also true that holding them back only makes matters worse.

A recent summary of evidence on grade retention in the U.S. concludes that "there are no benefits to student retention over promotion. Some studies reveal negative effects of grade retention, including lower academic achievement, higher socio-emotional maladjustment, and increased risk for school withdrawal."[19] Other analyses of the data on grade retention have focused on its discriminatory effect on poor youth of color. According to a review of the data by Hauser, Pager, and Solon, "by age 9, the odds of grade-retardation among African-American and Hispanic youth are 50 percent larger than among White youth," with most of this gap explained by economic inequalities." Writing in 2000, the authors warn that "the recent movement toward high stakes testing for promotion could magnify race-ethnic differentials in retention."[20] That indeed appears to be the case. If we now know the effects of grade retention are counter to its proclaimed intent, then something is wrong; and we must begin to question if overcoming achievement gaps is really what neoliberal reform discourses and machines are about—all of which creates a legitimation crisis in the system.

On a broader level, the failure of the machines of neoliberal reform to overcome or even significantly narrow class and race-based achievement gaps in public education—and in fact to widen these gaps, especially for poor urban youth—represents the failure of a commonsense cultural deficit theory of urban youth. Once we begin to define whole population of youth in terms of their deficiencies rather than their potentialities, and we start to talk about the need for remediation to compensate for their linguistic and cultural deficiencies, then (even if we think we are trying to help them get ahead) we cannot help but set them up for failure. In sum, we begin to lower our expectations for them and define them as at risk of failure and dropping out. Not surprisingly, perhaps, these collective institutional expectations become self-fulfilling. Student alienation, along with punitive high-stakes testing machines, sustain a culture of dropping-out.

These "failures" of urban school reform are ironically used to close schools that are not making adequate progress to raise test scores, and they are often replaced by for-profit public charter schools. Consequently, we can think of neoliberal machines as including "vulture capitalism" machines, picking up the pieces of a system of urban schooling that is being dismantled and creating in its place a new system without teacher unions or public oversight, and with test scores as the bottom line—even if these test scores will continue to mean little in the way of real learning or achievement. Such a privatized system of urban schooling will be even more narrowly focused on cost-effective instructional technologies and the teaching of economically functional, "basic" literacy and math skills; and we can expect socioeconomic and racial achievement gaps in public schools to widen further under such a system.

Picking Up the Pieces

What makes good democratic sense in responding to this bad sense of neoliberal reform? I want to conclude by pointing to three different types of responses, and suggest that each plays an important role in forging a counter-discourse on democratic educational renewal. The first of these is organized resistance. Over the past several years, resistance has been organized around a number of actions: teachers, often through their unions but also through social networks, have resisted teacher union-busting laws and stood up in opposition to high-stakes testing. Teachers have built alliances with parents in supporting an "opt out" movement against high-stakes testing. Teachers, with the support of many parents and students, went on strike in Chicago to resist school closings and for-profit charter schools. Teachers at a high school in Seattle refused to administer the state's high-states exam and won support throughout the nation. All of this is beginning to have an important educative role in changing public awareness of whose interests are being served by current reform models, and such movements link resistance in education to broader mobilized resistances against neoliberal hegemony that most recently has taken the form of Occupy Wall Street.

A number of critical theorists on the democratic left have argued that these types of resistance make use of the tools or machines of neoliberalism—the digital media and networking capacities—to work against the new "empire." Most notably perhaps, Hardt and Negri have argued that resistance to neoliberal hegemony is taking the form of the networked "multitude," mobilized through what is now a full-matrix global network of information flow that cannot effectively be policed since it has no center of power and communication can flow along an almost infinite number of paths. The multitude is to be imagined as a "swarm of ants or bees," as an "amorphous multiplicity" capable of striking at any time at any place, then dispersing again and becoming invisible to power.[21] During a "swarming," as with the Occupy Wall Street movement, a "swarm intelligence" begins to develop out of the multiplicity of communications; and this intelligence is capable of becoming more educated and knowledgeable, of overcoming its mis-education and realizing its fuller potential through re-education. Certainly, part of this re-education involves a recognition of the global, and simultaneously local, nature of the battle for the democratization of public life. Through circulation and travel across borders, both as embodied and virtual travelers, the multitude begins to develop an ethic of solidarity across boundaries and a language of a new "transversal" democratic movement that is postcolonial and hybrid. As the battle becomes globalized, it is also finding a basis for solidarity in collective action around class, for class struggles seem to be the most basic common denominator. As neo-liberalism has been the hegemonic discourse of the capitalist class, so it is mobilizing a global resistance that is heavily class-based, that takes on the capitalist class (the "one percent") as the enemy of democratization.

We might say that the multitude swarmed in Madison, Wisconsin, in February and March 2011, to occupy the Capitol in opposition to Governor Walker's anti-teacher union "budget repair bill;" and that "swarming" provides a good example of both the power and limitations of this type of resistance. Although teachers and their police and firefighter allies ultimately did not win the fight, they made a powerful statement. When word of the bill's likely passage got out, teachers and other public workers and their friends communicated through Facebook, Twitter, and email to announce a rally at the Capitol on February 15, which subsequently attracted 10,000 people. The governor had expected the usual resignation among teachers; instead he got activist teachers—and teachers who were learning how to network with others to increase their collective strength. For example, when the school superintendent threatened to fire any Madison teachers who "skipped school" to attend the protest, doctors from hospitals in the city set up a booth near the Capitol to provide "sick" teachers with medical notes covering their absence. At its peak, upwards of 100,000 people joined the multitude at the Capitol in solidarity with teachers.[22] The limitation of such resistance is that it is not accompanied by a coherent democratic counter-discourse to neo-liberalism, other than full funding of the current system; and the movement in Wisconsin did not effectively link the struggles of public employees with other workers, or with other education battles such as gender equity in schools and the rights of LGBT youth.

This is where a second response is needed: the forging of a progressive counter-discourse that can serve as a basis for re-launching democratic public education in new times. To some extent, this entails re-articulating neoliberal commonsense themes within a new, democratic discourse. As Michael Apple has argued, there is always some good sense along with bad sense in a hegemonic commonsense.[23] Otherwise, it would not have such a broad public appeal. The recent "value-added" reform discourse provides a good case in point. On the one hand, it makes good sense to expect that a democratic public education would add to young people's social and cultural capital so that they have more opportunities in life and more freedom to choose a life path regardless of race, class, gender, or sexual orientation. But this good sense becomes nonsense within the context of neoliberal reform discourse. The expansive, democratic meaning of "value-added" is reduced to a narrow means-ends, technical rationality. Even more damaging perhaps, once teachers and administrators learn to think "value-added" through this narrowly pragmatic lens, they also may come to believe that their primary "business" is adding value to the labor power of future entry-level workers so that they are at once more productive and disciplined. They are encouraged to forget that democratic education should be about something more.

To re-articulate the language of "value-added" with a progressive discourse would entail thinking of value differently. Certainly, it makes sense that democratic public schools should prepare young people for the world of work and gainful employment, without at the same time, sorting and channeling them for rungs in an inequitable labor force. Aside from a culturally relevant curriculum and a deep grounding in cultural histories and traditions, democratic public education is about adding values of equity, social justice, and human freedom to young people's lives as well as actively developing their civic and community engagement skills. These are the values that need to be added through a democratic education, and they cannot be quantified through standardized testing.

This forging of a new democratic discourse on the renewal of public education, in turn, is dependent upon building a broad-based democratic movement for change, linked to a political party that is capable of affecting change in the state—the third necessary response. As Antonio Gramsci argued, the "world outlook" of the party is essential in creating the conditions for a genuinely democratic "public spirit." The party is to be imagined as a "cell containing the germs of collective will," as an "awakener" that creates the conditions for the "public spirit" to emerge.[24] Slavoj Zizek has observed that, in the last days of the Soviet Bloc, multitudes did emerge throughout the Eastern Bloc. They were made up of a multiplicity of ideological-political orientations, including religious conservatives, human rights groups, business "liberals," and leftist trade unions. Those multitudes functioned well as long as they were united in opposition to the Party and the state apparatus, "but once they found themselves in power, the game was over," because they had no party ideology or coherent theory of how to govern.[25] Without a party that has a coherent counter-hegemonic discourse and strategy for rebuilding America, the multitude may slip into anarchistic tendencies and become fragmented and fractured.

The relationship between the multitude and the genuinely democratic party must be a dialectical one, with the party serving as an apparatus for translating the hopes, discontents, fears, and desires of the multitude into a counter-hegemonic leadership discourse and set of policy initiatives. It must lead the multitude toward a deeper and fuller understanding of what it will take to democratize public life and public education. Perhaps only through such a process is a multitude able to become a counter-hegemonic agent of a democratic will to power, capable of taking control of the state from neoliberal and neoconservative forces. If such a dialectic between the multitude and the party can be achieved, then perhaps the new global and local resistances will not be futile; for they would propose a discourse of democratic governmentality rather than critique and resistance alone.

What might such a democratic governmentality mean for public education? Certainly, any system of public education that is rebuilt out of the ashes must be something much different from the corporate bureaucratic system of schooling that has left its stamp on the educational imagination in the U.S. since the early 20th century. It would need to be a radically decentered and networked system, situating both teachers and students within evolving, transitory, transversal, poly-vocal learning communities, which emerge around pragmatic actions and projects and then disappear again into the environment. The school and the university would become nodes on a matrix, linking teachers and students to ever-expanding communities that bring the local and the global together. This implies, I believe, support for some system of public charter school networks and alliances, with teachers and students linked in synergistic ways to educate for social justice, human and animal rights, equity, and diversity. Teaching would need to be reconfigured within a set of relationships and networks in which knowledge is no longer unified or predetermined, but rather constructed and reconstructed within diverse language games and networks of dialogue and action.

Public schools, as sites for the induction of young people into interpretive communities and networks, would be situated within overlapping fields of local, regional, national, and transnational governmentality; and they would bring teachers and students together across overlapping political and cultural contexts.[26] At this point, networks of fully funded, public, non-profit charter schools might provide a counter-space for the development of such new forms of governmentality and dramatically new approaches to curriculum and pedagogy attuned to the changing times.[27] Teacher unions and professional associations might even organize networks of charter schools and learning communities—both virtual and material—to experiment with new forms of curriculum, pedagogy, and assessment that are more student-centered and culturally relevant.

However, these changes must remain just a possibility so long as they do not address widening income gaps and a corresponding decline in real equality of opportunity in America. In a system of deepening inequalities, it hardly makes sense to talk about democratic public education as something realizable now. As Derrida argued, in such a context it is only possible to talk of a "democracy to come," as a promise we make to the future, even though "the event of the promise takes place here, now, in the singularity of the here-now."[28] Here and now progressives can argue that, to genuinely overcome achievement gaps and leave no child behind, we will have to do much more than create better standardized tests or more effective methods of weeding out incompetent teachers. We will need to challenge the material structures, and the relations of power, that produce achievement gaps and that insure that millions of young people still get left behind.

Notes

1. See Carter G. Woodson, *The Mid-Education of the Negro* (New York: Tribeca, 2013, first published in 1933), and Angela Valenzuela, *Subtractive Schooling: U.S.-Mexican Youth and the Politics of Caring* (Albany: State University of New York Press, 1999).

2. The term "commonsense" is associated with Antonio Gramsci, whose theory of hegemony I am most indebted to in organizing my perspective on urban school reforms. See Gramsci, *Prison Notebooks* (New York: International Publishers, 1971).

3. Dennis Carlson, "Neoliberalism and Urban School Reform: A Cincinnati Case Study," in *The Destructive Path of Neoliberalism: An International Examination of Urban Education*, ed. Bradley Porfilio and Curry Malott (New York: Sense Publishers, 2008), 81–102.

4. I take the term "complicated conversation" from William Pinar, *What Is Curriculum Theory*, 2nd ed. (New York: Routledge, 2011). See also Dennis Carlson, "The Question Concerning Curriculum Theory," *Journal of the American Association for the Advancement of Curriculum Studies* (online journal http://www.uwstout.edu/soe/jaaacs/), 1 (2005).

5. Jacques Derrida, *Eyes of the University* (Stanford, CA: Stanford University Press, 2004), 83. For my critical reading of *Eyes of the University* and the responsibility of education faculty, see Dennis Carlson, "AESA Presidential Address: Conflict of the Faculties: Democratic Progressivism in the Age of 'No Child Left Behind,'" *Educational Studies* 43 (2008): 94–113.

6. Joel Spring, *The Sorting Machine Revisited: National Educational Policy Since 1945* (London: Longman, 1988).

7. Jacques Derrida, *The Work of Mourning*, trans. Pascale-Anne Brault and Michael Nass (Chicago: University of Chicago Press, 2001), 94

8. Derrida, *The Work of Mourning*, 40

9. See Christopher Jencks, *Inequality: A Reassessment of the Effect of Family and Schooling in America* (New York: Harper, 1981). Based on a detailed analysis of the available data, Jencks and his team concluded that the greatest thing that could be done to equalize educational outcomes by socioeconomic and racial background would be to guarantee every American a livable income.

10. Michel Foucault, *Discipline and Punish: The Birth of the Prison*, 2nd ed. (New York: Vintage, 1995).

11. The word "machines" is used in this expansive way by Gilles Deleuze and Felix Guattari in *Anti-Oedipus: Capitalism and Schizophrenia* (London: Penguin Classic, 2009).

12. This is a reference to Paul Willis' classic ethnography, *Learning to Labour: How Working Class Kids Get Working Class Jobs* (London: Ashgate, 1978). From the perspective of Willis and other neo-Marxists in the 1970s, learning to labor was the "hidden curriculum" of schooling, not the overt curriculum. That has changed with neoliberal reforms.

13. Michael Hardt and Antonio Negri. *Empire* (Cambridge, MA: Harvard University Press, 2000), 143.

14. Marlene Scardamalia, John Bransford, Bob Kozma, and Edys Queilmalz, "New Assessments and Environments for Knowledge Building," in *Assessment and Teaching of 21st Century Skills*, ed. Patrick Griffin, Barry McGaw, and Esther Care (New York: Springer, 2012), 248.

15. Cesare Casarino and Antonio Negri, *In Praise of the Common: A Conversation on Philosophy and Politics* (Minneapolis: University of Minnesota Press, 2008), 250–251.

16. Roland Barthes, *Mythologies* (New York: Hill and Wang, 1972), 153–154.

17. Michael Apple, "Education, Markets, and Audit Culture," *International Journal of Educational Policies* 1 no. 1 (2007), 4.

18. Diana Schemo and Ford Fessenden, "Gains in Houston Schools: How Real Are They?" *New York Times*, December 3, 2003, sec. A, 1, 27. See also my discussion of these and other findings in Dennis Carlson, "Are We Making Progress? The Discursive Construction of Progress in the Age of "No Child Left Behind," in Dennis Carlson and C. P. Gause (eds.), *Keeping the Promise: Essays on Leadership, Democracy, and Education*, ed. Dennis Carlson and C. P. Gause (New York: Peter Lang, 2007), 3–26.

19. Shane Jimerson and Jacqueline Brown, "Grade Retention," in *International Guide to Student Achievement*, ed. John Hattie and Eric Anderman (New York: Routledge, 2012), 141–142.

20. Robert Hauser, Devah Pager, and Solon Simmons, "Race-Ethnicity, Social Background, and Grade Retention," Center for Demography and Ecology, University of Wisconsin-Madison, Working Paper No. 2000-08 (2000), 2.

21. Michael Hardt and Antonio Negri, *Multitude* (Cambridge, MA: Harvard University Press, 2004), 56–57.

22. See Andrew Kersten, *The Battle for Wisconsin: Scott Walker and the Attack on the Progressive Tradition* (New York: Hill & Wang, 2011).

23. Michael Apple. *Educating the Right Way: Markets, Standards, God, and Inequality* (New York: Routledge, 2006).

24. Antonio Gramsci, (2007). *The Modern Prince and Other Writings* (New York: Synergy International of the Americas, 2007), 146–147.

25. Slavoj Zizek, "The Ideology of the Empire and Its Traps," in *Empire's New Clothes: Reading Hardt & Negri*, ed. Paul Passavant and Jodi Dean (New York: Routledge, 2004), 255–266.

26. Alan Luke, "Teaching After the Market: From Commodity to Cosmopolitan," *Teacher College Record* 7 (2004): 1429–1430.

27. I explore these issues further in Dennis Carlson, "Working the Contradictions: The Obama Administration's Educational Policy and Democracy to Come," in *The Phenomenon of Obama and the Agenda for Education: Can Hope Audaciously Trump Neoliberalism?* ed. Paul Carr and Brad Porfilio (Charlotte, NC: Information Age, 2011), 287–297; and "Democratic Public Education in the Age of Empire and the Multitude," in *Educating for Democratic Consciousness*, ed. Ali Abdi and Paul Carr (New York: Peter Lang, 2011), 108–122.

28. Jacques Derrida, *Negotiations: Interventions and Interviews, 1971–2001* (Stanford, CA: Stanford University Press, 2002), 180.

Contexts and Policy Implications

"We live in a society where every day millions of people are denied what should be their rights to respectful employment at a respectful wage, health care, decent housing, schools that are well funded and respectful both to the teachers and students who go to them and to the communities in which they are based, a respectful treatment of their histories and cultures, and a government that doesn't lie."
 —Michael W. Apple

"When I was a boy on the Mississippi River there was a proposition in a township there to discontinue public schools because they were too expensive. An old farmer spoke up and said if they stopped the schools they would not save anything, because every time a school was closed a jail had to be built."
 —Mark Twain

"The school is the last expenditure upon which America should be willing to economize."
 —Franklin Delano Roosevelt

CHAPTER FOUR

Subverting Learning and Undermining Democracy

A Structural and Political Economy Analysis of the Standards Movement

LAWRENCE C. STEDMAN

The standards movement has failed. In spite of a generation of efforts, from *A Nation at Risk* and Goals 2000 to state testing programs and No Child Left Behind (NCLB), little improvement has occurred (Stedman, 2010, 2011a, 2011b). Achievement has generally stagnated, especially at the high school level; most minority achievement gaps remain as large as they were in the late 1980s and early 1990s; and students still struggle in the major subjects. Civic literacy and workplace preparation remain poor. Class and racial inequalities—and segregation—remain vast and vexing problems. Even in the two areas where the standards movement achieved some success—lower-grade math achievement and academic course-taking in high school—there are grounds for skepticism. The gains were largely superficial, other forces such as teaching-to-the-test and social promotion were responsible, and serious deficiencies remain.

Beyond failing to improve achievement, standards-based accountability systems have constricted curricula and warped school culture. A new Taylorism and a ritualistic compliance with mandates are undermining learning and the development of civic literacy (Stedman, 2010). Testing and grades, not learning, drive instruction. School climates have worsened, with the effects stratified by race and class. During most of the standards era, dropout rates grew and reading of all types declined—NCLB has made things worse, not better. A fixation on its reading and math testing is short-changing social studies and the arts. Proficiency-based curricula and bureaucratic schooling are devastating the quality of life inside schools. Teachers have joined students in leaving school and are now dropping out at alarming rates.

It is time for a radically different approach, but one grounded in an understanding of why the standards movement failed. In part one of this analysis, I describe the movement's faulty premises and its failure to address the historical and structural problems of schooling. In part two, I examine its connections with the neoliberal reform project and capitalism. I describe the root problems of NCLB and Race to the Top and propose an alternative, democratic reform agenda.

Part I: An Educational and Historical Diagnosis

Faulty Premises

The standards movement was founded on two fictions: that there had been a major achievement decline in the 1960s and 1970s and that schools were responsible. Its proponents argued schools had embraced a soft, student-centered pedagogy, shifted from excellence to equity, and lowered standards (Copperman, 1978; Hirsch, 1987; Itzkoff, 1994; Ravitch, 1995). Repulsed by the social movements of the 1960s, many traditionalists were dismayed by an apparent loss of American excellence. The great test score decline, however, was largely a myth (Stedman, 1998, 2003). NAEP scores were generally level; College Board achievement scores had gone up in English, the sciences, and foreign languages; and a short version of the SAT, the PSAT, given to nationally representative samples, showed roughly flat trends.

While it was fashionable to blame open classrooms for the decline, few children experienced them and elementary school scores were stable or rising in the 1970s (Stedman & Kaestle, 1987). Using faulty evidence, *A Nation at Risk* decried a "curricular smorgasbord" in our high schools, but better data showed the claim was unjustified (Stedman & Smith, 1983), while the notorious SAT decline, caused mostly by demographic changes, also could not be linked to school changes (Stedman, 1998, 2011b). Investigators found that traditional high schools had SAT declines as large as those in experimental schools. Even the Advisory Panel on the SAT Decline (1977) concluded that political upheavals were the only way to explain the "suddenness and concentration" of the decline (pp. 37–38)—half came in just three years in the early 1970s (p. 6). The nation's students had been deeply affected by the Vietnam War, assassinations of popular figures, "burning cities," and Watergate (pp. 37–38).

Historical Myopia: A Century of Ignorance

Those who pushed the standards agenda often romanticized the schooling of earlier eras. Yet, even before the supposed retreat from standards in the late 1960s and 1970s, achievement was poor (Stedman, 2003). Nationwide assessments from the 1940s through the early 1960s revealed major deficiencies in student and adult knowledge (Stedman, 1998, 2011b). In 1960, for example, Project Talent studied a representative sample of 440,000 public high school students and found that seniors had trouble with passages from such classic writers as Austen, Conrad, and Verne and articles from *Look*, *Reader's Digest*, and *Time* (Flanagan, 1962, pp. 212–213). The typical student knew "relatively little about art" (Flanagan et al., 1964, p. 3–113)—only about half knew who painted the *Mona Lisa*—and most did not know basic constitutional legal terms (Flanagan et al., 1964, p. 3–114). In 1964, in the first international math assessment, even the country's best students—high school seniors in college-preparatory math programs—had major problems. They scored only 20% correct and were last by a large margin (Stedman, 2011b).

During the 1950s, Gallup repeatedly found serious weaknesses in adults' general knowledge. In 1955, for example, high school graduates now aged 25–36 averaged only 34–65%

on questions about domestic events, public figures, history, the humanities, geography, and science (Hyman, Wright, & Reed, 1975, p. 133). Those who have promoted certain types of cultural and academic literacy would be astounded by the gaps in their knowledge. Most high school graduates did *not* know who wrote *A Midsummer-Night's Dream* or who composed the "Messiah" (Hyman et al., 1975, Appendix B, Table 2.5). Only 61% knew who created Tom Sawyer or what the capital of Spain was. Only about half knew that Montana bordered Canada. A meager 8% knew that Rubens was a painter and only 6% which planet is closest to the Sun.

The difficulties predate the life-adjustment movement of the 1950s, the bête noir of earlier critics (Bestor, 1985; Hofstadter, 1962). In the early 1940s, first-year college students floundered so badly on a *New York Times* survey of basic historical information that Congress called for an investigation of the nation's schools (Fine, 1943). In the 1920s and 1930s, high school and college students were doing poorly across the curriculum (Learned & Wood, 1938; Stedman, 2003).

Some standards advocates took an even longer view. They blamed the 1918 Cardinal Principles of Secondary Education report for a century-long retreat from academic excellence (Hirsch, 1987; Ravitch, 1995). Low achievement, however, was widespread even before then (Stedman, 2003, 2011b). During the early years of the 20th century, high school students struggled greatly in math and social studies and even the tiny, elite group of college-bound seniors regularly failed their College Board entrance exams (Fiske, 1920). Such weak achievement helped fuel the growth of progressive education because it showed that traditional schooling, with its emphasis on tests, facts, and memorization, was failing.

The Structural and Political Roots of the Failure

Poor achievement, then, is a long-standing problem and not one caused by a modern collapse of standards. While social forces beyond the school, such as anti-intellectualism and consumerism, sustain it, its persistence also implicates the deep structure of schooling: assembly-line teaching, encyclopedic curricula, test-based accountability, and impersonal institutions. Textbooks and chalk-and-talk methods have dominated teaching for over a century. Schools remain obsessively concerned with measuring, controlling, and classifying students. Most high schools still have madcap 40-minute periods and excessive teacher workloads—120 students or more—that hamper sustained, engaging instruction. The international assessments have repeatedly shown that the United States has superficial teaching and a shallow curriculum (Stedman, 1997).

Ignoring these realities produced misguided school reform. In the 1980s, the major reform reports exaggerated the test-score decline and advocated a return to old-fashioned practices and standards. In the early 1990s, Goals 2000 and the Improving America's Schools Act (IASA)—and later NCLB—echoed and legislated their appeals. Under the sway of the conservative restoration, politicians promoted work intensification and accountability in schools (Apple, 2000; Shor, 1992). It would be a mistake, though, to construe this as simply a conservative effort. The political shift to the right spanned both parties, and both neoconservatives and neoliberals supported the standards movement (Apple, 2006). Yet, in spite of a bipartisan national effort over the past quarter-century, standards-based policies have failed to produce academic quality.

The reform effort was deeply flawed from the outset. Policy makers and educators conceived of standards in narrow test-score terms. They focused on benchmarking student performance while ignoring school culture, student engagement, and physical conditions. Even if one embraces their necessity, standards could have been much richer and multi-dimensional. There could have been criteria for quality of student and teacher life, community involvement, aesthetics, cultural pluralism, and democratic governance. Contemplating these gaps shows starkly how conservative and limiting the *standards* approach to standards has been.

Other political and bureaucratic factors contributed to the movement's failure. Originally, *national* standards were conceived of as a combination of content, performance, and opportunity-to-learn standards (Ravitch, 1995). That effort soon unraveled. What were supposed to have been rich, *voluntary* standards that would permeate school culture and reshape teaching, as had started to happen with the standards promoted by the National Council of Teachers of Mathematics (NCTM), became *compulsory* standards of a vastly different nature. State curricular standards ended up becoming sprawling lists of skills and knowledge that lacked intellectual rigor. Most students received low marks (Finn, Petrilli, & Julian, 2006). With their bizarre amalgam of academic trivia and age-inappropriate benchmarks, the standards were justifiably satirized (Ohanian, 1999). The third element—equity in resources—did not fit the excellence agenda and was largely discarded, helping keep achievement gaps wide. Legislators rejected national resource standards because they worried about too much government involvement and wanted to preserve federalism (Ravitch, 1995). Ironically, however, they still passed IASA and NCLB with far greater federal intrusion into local and state schooling. Testing and "excellence" had trumped equity.

As the accountability push spread, state and local systems became more tightly coupled, thus focusing teaching even more on the tests (Fusarelli, 2002). The original call for authentic assessment gave way to low-level, multiple-choice testing. To achieve higher success rates for NCLB, many states dumbed down their tests and lowered passing standards (Darling-Hammond, 2004), and inside schools, teachable moments and long-term projects were sacrificed at the altar of drill and test preparation (Fragnoli, 2003; Mathison & Freeman, 2003). The resulting system has diminished curricula, deskilled and demoralized teachers, increased dropouts, and further centralized power in state bureaucracies (Mathison & Ross, 2004; Ross, 1996).

Part II: A Political Economy Analysis

The Audit Culture

Some argue it is a mistake to equate the standards movement with the bureaucratic, test-driven accountability nightmare that has arisen (Ravitch, 2010). To be sure, it is worth distinguishing the initial curricular efforts of the professional subject matter organizations such as NCTM from much of what has gone on. At the same time, however, we must remember that, even at the outset, the standards movement was more than a beneficent pedagogical endeavor and was deeply intertwined with accountability. In *A Nation at Risk*, for example, the National Commission on Excellence in Education (1983) had proposed "more rigorous and measurable standards" and standardized testing "at major transition points" (pp. 73–74). The federal government itself had funded the subject matter organizations to write standards documents as part of an overall Bush-Clinton strategy of accountability and school reform (Stedman,

2011b). Leading figures in the standards movement also considered testing and performance standards essential to its success (Ravitch, 1995). The past generation, however, has shown us that test-driven reform has failed in the real world and even made things worse. In spite of that, some policy makers, including NCLB's architects, still promote testing and accountability (Stedman, 2009, 2010). We must look closely at this mindset and how it has reshaped the work of schools.

Contemporary standards-based accountability systems are part of a pernicious "audit culture" that emphasizes enumeration and regulation (Apple, 2006). They have turned learning into a commodity (Kozol, 2005) and produced what Freire (2001) calls "bureaucratized" minds (p. 42). Within schools, institutionalized accounting schemes have transformed teacher and student work into data-driven quests to meet targets, much the way modern corporations seek to meet monthly or quarterly sales goals. Such systems depend upon the alienated labor of both students and teachers (Kesson, 2004). Professional learning communities have degenerated into "data teams" with a singular focus on raising scores and improving the *numbers* (Mikoda, 2009; Servage, 2008). Curiosity is suffocated and social problems are recast as issues of test performance. Few standards advocates understand that centralized standards threaten community, autonomy, and liberty in fundamental ways (Strike, 1997). Few recognize the need for regional and variable standards. One size, indeed, fits few (Ohanian, 1999).

The roots of the standardization-accountability movement can be found in the early 20th century (Callahan, 1962; Krug, 1964; Tyack 1974). Ironically, modern neoconservative reform efforts embody two key strands of progressivism: social efficiency and scientific management. What we are witnessing today is nothing other than the logical unfolding of early administrative progressives' efforts to use standardized tests to classify, rank, and determine children's futures.

The problems with regimentation and an excessive zeal for standardization, however, have been long recognized. In a 1923 article for the *New York Times*, Charles W. Eliot, former president of Harvard University and chair of the 1893 Committee of Ten, decried the pernicious effects of standardization on American education and life:

> A new blight is afflicting education and industries in the United States.... Its name is standardization, and there is a very general movement to give it application in a great variety of American activities. The blight seems to have started in the industrial domain.... Soon standardization began to affect the school and college programmes, the conditions of admission to college, and the qualifications for degrees. It limited injuriously freedom of election of studies in both school and college. (As quoted in Krug, 1972, p. 195)

Eliot would be appalled by what passes today for school reform. Test-driven instruction and regimented schooling have undermined what he once described as the major successes of progressive reform: "the motive of joy through achievement," wholesome working conditions for both teachers and students, and self-discipline through the exercise of freedom, which he saw as the key to preparing students for democracy (Eliot, 1901).

Repealing No Child Left Behind

NCLB is the embodiment of what has gone wrong. It has imposed a counter-productive accountability system that substitutes testing for education, promotes privatization, subverts democratic participation, and ignores long-standing inequalities (Darling-Hammond, 2004;

Kohn, 2004; Meier, 2004). It needs to be repealed. While the backers of NCLB and test-driven schooling celebrate inconsequential gains on NAEP and state tests, savage inequalities are devastating communities and schools, and deeply scarring students, families, *and* teachers (Anyon & Greene, 2007; Kozol, 2005). The spectacle is jarring. With each new release of NAEP results, NCLB supporters proclaim success, no matter how small the gains (Stedman, 2009, 2010). In 2004, for example, in spite of weak results, Secretary of Education Spellings claimed long-term NAEP trends were "proof that *No Child Left Behind is* working" (U.S. Department of Education, 2005). In 2008, though little had changed, she still asserted, "It shows that we are on the right track…. It proves the 'policy principle' and that 'accountability is working'" (Glod, 2009).

A fundamental problem is that proponents of test-driven schooling accept score gains as *prima facie* evidence of improved learning. Yet, given all the testing mandated by states and NCLB, such gains often reflect teaching-to-the-test rather than genuine learning. Even NAEP scores are increasingly suspect as state education departments have promoted the use of NAEP test items in classroom instruction (Stedman, 2010). In general, NCLB's drill-based score gains are low quality and short-lasting, limited to a few test areas and ages, and not worth their social, fiscal, and educational costs (Stedman, 2011b). Even leading standards advocates have spoken out against it. Ravitch (2009a) calls NCLB "ruinous," "harshly punitive," and "a costly failure."

NCLB has had a questionable impact on civics education. While its "Education for Democracy Act" promoted instruction in the Bill of Rights, it included equal funding for economics education (Stedman, 2011a). Congress had placed an understanding of the free enterprise system on an equal footing with the promotion of democracy. But the initial support for both efforts was a paltry $30 million, compared to an overall appropriation of $11.6 billion for NCLB's main activities (National Center for Education Statistics, 2004, p. 446). Of greater consequence, NCLB included provisions that opened up high schools to invasive military recruitment activities, ones that have disproportionately affected minority students (Stedman, 2011b). This has furthered the militarization of schooling (Saltman & Gabbard, 2003).

Gibson (2008) rightly decries NCLB's "assaults on educators and kids." Teachers are treated like factory workers, while students are regimented into training mills. Social studies, the arts, and now even recess are being sacrificed at the altar of test drilling (Stedman, 2011b). Tinkering with NCLB will not fix its profound flaws. There is a vast difference between a bureaucratic system fixated on raising test scores without regards to their meaning and a collaborative effort focused on democracy and social justice—and ensuring that engaging teaching is taking place. The latest effort, however, is to re-label and re-market NCLB, as if its problems were ones of image rather than misguided policymaking. Even Arne Duncan, President Obama's Secretary of Education, has said, "Let's rebrand it. Give it a new name" (Dillon, 2009).

Stopping the Neoliberals' Race to the Top
Educators must understand that standards-based reform is part of a larger managerial and neoliberal project that diverts democracy and sustains capitalism (Apple, 2006; Ross, 1996, 2004). Supported by neoconservatives and a new professional middle class, the effort combines accountability and social control (high-stakes testing, merit pay, and centralized curriculum) with choice and the market (transfer rights, vouchers, and charter schools). What many of us perceive as a failure due to its damaging effects on school culture is, in fact, a success in mana-

gerial terms. A proficiency-driven, command-and-control, authoritarian type of schooling was, in fact, a central goal of the reforms and serves capital's interests well.

The Obama administration's major educational initiative, Race to the Top, continues this project and reflects key elements of modern bureaucratic capitalism: competition, control and benchmarking (now of teachers as well as students), technical workplace and career preparation, and a valuing of the market over democracy (McKenna, 2009). It further entrenches the noxious features of NCLB: auditing through false metrics, accountability without regard to circumstance, distrust of teachers, and a fixation on test scores instead of learning. Those in charge remain out of touch with the real world of schooling and the lives of children. As Ravitch (2009a) explains, the Obama administration has driven away veteran educators and progressive reformers, favoring instead entrepreneurs and think-tank experts who are ill-equipped to understand public schools and help them improve. She aptly derides the Obama-Duncan approach:

> Now that President Obama and Secretary Arne Duncan have become the standard-bearer for the privatization and testing agenda, we hear nothing more about ditching NCLB, except perhaps changing its name. The fundamental features of NCLB remain intact regardless of what they call it.
>
> The real winners here are the edu-entrepreneurs who are running President Obama's so-called "Race to the Top" fund and distributing the billions to other edu-entrepreneurs, who will manage the thousands of new charter schools and make mega-bucks selling test-prep programs to the schools. (Ravitch, 2009b)

New Directions for Reform

Real reform, therefore, requires a fundamentally different philosophy of education and the challenging of vested interests. We would be served well by blending Dewey's (1916, 1938) democratic education and philosophy of experience, Noddings' (2002, 2007) ethic of care, and Freire's (1970, 2001) pedagogy of *conscientization*. We need to replace social control and transmission models with a caring, dialogic, experience-based pedagogy that involves authentic learning, respects student autonomy and teacher professionalism, and embraces intervention in the world.

We should be educating through vibrant, *democratic* communities, where students and teachers work together to solve real social problems (Apple & Beane, 2007; Dewey, 1938). We need to forcefully remind politicians that education is about more than high test scores and meeting bureaucratic standards. Dewey (1938) rightly—and pointedly—deconstructed the traditional conception of academic preparation:

> What avail is it to win prescribed amounts of information about geography and history, to win ability to read and write, if in the process the individual loses his own soul: loses his appreciation of things worthwhile, of the values to which these things are relative; if he loses desire to apply what he has learned and, above all, loses the ability to extract meaning from his future experiences as they occur? (p. 49)

We want, and need, students to develop their imaginations and intellectual passions, not just cram material for a state test. We should echo Einstein's advice to the New York State Department of Education that the "accumulation of material should not stifle the student's independence" (Isaacson, 2007, p. 6). He also believed that "imagination is more important than knowledge" (p. 7). While both are crucial and not in opposition, his remark is a healthy antidote to the imbalance in today's schools where creativity and imagination are short-changed and knowledge is treated as information that is packaged for transmission instead of arising from student exploration and reflection (Anyon, 1981, 2006; Dewey, 1938).

Democracy remains marginalized. "Preparation for democracy" has become a timeworn cliché that needs resurrecting in progressive forms. Although most policy initiatives of the standards era included civic literacy rationales, they were defined in narrow economic and hegemonic terms (Stedman, 2011a). *A Nation at Risk*, for example, highlighted the Jeffersonian idea of education for democracy, but blended it with a much different purpose, that "education is one of the chief engines of a society's material well-being" (NCEE, 1983, p. 21). It spoke of "productive citizenship" (p. 81) that would help create a "strong economy" (p. 21). Similarly, Goals 2000 cast civic literacy as "responsible citizenship" with the aim of "productive employment in our Nation's modern economy" (NEGP, 1997, p. vi). Even when the initiatives have gone past rhetoric and included civics programs, the efforts were dwarfed by the funding and support for the accountability regime. Policymakers and neoconservative school critics have simply failed to take schools' responsibilities toward democracy seriously (Stedman, 2011a).

Instead of thinking of education in terms of standards and test scores, we should be discussing whose interests the current arrangements serve and how to redesign schools to develop meaningful, participatory democracy (Stedman, 2011b). It is not a matter of students acquiring a potpourri of civics knowledge and learning how to read a sample ballot. As Dewey (1916) explained, "Democracy is more than a form of government; it is primarily a mode of associated living, of conjoint communicated experience" (p. 101). Authoritarian, test-centered, bureaucratic schools cannot educate well and cannot prepare students well for their roles in democracy.

In an increasingly diverse society, we need students who relate well to others and know well the people, struggles, and literary works that have shaped our multicultural nation. *We want our students to be well read, not just read well—and to engage with the world.* We will serve democracy, the nation, and the planet much better by designing schools to turn out imaginative, well-informed, and socially dedicated graduates. As global warming transforms the Earth, we should aim for a scientifically literate people who will confront the self-serving arguments of economic interests and fashion creative solutions. In an era when civil liberties have been subverted in the name of homeland security, we need a constitutionally literate and activist public who will work to overturn the Patriot Act and restore basic democratic principles.

Habits of mind, tolerance, literary activity, and civic participation, however, cannot be commanded; they must be nurtured. We need to make schools places where students *and* teachers want to be. Large, modern high schools are characterized by anonymity and powerlessness (Clark-Pope, 2001), yet spaces for learning should embody democratic values and be inviting to their participants (Lamash, 2007). School reforms and accountability systems that do not centralize such matters are doomed to failure.

Confronting Capitalism and the Stratification of Reform

Our reform efforts, however, should not be based on utopian thinking or isolated demonstration projects; rather, they should be grounded in a critical-historical analysis of capitalism (Engels, 1970. We must understand how the interests of capital shape educational reform and how schools reflect the social relations of production (Anyon, 1981, 2006; Bowles & Gintis, 1976, 2001; Gibson, 2008). To be sure, schools have always had more positive purposes, such as egalitarian and developmental ones, but these are in tension with reproducing the existing order (Bowles & Gintis, 1976). Institutions of acculturation work to perpetuate a society's existing social and economic arrangements, and, so, the schools' mission remains political socialization, workplace training, and class reproduction. The interests of capital dominate. That reality must be confronted if we are to establish a new school reform agenda.

The standards movement originated, in large measure, as a response to a crisis in capitalism. Its architects hoped to address a shortfall in human capital that corporations faced in a globalized economy. In the United States, the movement was also a reaction to the erosion of the country's economic dominance. That is a key reason the reform commissions of the early 1980s highlighted declining student skills, the weak standing of the U.S. in the international assessments and emerging global markets, and the value of education for economic growth and prosperity (Stedman, 1987). It is also why Goals 2000 called for the U.S. to be first in the world in math and science achievement (National Education Goals Panel, 1997). Later legislative efforts, specifically IASA (1994) and NCLB (2001), focused even more explicitly on improving students' human capital skills and imposed accountability measures to attempt to make that happen.

Through these external control and accountability systems, schools were recommitted to the business of producing a well-trained, compliant workforce—one that would acquire the relevant technical skills, and, for the higher echelons, internalize capitalist values and aggressively pursue corporate interests. Schools play a central role in the reproduction of this consciousness. Students are socialized to accept alienation, compete for external rewards, and pledge allegiance to the State and corporate system (Gibson, 2008; Kesson, 2004; Kozol, 2005). Knowledge has been commodified and a "pervasive corporate indoctrination" characterizes school culture, language, and practices (Kozol, 2005, pp. 94–97).

Yet, this socialization is not done monolithically. It reflects the hierarchical division of labor in modern capitalism and the racist history of the U.S. and, so, it is tailored to students' class and race. Decades ago, Bowles and Gintis (1976) outlined a correspondence between the social relations of production and schooling. They identified three modes of workplace activity that varied by position in the economic hierarchy—rule-following, dependability, and internalization—and documented how these were mirrored in the schooling students received. More recently, they have presented evidence that their insights about schooling in capitalist America still hold true (Bowles & Gintis, 2001). In her classic study, Anyon (1981) richly documented how social and economic stratification is reflected in teaching and curricula. Working-class schools, for example, emphasized rules, disconnected facts, and simple skills, while executive elite schools were pressure-cookers that stressed research, high performance, and cultural capital. She, too, has recently argued that such stratification is even more clearly present today (Anyon, 2006).

These differentiated forms of schooling are strikingly similar to those the standards movement has created in urban-poor schools and professional-suburban ones (Clark-Pope, 2001; Humes, 2003; Kozol, 2005; Stedman, 2010). A growing bifurcation in the economy is reflected in an increasing bifurcation of the schooling given to the masses and elites (Anyon, 2006).

While we should not overstate this economic determinism, the relative autonomy of schools is eroding as they become more tightly aligned with State demands and the needs of capital. Given this reality, we will not overcome the standards movement or transform the structure of schooling unless we confront their hegemonic functions and relationship to the overall political economy. As Gibson (2008) admonishes us,

> Anyone interested in confronting our conditions today must follow Hegel's dictum: "The truth is in the whole." The whole is capitalism.... The failure to create a mass base of class conscious people, which is our life and death high stakes test, remains the Achilles Heel of nearly every social movement in the US. It follows we need to openly talk about what capitalism is, why class struggle takes place, what of CAPITALIST schooling, what can be done, and what a better future might be.

Schools will not be fundamentally changed until educators take this message to heart and work in tandem with popular movements that are addressing the inherent contradictions between capitalism and participatory democracy and between the purposes of capital and the needs of learners and their families.

Educators who seek fundamental reform, therefore, should dedicate themselves to critical-historical analysis and comprehensive social change. To succeed, we will have to join forces with those seeking social justice, democratic voice, and new forms of community, institutional, and economic life. As Counts (1932) pointed out so long ago, capitalism "no longer works"; it is "not only cruel and inhuman; it is wasteful and inefficient" (p. 44). He was right in his call for progressive, democratic reform; it is finally time that we dared to build a new social order.

Acknowledgments

This chapter was adapted from Stedman (2011b below). It was published by *Critical Education* under a Creative Commons License, wherein the author holds the copyright and has exclusive rights to its commercial reproduction and adaptation. Nevertheless, the author appreciates the support of *Critical Education*'s editor, E. Wayne Ross, who backed its initial publication and heartily endorsed its adaptation for inclusion in this volume.

My thanks go as well to five doctoral students for their insights during several conversations, e-mails, and seminars. Aleksey Tikhomirov highlighted the linkage of tight-coupling and the standards movement and is a continual font of ideas about leadership and school reform. Marianne Lawson pointed out Freire's phrase "bureaucratized minds" and provided a fresh look at how Marx's concept of alienation applies to traditional schooling. With passion and forthrightness, Carol Mikoda and Betta Borelli, veteran secondary school teachers, described in wonderfully rich detail their first-hand experiences with so-called "professional learning communities." Amanda McKenna skillfully analyzed the connections between Race to the Top and the principles of modern bureaucratic capitalism. All five graciously gave me permission to include their ideas in this work.

References

Advisory Panel on the Scholastic Aptitude Test Score Decline. (1977). *On further examination*. New York: College Board.

Anyon, J. (1981). Social class and school knowledge. *Curriculum Inquiry, 11*(1), 3–42.

Anyon, J. (2006). Social class, school knowledge, and the hidden curriculum: Retheorizing reproduction. In L. Weis, C. McCarthy, & G. Dimitriadis (Eds.), *Ideology, curriculum, and the new sociology of education* (pp. 37–46). New York: Routledge.

Anyon, J., & Greene, K. (2007). No Child Left Behind as an anti-poverty measure. *Teacher Education Quarterly, 34*(2), 157–162.

Apple, M. (2000). *Official knowledge: Democratic education in a conservative age* (2nd ed.). London: Routledge.

Apple, M. (2006). *Educating the "right" way: Markets, standards, god, and inequality* (2nd ed.). New York: Routledge.

Apple, M., & Beane, J. (Eds.) (2007). *Democratic schools: Lessons in powerful education* (2nd ed.). Portsmouth, NH: Heinemann.

Bestor, A. (1985). *Educational wastelands: The retreat from learning in our public schools* (2nd ed.). Chicago: University of Illinois Press.

Bowles, S., & Gintis, H. (1976). *Schooling in capitalist America: Educational reform and the contradictions of economic life*. New York: Basic Books.

Bowles, S., & Gintis, H. (2001). *Schooling in capitalist America revisited*. Retrieved from http://www.umass.edu/preferen/gintis/soced.pdf

Callahan, R. (1962). *Education and the cult of efficiency*. Chicago, IL: University of Chicago Press.

Clark-Pope, D. (2001). *Doing school: How we are creating a generation of stressed out, materialistic, and miseducated students*. New Haven, CT: Yale University Press.

Copperman, P. (1978). *The literacy hoax: The decline of reading, writing, and learning in the public schools and what we can do about it*. New York: William Morrow.

Counts, G. (1932). *Dare the school build a new social order?* Carbondale,: Southern Illinois University Press.

Darling-Hammond, L. (2004). From "separate but equal" to "No Child Left Behind": The collision of new standards and old inequalities. In D. Meier & G. Wood (Eds.), *Many children left behind* (pp. 3–32). Boston: Beacon Press.

Dewey, J. (1916). *Democracy and education*. New York: Macmillan.

Dewey, J. (1938). *Experience and education*. New York: Macmillan.

Dillon, S. (2009, February 22). Rename law? No wisecrack is left behind. *New York Times*. Retrieved from http://www.nytimes.com/2009/02/23/education/23child.html

Eliot, C. (1901). Remarks in response to N. Butler's paper, "Status of Education at the Close of the Century" in Chapter VIII of *Report of the Commissioner of Education for the year, 1899–1900, Volume I*, 569–571. Washington, D.C.: U.S. Government Printing Office.

Engels, F. (1970). *Socialism: Utopian and scientific*. Delhi, India: Progress Publishers. (Original work was published in 1880.)

Fine, B. (1943, April 4). Ignorance of U.S. history shown by college freshmen. *The New York Times*, 1.

Finn, C., Petrilli, M., & Julian, L. (2006). *The state of state standards 2006*. Washington, DC: Thomas B. Fordham Foundation.

Fiske, T. (1920). *Twentieth annual report of the secretary*. New York: College Entrance Examination Board.

Flanagan, J. (1962). Maximizing human talents. *The Journal of Teacher Education, 13*(2), 209–215.

Flanagan, J., Davis, F., Dailey, J., Shaycroft, M., Orr, D., Goldberg, I., & Neyman, C. (1964). *The American high-school student*. Pittsburgh: Project TALENT.

Fragnoli, K. (2003). *Externally imposed testing in the elementary classroom: A critical analysis of teachers' pedagogical negotiations* (Doctoral dissertation). State University of New York, Binghamton.

Freire, P. (1970). *Pedagogy of the oppressed*. New York: Seabury Press.

Freire, P. (2001). *Pedagogy of freedom: Ethics, democracy, and civic courage*. Lanham, MD: Rowman & Littlefield.

Fusarelli, L. (2002). Tightly coupled policy in loosely coupled systems. *Journal of Educational Administration, 40*(6), 561–575.

Gibson, R. (2008, August). *Chicago, Detroit, schools, and the election spectacle*. Retrieved from http://www.richgibson.com/chicago-detroit-schools-election.htm

Glod, M. (2009, April 29). "Nation's report card" sees gains in elementary, middle schools. Since NCLB, math and reading scores rise for ages 9 and 13. *Washington Post*. Retrieved from http://www.washingtonpost.com/wp-dyn/content/article/2009/04/28/AR2009042801244.html

Hirsch, E. D. (1987). *Cultural literacy*. Boston: Houghton Mifflin.

Hofstadter, R. (1962). *Anti-intellectualism in American life*. New York: Random House.

Humes, E. (2003). *School of dreams: Making the grade at a top American high school*. New York: Harcourt.

Hyman, H., Wright, C., & Reed, J. (1975). *The enduring effects of education*. Chicago: University of Chicago Press.

Improving America's Schools Act of 1994, Pub. L. No. 103-382. (1994).

Isaacson, W. (2007). *Einstein: His life and universe*. New York: Simon & Schuster.

Itzkoff, S. (1994). *The decline of intelligence in America: A strategy for national renewal*. Westport, CT: Praeger.

Kesson, K. (2004). Inhuman powers and terrible things: The theory and practice of alienated labor in urban schools. *Journal for Critical Education Policy Studies, 2*(1), 40–72.

Kohn, A. (2004). NCLB and the effort to privatize public education. In D. Meier & G. Wood (Eds.), *Many children left behind* (pp. 79–100). Boston: Beacon Press.

Kozol, J. (2005). *The shame of the nation: The restoration of apartheid schooling in America*. New York: Three Rivers Press.

Krug, E. (1964). *The shaping of the American high school, Volume 1, 1880–1920*. Madison: University of Wisconsin Press.

Krug, E. (1972). *The shaping of the American high school, Volume 2, 1920–1941*. Madison: University of Wisconsin Press.

Lamash, L. (2007). *The story of a school building: Spatial representations of educational change* (Doctoral dissertation). State University of New York, Binghamton.

Learned, W., & Wood, B. (1938). *The student and his knowledge: A report to the Carnegie Foundation on the results of the high school and college examinations of 1928, 1930, and 1932*. New York: Carnegie Foundation for the Advancement of Teaching.

Mathison S., & Freeman, M. (2003). Constraining elementary teachers' work: Dilemmas and paradoxes created by state mandated testing. *Education Policy Analysis Archives, 11*(34).

Mathison S., & Ross, E. W. (Eds.). (2004). *Defending public schools, Volume IV: The nature and limits of standards-based reform and assessment*. Westport, CT: Praeger.

McKenna, A. (2009). *"Race to the Top": A political economy analysis*. Unpublished paper.

Meier, D. (2004). NCLB and democracy. In D. Meier & G. Wood (Eds.), *Many children left behind* (pp. 66–78). Boston: Beacon Press.

Mikoda, C. (2009). *Professional learning communities: A policy analysis*. Unpublished paper.

National Center for Education Statistics. (2004). *Digest of education statistics 2003*. U.S. Department of Education. Washington, DC: U.S. Government Printing Office.

National Commission on Excellence in Education. (1983). *A nation at risk*. Washington, DC: U.S. Government Printing Office.

National Education Goals Panel. (1997). *The national education goals report: Building a nation of learners 1997*. Washington, DC: U.S. Government Printing Office.

No Child Left Behind Act of 2001, Pub. L. No. 107-110. (2002). 115 STAT. 1425.

Noddings, N. (2002). *Educating moral people: A caring alternative to character education*. New York: Teachers College Press.

Noddings, N. (2007). *Philosophy of education*. Boulder, CO: Westview Press.

Ohanian, S. (1999). *One size fits few: The folly of educational standards*. Portsmouth, NH: Heinemann.

Ravitch, D. (1995). *National standards in American education: A citizen's guide*. Washington, DC: The Brookings Institution.

Ravitch, D. (2009a, February 23). In education, the new administration is as ruinous as the old. *The Arena*. Retrieved from http://www.politico.com/arena/perm/Diane_Ravitch_ED3CC65A-1240-42E1-9716-8DB5FD3426D8.html

Ravitch, D. (2009b, August 23). Obama's awful education plan. *Huffington Post*. Retrieved from http://www.huffingtonpost.com/diane-ravitch/obamas-awful-education-pl_b_266412.html

Ravitch, D. (2010). *The death and life of the great American school system: How testing and choice are undermining education*. New York: Basic Books.

Ross, E. W. (1996). Diverting democracy: The curriculum standards movement and social studies education. *International Journal of Social Education, 11*(1), 18–39.

Ross, E. W. (2004). General editors introduction: Defending public schools, defending democracy. In D. Gabbard & E. W. Ross (Eds.), *Defending public schools, Volume 1: Education under the security state* (pp. xi-xviii). Westport, CT: Praeger.

Saltman, K., & Gabbard, D. (Eds.). (2003). *Education as enforcement: The militarization and corporatization of schools*. New York: Routledge.

Servage, L. (2008). Critical and transformative practices in professional learning communities. *Teacher Education Quarterly, 35*(1), 63.

Shor, I. (1992). *School and society in the conservative restoration*. Chicago: University of Chicago Press.

Stedman, L. (1987). The political economy of recent educational reform reports. *Educational Theory, 37*(1), 69–76.

Stedman, L. (1997). International achievement differences: An assessment of a new perspective. *Educational Researcher, 26*(3), 4–15.

Stedman, L. (1998). An assessment of the contemporary debate over U.S. achievement. In D. Ravitch (Ed.), *Brookings papers on education policy: 1998* (pp. 53–121). Washington, DC: The Brookings Institution.

Stedman, L. (2003). U.S. educational achievement in the 20th century: Brilliant success and persistent failure. In R. Weissberg, H. Walberg, M. O'Brien, & C. Bartels-Kuster (Eds.), *Long-term trends in the well-being of children and youth* (pp. 53–76). Washington, DC: Child Welfare League of America Press.

Stedman, L. (2009). *The NAEP long-term trend assessment: A review of its transformation, use, and findings.* Washington, DC: National Assessment Governing Board.

Stedman, L. (2010). How well does the standards movement measure up? An analysis of achievement trends and student learning, changes in curriculum and school culture, and the impact of No Child Left Behind. *Critical Education, 1*(10).

Stedman, L. (2011a). In the name of democracy: Educational policy and civics achievement in the standards era. In J. DeVitis (Ed.), *Critical civic literacy: A reader* (pp. 43-62). New York: Peter Lang.

Stedman, L. (2011b). Why the standards movement failed. An educational and political diagnosis of its failure and the implications for school reform. *Critical Education, 2*(1).

Stedman, L., & Kaestle, C. (1987). Literacy and reading performance in the United States, from 1880 to the present. *Reading Research Quarterly, XXII*(1), 8–46.

Stedman, L., & Smith, M. (1983). Recent reform proposals for American education. *Contemporary Education Review, 2*(2), 85–104.

Strike, K. (1997). Centralized goal formation and systemic reform: Reflections on liberty, localism and pluralism. *Education Policy Analysis Archives, 5*(11).

Tyack, D. (1974). *The one best system: A history of American urban education.* Cambridge, MA: Harvard University Press.

U.S. Department of Education. (2005). Spellings hails new national report card results: Today's news "Proof That No Child Left Behind Is Working" [Press release]. Retrieved from http://www.ed.gov/news/pressreleases/2005/07/07142005.html

CHAPTER FIVE

"It Need Not Have Been This Way"

School Reform Around the Socially Just School in Australia and Lessons from the Finnish Educational Miracle

JOHN SMYTH

...it is an inescapable fact that most successful economies are those where teaching is a prestigious and valued profession. Teaching, at least in government schools, is not a valued and prestigious profession in Australia. (Davidson, 1993)

What Has Been Happening Under the Neoliberal Reform Agenda?

The opening quote by one of Australia's most fearless economic journalists points to a deep underlying malaise not being addressed around the world by the zealots who believe schooling ought to be the engine of the economy.

It is time we stopped being delusional and faced up to the reality that the ill-conceived neoliberal school reform experiment of the past four decades that has been unleashed with such ferocity in countries such as the USA, UK, Australia, New Zealand and Canada has been a dismal failure and an unmitigated disaster. Not only has it demonstrably failed to deliver on its own extravagant promises—what one of its celebrants has labeled "the modern management mantra—faster, cheaper, better" (Schwartz, 2012), but it has also brought with it untold damage to the lives and life chances of a generation of young people. So, there we have it—it is now out in the open; when we strip it back to its essentials, it is all about a management ideology that is masquerading as an authoritative voice purporting to be able to do things better educationally, without the pesky encumbrances of democratic dialogue and debate, and at a cheaper price.

In the real world, when football coaches, Olympic officials, and athletes don't deliver, the punishment is sure and swift—we dispense with them. Being punitive is a central defining pillar of the neoliberal ideology. It believes passionately that under-performance has to be ruthlessly confronted and punished through the technocratic operation of market forces. The odd exception seems to be that this does not apply to an under-performing ideology! If we were to use the withering on the vine metaphor, then the failed neoliberal ideology as it has been blisteringly applied to education would have been unceremoniously dumped decades ago. Instead, and in light of its own immovable commitment to 'hard data' arranged in the form of punitive international league tables, it is clear that the countries that have been the most wedded to the fantasy of the market as being the single way to deliver educational improvements are also the ones that have been the worst performers. It is very strange indeed that instead of jettisoning this underperforming and underwhelming ideology—to borrow from Adorno (1994), 'an uncouth interloper…[that is] arrogant, alien and improper' (p. 23)—what we have had instead is a metaphorical case of a hardening of the arteries and an application of even larger doses of the same medicine.

Even one of the high priests of the neoliberal market ideology for education—the Organisation for Economic Co-operation and Development (OECD)—has seemingly backed off a little. For example, in one of its most recent documents, *Equity and Quality in Education: Supporting Disadvantaged Students and Schools* (OECD, 2012), there is a change of tone in the title. The word "equity" appears and it is placed after the word "quality," and the word "disadvantaged" appears. Even the preface makes the right kind of flourishes, albeit rhetorically:

> The highest performing education systems are those that combine equity with quality. They give all children opportunities for a good quality education. (p. 3)

We don't have to delve far into this document to realize that this tiger has not changed its stripes—the same underlying deficit, economic, labor market-driven, punitive ideology is well ensconced; the hackneyed language employs the same old hoary clichés—"economic competitiveness," "school choice," responsive "funding strategies," "school leadership," "school climate," "effective classroom learning strategies" and "school effectiveness"—that produced the problem in the first place. The overwhelming argument in the document, in short, is that we need to address equity issues because it is good for the economy.

If we go back only a little over a decade and a half, we find the OECD (1994) celebrating the virtues of the emergence of a new era:

> Greater choice of school by parents and pupils is changing the balance of power in education, away from "producers" [read "teachers"] and towards "consumers" [read "parents"].… (p. 7)

The supposed rationale for this new "market-oriented view of educational provision"

> …is the "choosiness" of a growing number of parents and pupils, who wish to make their own judgments about the desirability of attending a given school.… (p. 7)

While admitting that they were a long way from connecting the dots as to how school choice was going to be "proven" in terms of school performance, the OECD (1994), in its *School: A Matter of Choice,* had no such qualms in stepping out and making the direct connection to their long-preferred and oft-touted solution of "school effectiveness":

> There is no direct evidence that…competition improves school performance.… However, the dynamic of competing for pupils typically enhances some school characteristics associated with effectiveness, such as strong leadership and sense of mission. (p. 7)

That is, the way to handle the inevitable disfigurement and scarring of the social landscape produced by the grotesque working of the market alluded to here is to genuflect to what Barack Obama (SBS News, Aug 13, 2012) recently dubbed the "trickle-down fairy dust" effect. In the words of the OECD (1994):

> Unequal opportunities in choosing popular schools may be addressed by policies that offer disadvantaged groups more information, more help with transport and possibly [note the equivocation] privileged access to certain schools. (p. 7)

It is fascinating, after decades of celebrating, eulogizing and proselytizing the virtues of improving education through the ideology of the market, that the OECD, as one of the major protagonists, has come to the belated recognition that the strongest-performing countries educationally are the ones that have largely shunned the market model or have at least been only nominal enthusiasts. Instead, countries such as Finland (the standout example) have pursued more democratic and inclusive approaches that have placed students, teachers and parents at the centre—the latter, as activist "citizens" rather than self-seeking "consumers."

The intellectual hegemony of the ideas that have been orchestrated through organizations such as the OECD to educational systems, allegedly as "world's best practice," have come from ideas that have been incubated and warehoused by international predator organizations such as the World Bank, IMF and the WTO. The effect, as one observer cryptically put it, has been a kind of "Tarzan style of policy making":

> A group of hairy-chested individuals swing down from the trees, uttering cries of "efficiency," "competition," "market discipline"; they tip all the huts over, then they swing back into the trees, leaving the villagers to clean up the banana peels. (Connell, 1996)

It is from these quarters that the business and corporate sector have been able to derive their legitimation in clamoring for managerialist policies with which to supposedly fix the problem. Their claim is that

> …education being one of the largest employers in first world countries, has for far too long been treated as a sheltered workshop, and is desperately in need of a shot of realism in the form of fiscal austerity and discipline from market forces. (Smyth & Shacklock, 1998, p. 61)

In a controversial report I wrote for the International Labour Organization over two decades ago (Smyth, 1993), I pointed out what was likely in store for us educationally if we continued down this ill-advised path. As I later commented:

> It does not take a lot of sophisticated investigation or analysis to ascertain what these [neoliberal] policies have done in the Third World, and what we can expect from them as a consequence in developed countries like Australia (Smyth & Shacklock, 1998, p. 62).

In the words I wrote in the draft commissioned report at the time:

> These are the same policies that were "found guilty" of producing a "dramatic deterioration of the living standards in the Third World" (West Africa, 1988, pp. 1942–3) by the 13-man jury of the Permanent People's Tribunal in West Berlin in September 1988, whose job it was to investigate the effects of the IMF and the World Bank on the disastrous situation in the Third World resulting in over 950 million people living in absolute poverty. This tribunal found that rather than alleviating the problem, these interna-

tional agencies through their policies has *intensified the problem* such that "the majority of humankind is worse off now than 10 years ago" (West Africa, 1988, p. 1942). Furthermore, the policies that seem to have produced this situation have been ones of structural adjustment; namely—cuts in public expenditures, especially in those areas which seem not to be productive, for example social services; cuts in wages; in privatization . . . [of the public sector]; liberalization of imports to stimulate competition; devaluation of the currency . . . (West Africa, 1988, pp. 1942–3)

In short, while we might need to hedge such connections with a few qualifiers, the overall effect and direction seems clear enough:

There is no doubt that the IMF and the World Bank as international institutions for the regulation of crisis management have failed and that they are therefore responsible for the dramatic deterioration in the living conditions of the peoples in many parts of the world. They serve the interests of the creditors rather than functioning for the benefits of the people of the world (West Africa, 1988, p. 1943) (Smyth, 1993, pp. 5–6).

My later reflection on what was occurring at the time and which has largely come to pass, was that:

The effect of these policies are a blight on humanity that ought to be roundly and loudly condemned. And, it is out of this same ideological warehouse that equally devastating policies are being wrought on education systems around the world aimed at destroying the very notion of state provided education as we know it (Smyth & Shacklock, 1998, p. 63).

These ideas were ones that I canvassed some time ago and the conditions have worsened immeasurably as a result of the Global Financial Crisis (GFC). Without wishing to labor the point excessively, there is an important follow-on question that needs to be posed before we can look to the alternatives.

Why Have We Allowed This to Happen?

I have argued elsewhere (Smyth & Shacklock, 1998) that these policies have been allowed to occur and evolve through a carefully contrived process of constructing "a moral panic about the supposed failure of western economic systems and the implications for schools…" (p. 68). I point to the OECD's (1995) *Governance in Transition: Public Sector Management Reform* as being particularly illustrative of how "concerns" are aired, incubated, constructed and massaged in ways that ensure they are then "picked up and acted upon by policy makers in education (and other social areas) around the world…"(p. 68).

The message and the argument is unerringly the same and has not shifted dramatically for decades: there has been a decline in public confidence in public provision; the mode of operation of the public sector is deemed to be inferior to that of the private sector; therefore we need to reign in budgets; alongside this fiscal austerity we need to foster efficiency and productivity by unproblematically following a mantra of self-evident (but unchallengeable) truths: "client-focused services, best practice, benchmarking, contracting out, corporatization, and privatization of many government services" (Mitchell, 1996, p. 17). Countries that have signed up to this neoliberal agenda have pursued and doggedly implemented a cache of ideas regardless of the effects:

- public sector organisations are conceived of as producers that convert inputs into outputs of goods and services;

- the public act as "consumers" or "customers" who consume these outputs;

- the efficient delivery of outputs is the principal measure of success, where greater efficiency is produced by reducing the resource cost of producing a given quality of goods and services; and

- competition among providers or producers is the best way of maximizing efficiency. (Hamilton, 1996, pp. 29–30)

Is the Neoliberal Way the Only Way?

To argue that there is no other game in town is to be mischievous, ideologically blind, or willfully bent on countenancing only one option. The current problem with school reform is a combination of all three. The reality is that there are some extremely compelling alternative options available, some of which are demonstrably out-competing the dominant neoliberal model even from within its own warped measurable outputs ideology. But before I come to these, a little ground-clearing needs to occur.

It is becoming very clear that the entire foundation of the neoliberal reform project is crumbling under the weight of its own ineptitude and is in deep trouble because of its disconnectedness from the real world of schools and young people's lives. There can be no more damning indictment of this than the major and very public recantation and critique of the whole neoliberal school reform panoply by sometime ardent supporter and "true believer" Diane Ravitch (2010), the high-profile former US Assistant Secretary of Education under President G.W. Bush. In her words, it failed the reality test—"I [lost] confidence in these reforms.... [M]y views changed as I saw how these ideas were working in reality" (p. 2). Ravitch explained how, as a policy maker, she had unwittingly become so easily seduced:

> There is something comforting about the belief that the invisible hand of the market, as Adam Smith called it, will bring improvements through some unknown force. In education, this belief in market forces lets us ordinary mortals off the hook, especially those who have not figured out how to improve low-performing schools or break through the lassitude of unmotivated teens. (p. 11)

In a piece I wrote recently entitled 'Speaking the Unpleasant' (Smyth & McInerney, 2012—with acknowledgements to Chavez & O'Donnell, 1998), I alluded to Ravitch's deep unease around the "distractions, wrong turns, and lost opportunities" (Ravitch, 2010, p. 225) taken by the neoliberal reformists. She argued there needed to be a major policy reversal around a litany of key reasons why schools could not be improved under the current policy trajectory—most notably, *if*:

- We continually reorganize their structure and management without regard for their essential purpose (p. 225).

- Officials intrude into pedagogical territory and make decisions that properly should be made by professional educators (p. 225).

- We continue to focus only on reading and mathematics while ignoring other studies (p. 226).

- We value only what tests measure (p. 226).

- We rely exclusively on tests as the means of deciding the fate of students, teachers, principals, and schools (p. 226).

- We continue to close neighborhood schools in the name of reform (p. 227).

- We entrust them to the magical powers of the market (p. 227).

- Charter schools [academies or their equivalents] siphon away the most motivated students and their families in the poorest communities from the regular public schools (p. 227).

- We expect them to act like private, profit-seeking enterprises (p. 227).

- We continue to drive away experienced principals and replace them with neophytes who have taken a leadership training course but have little or no experience as teachers (p. 228).

- We blindly worship data (p. 228).

- We listen to those who say that money doesn't matter (p. 228).

- We ignore the disadvantages associated with poverty that affect children's ability to learn (p. 229).

- We use them as society's all-purpose punching bag, blaming them for the ills of the economy, the burdens imposed on children by poverty, the dysfunction of families, and the erosion of civility (p. 229). (Smyth & McInerney, 2012, p. 25)

Despite its rhetorical posturing about being wedded to notions of "evidence-based" approaches, one thing the neoliberal project dislikes intensely is "evidence"—unless of course it is evidence that supports its own warped and flawed ideology. Evidence of the kind that supports the idea that neoliberal projects are better for children (for example, when they compete against each other; when the focus is on management and governance rather than teaching; the fanciful notion that high-stakes testing improves learning; and that somehow schooling is better for children when it is driven by market forces) is hard, if not impossible, to come by. Continuing to harp on about the only evidence that counts being that of a "hard" or "randomized controlled-experimental" kind is really quite cute. The bad news for the neoliberal zealots is that, in the real world, as distinct from the isolated thought bubble they live in, (and whether they like it or not), evidence comes into existence in all kinds of ways, not just in the elitist singular form they recognize.

I want to spend the rest of this chapter canvassing some alternative "evidence"—first of a "macro" kind, around what has occurred in Finland; and second, of a "micro" kind, at the school level, around research I have been doing over the past 30 years that presents a more democratic face and that fits under the rubric of the *socially just school*, in disadvantaged schools in Australia. In both cases, it is important that I be very clear that I do not want to overly romanticize what has occurred in either instance (cf. Simola, 2005, "the Finnish miracle"; Hargreaves, 2011, "unFinnished business"; and Sahlberg, 2010, "Finnish lessons" to the rest of the world), because the reality has been that democratic alternatives have had to struggle mightily against the crushing and powerful prevalence of the dominant neoliberal reform project, and this has not been without tangible consequence.

Finland is the single standout case the rest of the world—particularly, the US, UK, Australia, New Zealand and Canada—would prefer did not exist because its mere presence totally demolishes and undermines all of the neoliberal claims to legitimacy. On almost every set of indicators—achievements measured on PISA testing scales; equity of educational treatment; "dropout" and school completion rates; transition rates into higher education; grade retention; performance of immigrant and low SES students—Finland either leads the world or is up there with a small number of similar-minded countries such as Korea and other Nordic countries (see OECD, 2012) that have gone down a very different reform path. The question of how they have been able to avoid embracing the tenets of neoliberalism that have gripped other parts of the world with such devastating and disfiguring results lies very much, in the case of Finland, in the nature of the Finnish people and their history of struggle and resistance within a strong national culture and sense of identity. I will turn to this later in the context of the *socially just school*.) As I have elsewhere summarized their situation:

> Finland has none of the trappings of…league tables, national testing, and school audits, and while it has not been immune from the global tendencies …[it] has chosen to mediate this particular global policy trend in quite a different way. As Rinne et al. (2002) put it, in Finland the embrace of "privatization" and "school choice" has been "slow and clumsy" and the "partial failure of the neo liberal invasion is to be found in the national history of Finland" which has had a "stubborn mentality" (p. 655) of standing its ground on equity issues even in the face of slick international educational policies. (Smyth, 2011, p. 108)

According to Rinne, Kivirauma, and Simola (2002), "The market-based rhetoric and practices have not been able to take root in the core areas of the traditional Nordic welfare state—education, social services and health—as easily in other areas of society" (p. 655).

This "partial failure of the neo-liberal invasion" (p. 655) resides in the ability Finland developed as part of its history, of opposing and defying repressive regimes such as the attempts at Czarist "Russianization" (p. 655). In short:

> Throughout its history, Finland has learned to keep a balance during many waves of invasion…. The national culture and the educational policies of the country have always undulated between the slick turns of the helm by the power elite and a form of "national conservatism"…. The swiftest errand boys of the elite have speedily adapted the exhortations of the centre of power…and [orchestrated] the [radical] turn of the helm…[but the] ship does not change course at the same speed. (p. 655)

It seems that an inherent national conservatism, grounded in a sense of decency, has enabled two quite different games to be played out in Finland, without the synthetic one of making money being allowed to drown out issues of sensibility and decency. Rinne et al. (2002) explain it as follows:

> Although the economic elite of Finland has edged into a top position in the world market through IT developments and its leading marketing enterprise Nokia, and even though the political and educational elite of Finland is trying to play the role of model student in the family of the European Union, the mentality and actions of the nation follows these changes at a slow and lazy pace. (p. 655)

In the international rush to find the formula behind the Finnish "miracle," or the "Finnish Way" (Sahlberg, 2011), something that is clearly impossible, we need to be extremely mindful that what has occurred there has been culturally and historically unique and cannot be rendered down to a list of attributes to be borrowed or applied. That is not to say that there are not lessons that can be learnt, but it cannot be reduced to the equivalent of some "international spectacle" (Simola, 2005, p. 455). As Sahlberg (2011) puts it, invoking Vilho Hirvi, one of the Finnish educational pioneers of the 1990s: "An educated nation cannot be created by force" (p. 2), with the result that "reforming schools is a complex and slow process" (p. 3). Part of the explanation lies in the dual approach of a commitment to providing "educational opportunities in an egalitarian manner" in a way that "makes efficient use of resources" (p. 1).

The starting point has to be the reality that "the Finns transformed their educational system from mediocre in the 1980s to one of the models of excellence today" (Sahlberg, 2011, p. 1); but they did not do it in the tough muscular way other countries have attempted reforms, notably by "tightening control over schools, stronger accountability for student performance, firing bad teachers, and closing down troubled schools...tougher competition, more data, abolishing teacher unions, opening more charter schools, or employing corporate-world management models in education" (pp. 4–5). Quite the opposite: the driving ideas have been around "improving the teaching force, limiting student testing to a necessary minimum, placing responsibility and trust before accountability, and handing control over school-and-district-level leadership to education professionals" (p. 5). Furthermore, this has all been done with modest resourcing and during "the worst economic crisis that Finland has experienced since World War II" (p. 6). At the core of the transformation—and essential to our understanding of it—has been a concerted and long-term commitment to "building on teacher strengths, securing relaxed and fear-free learning for students, and gradually enhancing trust within education systems" (p. 6).

Some of the proximal indicators of Finland's education success are that teachers are extremely highly regarded and respected by the public and they themselves have a highly developed sense of professionalism, with teacher education a prized occupational pathway that is more difficult to get into than medicine and law and with all teachers, including primary teachers, being required to hold a master's degree.

What Then Can Be Done?

The kind of educational thinking driving the reform process in Finland is not especially radical or novel. What makes their ideas stand out is that they have been institutionalized, systematically adopted, and have become culturally embedded. In some respects this standout quality is also the greatest impediment to emulating such reform models—they have unique contexts and histories that cannot be transplanted. Possibly of more relevance are local or indigenous instances of resistance and struggles against the dominant neoliberal school reform model, because it is within those instances that we can more readily see how constraints are being rubbed up against, and with what level of success or failure. As Connell (2011) puts it, the challenge in places like the US, UK and Australia is creating a movement against "a monopoly that installs a privileged set of diagnoses [deemed appropriate] for the whole world" (p. 5).

To be clear about what has to be struggled against, Connell (2011) identifies two sharp edges. First, the policy and research infatuation with "school and teacher "effectiveness" that

treats schools and teachers as bearers of variables (attitudes, qualifications, strong leadership, etc.) to be correlated with pupil outcomes, measured on standardized tests...[leading to the notion] that there is always a "best practice" that can be instituted and audited from above. (p. 77)

Second, and coupled with this, is what Connell (2011) refers to as the "neoliberal governance of teaching itself" that derives from the market-oriented nature of neoliberalism, which "is profoundly suspicious of professionalism…[and which it regards] as anti-competitive" (p. 77). This highly distrustful view of teachers means that they have to be closely controlled, endlessly audited, and made capable of comparison, so that schools can be forced to compete against one another.

One of the triggers in the push for a counter-narrative is confronting the realities of the disgraceful inequities consistently spawned by this model of school reform (for an illustration of this see Kozol, 1992, 1995, 2005, 2012). There is a sense that there is something fundamentally wrong with the educational trajectory in countries such as the US (see Berliner, 2006, 2009, 2013) and Australia (see Argy, 2007; ACOSS, 2012).

While it is not possible for schools on their own to reverse the social scarring produced by social and political structures, they need to be a crucial part of the mix to create a more democratic and just society.

For some three decades, in my research, I have been exploring what an alternative archetype that I refer to as the *socially just school* (Smyth, 1994, 2004, 2012a, 2013) might look like—which in its conceptual underpinnings is not that far removed from what is happening existentially in Finland. Schematically, and briefly, the *socially just school* has ten broad qualities, inflections or attributes that give it an orientation that marks it out from its neoliberal counterpart as follows:

1. They have a clear and decisive mission or philosophy as to what they exist for—to improve the life chances of the most excluded and marginalized. They have a very well-developed sense of justice, and a deep understanding of injustice.

2. They regard themselves as having agency. They don't allow themselves to be constructed as victims, nor do they see themselves as being primarily beholden to, or being driven unthinkingly, by outsiders' agendas. In a sense, they regard their students and families as having been put in the state they are in because of the playing out of the social, political and economic agenda of others who are more powerful. In this respect they operate strategically—one might argue, courageously and fearlessly—in advancing the interests of their students and communities in ways that try to minimize further damage or ameliorate the worst excesses of what has been done to them. Far from benign or neutral, these schools have a clear sense of the political work they are engaged in.

3. They do not have an overblown or overwhelming concern or preoccupation with their own self-image or self-importance—which is stunningly refreshing in this synthetic era of posturing and image and impression management aimed at ensuring "market share." They understand who they are, they are comfortable and secure with this image, and unashamedly present themselves to the outside world for what they authentically are rather than as facsimiles.

4. The unassailable dispositional attribute that distinguishes the socially just school from other schools is that they regard disadvantage as being socially constructed. That is to say, they do not regard it as a natural state of affairs that students, parents and the community have deficits that have to be remedied or fixed. Rather, they think in terms

of the need to locate the sources of the forces that have made them the way they are, of the need to better understand how these forces work, how they need to be confronted, and in the end transformed. In that regard, these schools are activist places.

5. Rather than seeing their students and families as "clients" or "customers"—both of which bring with them dependency status, on the one hand of "being serviced," and on the other of engaging in an extractive transaction—these schools regard their constituents as "valued members." This means adopting a personal rather than an institutional relationship in which the school gets to intimately know the strengths, struggles, aspirations, and histories that students and their families bring to the school.

   Put another way, these are schools that bring people's lives into the school—students, parents, and members of the community—rather than creating walls and moats around the institution of the school. They are places that value diversity and their constituents view this as a major and undeniable aspect of their strength, rather than seeing it in terms of deficits. They see troubling inheritances as challenges to be worked with, rather than insurmountable interferences or obstacles.

6. The socially just school has a "success-oriented approach" to learning. That is to say, they regard students and communities as capable of learning and achieving despite much handwringing by others outside these schools about alleged under-performance.

   The problem with benchmarks and standards is that they demonstrably fail to take account of context, skill sets, attributes, ways of learning, and strengths that don't always fit with conventional methods. To that extent, these are schools that are intent on celebrating and re-making an identity that is much more consistent with the richness of the resources and histories that communities of disadvantage bring, while also being mindful of where they have come from. There is a strong sense that these schools regard their students and families as vibrant and rich sources of resources, rather than bundles of pathologies to be remedied or rectified.

7. One element that goes to the very essence of the socially just school is the commitment to working in innovative ways—and for good reason. Conventional ways simply do not work in these schools, and they have to be adept at analyzing their contexts, pinpointing the issues, recasting things, and devising local solutions that often constitute radically different ways of operating to improve the life chances of their students.

   Approaches that work in middle-class schools and that rely on docile forms of compliance, even boredom, are unlikely to have much currency in settings of disadvantage. The starting point in socially just schools is altogether different. They recast themselves as listening organizations with a commitment to giving students, parents, and families authentic voice in shaping their futures and how they go about learning.

8. In respect of externally generated educational policy, they recast the external initiative around their guiding question: how might this work in the interests of the least advantaged? In other words, rather than outright resistance, their approach is one of getting inside whatever the policy is and re-working it in the interests of their students and communities.

9. They approach classroom discipline differently. The conventional view is that this is a behavior management issue, and the way to handle it is to bear down harshly on

recalcitrant students and demand conformity. The socially just school, for the most part, recasts discipline issues in quite a different way—it regards student disengagement from classroom learning as typically an indication of a disengaging curriculum.

In other words, responsibility is directed to what is on offer to students and how it should change, rather than always on the student to alter their actions. When students cannot see the relevance of the curriculum to their lives, or that of their families and communities, it follows that there is an enhanced likelihood of disengagement and disconnection. No amount of haranguing and chastising is likely to work in the long term if the curriculum is inappropriate.

10. They confront and puncture myths. For example, "these kids are not capable of academic learning, and therefore must be forced to endure an inferior vocational alternative." Socially just schools are able to see through the class-based sorting mechanism that lies at the heart of much so-called vocational education, and they disavow this by engaging their students with a rigorous and relevant curriculum.

11. A particular challenge is developing sophisticated ways of making connections from where students are at in their lives, and developing an educational imagination around "big ideas"—and they don't see these as mutually exclusive. In other words, they are not schools that give in to the inevitability of a dumbed-down vocational curriculum that equips their students only for low-level, insecure, poorly paid, menial, or non-existent jobs. They regard such a degraded response as an abrogation of their moral responsibility and as a mark of institutional failure on their part (Smyth, 2012a, pp. 12–14; Smyth, 2012b).

Conclusion

In this chapter I have attempted four things. First, I have confronted the neoliberal model of school reform that has both assaulted and gripped education in the western world. Second, I have addressed the provocation of why we have allowed this to happen. Third, I have punctured the myth that there "is no other way" by referring to the macro-case of Finland. Finally, I have alluded to the existence of what I have referred to in my own Australian research as the archetype of the "socially just school."

The question remains as to whether we have the courage to speak out louder in condemning a grossly unjust trajectory, or whether we will continue in the comfort of being "done to."

References

Adorno, T. (1994). *Minima moralia: Reflections from damaged life*. London: Verso. (Original work published 1974.)

Argy, F. (2007). Education inequalities in Australia *Institute of Advanced Studies, Paper No. 5, May*.

Australian Council of Social Service. (2012). *Poverty in Australia: ACOSS Paper 194*.

Berliner, D. (2006). Our impoverished view of educational reform. *Teachers College Record, 108*(6), 949–995.

Berliner, D. (2009). *Poverty and potential: Out-of-school factors and school success*. Tempe: AZ: Education Policy Research Unit, Arizona State University and Boulder Education and the Public Interest Center, University of Colorado.

Berliner, D. (2013). Effects of inequality and poverty vs teachers and schooling on America's youth. *Teachers College Record, 116*(1). Retrieved from http://www.tcrecord.org

Chavez, R., & O'Donnell, J. (Eds.). (1998). *Speaking the unpleasant: The politics of (non) engagement in the multicultural education terrain*. Albany: State University of New York Press.

Connell, R. (1996, August). *Prepare for interesting times: Education in a fractured world*. Inaugural professorial address, University of Sydney, Australia.

Connell, R. (2011). *Confronting equality: Gender, knowledge and global change*. Cambridge, UK: Polity Press.

Davidson, K. (1993, October 30). Is this man trying to do to health what Victoria did to education? *The Age*, p. 9.

Hamilton, C. (1996). "Misotely" and the National Commission of Audit. In Australia Institute (Ed.), *What should governments do? Auditing the National Commission of Audit* (pp. 26–39). Canberra: Australia Institute.

Hargreaves, A. (2011). Foreword: unFinnished business. In P. Sahlberg (Ed.), *Finnish lessons: What can the world learn from educational change in Finland?* (pp. xv–xx). New York: Teachers College Press.

Kozol, J. (1992). *Savage inequalities: Children in America's schools*. New York: Harper Perennial.

Kozol, J. (1995). *Amazing grace: The lives of children and the conscience of a nation*. New York: Harper Collins.

Kozol, J. (2005). *The shame of the nation: The restoration of apartheid schooling in America*. New York: Crown.

Kozol, J. (2012). *Fire in the ashes: Twenty-five years among the poorest children in America*. New York: Crown.

Mitchell, D. (1996). Social policy and the National Commission of Audit: Old whines in new bottles? In Australia Institute (Ed.), *What should government do? Auditing the National Audit Commission* (pp. 17–28). Canberra: Australia Institute.

OECD. (1994). *School: A matter of choice*. Paris: Author.

OECD. (1995). *Governance in transition: Public management reforms in OECD countries*. Paris: Author.

OECD. (2012). *Equity and quality in education: Supporting disadvantaged students and schools*. Paris: Author.

Ravitch, D. (2010). *The death and life of the American school system: How testing and choice are undermining education*. Philadelphia: Basic Books.

Rinne, R., Kivirauma, J., & Simola, H. (2002). Shoots of revisionist education policy or just slow readjustment? The Finnish case of educational reconstruction. *Journal of Education Policy, 17*(6), 643–658.

Sahlberg, P. (2011). *Finnish lessons: What can the world learn from educational change in Finland?* New York: Teachers College Press.

Schwartz, S. (2012, August 9). Don't let unis hike their fees, make them efficient. *Australian Financial Review*. http://www.afr.com/p/opinion/don_let_unis_hike_their_fees_make_0K0mRMn37N0MfieXobaOkM

Simola, H. (2005). The Finnish miracle of PISA: Historical and sociological remarks on teaching and teacher education. *Comparative Education, 41*(4), 455470.

Smyth, J. (1993 December). *A study of participation, consultation and collective bargaining in the teaching profession in Australia* (Draft Commissioned Paper). Geneva: International Labour Organization.

Smyth, J. (1994, November). *Opening address to "Touchstones of Socially Just School Conference."* Paper presented at the Touchstones of Socially Just School Conference, Flinders University, Adelaide.

Smyth, J. (2004). Social capital and the "socially just school." *British Journal of Sociology of Education, 25*(1), 19–33.

Smyth, J. (2011). The *disaster* that has been the "self-managing school"—its genesis, trajectory, undisclosed agenda, and effects. *Journal of Educational Administration and History, 43*(2), 95–117.

Smyth, J. (2012a). The socially just school and critical pedagogies in communities put at a disadvantage. *Critical Studies in Education, 53*(1), 9–18.

Smyth, J. (2012b, October). *Young people and the socially just school: Re-thinking the nexus between education and social justice*. Paper presented at the Youth Research Centre and Melbourne Graduate School of Education seminar, University of Melbourne, Australia.

Smyth, J. (2013). Losing our way? Challenging the direction of teacher education in Australia and re-framing it around the *socially just school*. *Asia-Pacific Journal of Teacher Education, 41*(1), 111–122

Smyth, J., & McInerney, P. (2012). *From silent witnesses to active agents: Student voice in re-engaging with learning*. New York: Peter Lang.

Smyth, J., & Shacklock, G. (1998). *Re-making teaching: Ideology, policy and practice*. London: Routledge.

West Africa (1988). IMF found guilty. *West Africa* (October 17-23), 1942-1943.

CHAPTER SIX

Schooling in Disaster Capitalism

How the Political Right Is Using Disaster to
Privatize Public Schooling

KENNETH J. SALTMAN

A round the world, disaster is providing the means for business to accumulate profit. From
the Asian tsunami of 2005 that allowed corporations to seize coveted shoreline properties
for resort development to the multibillion-dollar no-bid reconstruction contracts in Iraq and
Afghanistan, from the privatization of public schooling following Hurricane Katrina in the
Gulf Coast to the ways that No Child Left Behind sets public schools up to be dismantled
and made into investment opportunities—a grotesque pattern is emerging in which business
is capitalizing on disaster. Naomi Klein has written of

> … the rise of a predatory form of disaster capitalism that uses the desperation and fear created by ca-
> tastrophe to engage in radical social and economic engineering. And on this front, the reconstruction
> industry works so quickly and efficiently that the privatizations and land grabs are usually locked in
> before the local population knows what them.[1]

Despite the fact that attempts to privatize and commercialize public schools proceed at a
startling pace,[2] privatization increasingly appears in a new form that Klein calls "disaster capitalism" and that David Harvey terms "accumulation by dispossession." This article details
how in education the political Right is capitalizing on disaster from Chicago's Renaissance
2010 to the federal No Child Left Behind Act, from educational rebuilding in the Gulf
Coast of the U.S. to education profiteering in Iraq. The new predatory form of educational
privatization aims to dismantle and then commodify particular public schools. This conservative movement threatens the development of public schools as necessary places that foster engaged critical citizenship. At the same time, it undermines the public and democratic
purposes of public education; it amasses vast profits for few, and even furthers U.S. foreign
policy agendas.

Educators committed to defending and strengthening public education as a crucial public sphere in a democratic society may be relieved by several recent failures of the educational privatization movement. By 2000 business publications were eyeing public education as the next big score, ripe for privatization and commodification, likening it to the medical and military industries and suggesting that it might yield $600 billion a year in possible takings.[3] However, it has become apparent that only a few years later, Educational Management Organizations (EMO) that seek to manage public schools for profit have not overtaken public education (though EMOs are growing at an alarming rate of a five-fold increase in schools managed in six years). The biggest experiment in for-profit management of public schooling, The Edison Schools, continues as a symbol, according to the right-wing business press, of why running schools for profit on a vast scale is not profitable.[4] The massive EMO Knowledge Universe, created by junk bond felon Michael Milken upon his release from prison from nearly a hundred counts of fraud and insider trading, is in the midst of going out of business.[5] By the autumn of 2005, the school voucher movement, which the Right has been fighting to implement for decades, had only succeeded in capturing the Washington, D.C. public schools (through the assistance of Congress), and that experiment is by all accounts looking bad. The charter school movement, which is fostering privatization by allowing for publicly funded schools managed by for-profit companies, and is being pushed by massive federal funding under No Child Left Behind, has also taken a hit from NAEP scores that, in traditional terms of achievement, suggest charters do not score as high as the much-maligned public schools. Even school commercialism has faced a sizable backlash from a public fed up and sickened by the shameless attempts of marketers to sell sugar-laden soft drinks and candy bars to U.S. schoolchildren who are suffering epidemic levels of type II diabetes and obesity. Although commercialism continues putting ads in textbooks and playing fields, on buildings and buses, a growing number of cities, states, and provinces have put in place anticommercialism laws. Such laws limit the transformation of public space into yet more commercial space for corporations, which have succeeded in infiltrating nearly every bit of daily life with advertisements and narratives that proselytize the elements of corporate culture: celebrating consumerism, possessive individualism, social Darwinism, authoritarianism, and a corporate vision for the future of work, leisure, politics, and the environment.

It would be difficult to assert that most public schools currently foster the best alternative to corporate culture, that is, democratic culture, what Dewey called "creative democracy." Nurturing a democratic culture and a democratic ethos demands of educators continual work, practice, and attention.[6] The present historical moment is seeing the radical erosion of democratic culture by not only the aforementioned onslaught of commercial culture but also the state-led dismantling of civil liberties under the new dictates of the security state, the resurgence of jingoistic patriotism under the so-called "war on terror," and demands for adhesion to a militarized corporate globalization.[7] If many public schools do not presently foster a democratic ethos necessary for developing in citizens habits of engaged public criticism and participation, the public nature of public schools makes them a crucial "site and stake" of struggle for the expansion of democratic social relations. Privatizing public schools does not simply threaten to skim public tax money to provide rich investors with profit. Public schools differ from privately controlled schools in that they harbor a distinct potential for public deliberation and oversight that privately owned and controlled educational institutions limit. Privately controlled institutions are captured by private interests.

For example, freedom of speech is protected on the public space of a town common but is privately regulated in a shopping mall. In a public school, learning and knowledge can be engaged in relation to pressing public problems in ways that can be limited within privatized schools. Consider, for example, the following threats to the public: the threats posed by the expanded corporate control over a biotechnology giant such as Monsanto that can patent life, own and control the genetic makeup of all crops, and infect biodiverse crops with potentially devastating genetically modified Franken-food; the threats posed to the global environment by a multinational corporation such as McDonald's that participates in destroying the rainforests for cattle grazing land; the threats to public life as a national security state expands to enable the U.S. government to continue to surround strategically the world's oil supplies with permanent military bases to benefit oil corporations, military corporations, and to continue to project a capitalist model of development that is most often, despite the rhetoric, thoroughly at odds with democracy, particularly in the states alleged to be U.S. allies: Egypt, Pakistan, Jordan, Uzbekistan, etc. When a for-profit corporation runs schools, it will share ideological commitments to corporate globalization that frame public problems in ways compatible with ever-expanding corporate profit despite the risks to people. Public problems such as the weakening of the public sphere resulting from the corporate takeover of knowledge and schooling is not likely to be taught by corporations such as The Edison Schools. At stake in the struggle for public education is the value of critical and public education as a foundation for an engaged citizenry and a substantive democracy.

Capitalizing on Disaster in Education

Despite the range of obvious failures of multiple public school privatization initiatives, the privatization advocates have hardly given up. In fact, the privatizers have become far more strategic. The new educational privatization might be termed "back door privatization"[8] or maybe "smash and grab" privatization. A number of privatization schemes are being initiated through a process involving the dismantling of public schools followed by the opening of for-profit, charter, and deregulated public schools. These enterprises typically despise teachers' unions, are hostile to local democratic governance and oversight, and have an unquenchable thirst for "experiments," especially with the private sector.[9] These initiatives are informed by right-wing think tanks and business organizations. Four examples that typify back-door privatization are (1) No Child Left Behind, (2) Chicago's Renaissance 2010 project, (3) educational rebuilding in Iraq, and (4) educational rebuilding in New Orleans.

No Child Left Behind

No Child Left Behind sets schools up for failure by making impossible demands for continual improvement. When schools have not met Adequate Yearly Progress (AYP), they are subject to punitive action by the federal government, including the potential loss of formerly guaranteed federal funding and requirements for tutoring from a vast array of for-profit Special Educational Service providers. A number of authors have described how NCLB is a boon for the testing and tutoring companies, while it does not provide financial resources for the test score increases it demands.[10] (This is aside from the cultural politics of whose knowledge these tests affirm and discredit.[11]) Sending billions of dollars of support toward the charter school movement, NCLB pushes schools that do not meet AYP to restructure in ways that encourage privatization, discourage unions, and avoid local regulations on crucial matters. One study has found that by 2013 nearly all of the public schools in the Great Lakes region of the U.S. will be declared failed public schools and subject to such reforms.[12] Clearly, NCLB is designed to accomplish the implementation of privatization and deregulation in ways that open action could not.

A study of the Great Lakes region of the U.S. by educational policy researchers found that 85 to 95 percent of schools in that region would be declared "failed" by NCLB AYP measures by 2014.[13] These implications are national. Under NCLB, "The entire country faces tremendous failure rates, even under a conservative estimate with several forgiving assumptions."[14] Under NCLB, in order for Illinois, for example, to get much needed federal Title I funds, the school must demonstrate adequate yearly progress. Each year Illinois has to get higher and higher standardized test scores in reading and math to make AYP. Illinois schools, and specifically Illinois schools already receiving the least funding and already serving the poorest students, are being threatened with: (1) losing federal funds; (2) having to use scarce resources for under-regulated and often unproven supplemental educational services (SESs) (private tutoring) such as Newton, a spin-off company of the much criticized for-profit Edison Schools; or (3) being punished, reorganized, or closed and reopened as a "choice" school (these include for-profit or nonprofit charter schools that do not have the same level of public oversight and accountability, that often do not have teachers' unions, and that often have to struggle for philanthropic grants to operate). Many defenders of public education view remediation options 2 and 3 under NCLB as having been designed to undermine those public schools that have been underserved in the first place in order to justify privatization schemes.[15] Public schools need help, investment, and public commitment.

NCLB is setting up for failure not just Illinois public schools but public schools nationally by raising test-oriented thresholds without raising investment and commitment. NCLB itself appears to be a system designed to result in the declaration of wide-scale failure of public schooling to justify privatization.[16] Dedicated administrators, teachers, students, and schools are not receiving much needed resources along with public investment in public services and employment in the communities where those schools are situated. What they are getting instead are threats.

The theoretically and empirically dubious underlying assumption of NCLB is that threats and pressure force teachers to teach what they ought to teach, force students to learn what they ought to learn. In terms of conventional measures of student achievement, Sharon Nichols, Gene Glass, and David Berliner found in their empirical study, *High-Stakes Testing and Student Achievement: Problems for the No Child Left Behind Act*, that "there is no convincing evidence that the pressure associated with high-stakes testing leads to any important benefits for students' achievement… [The authors] call for a moratorium on policies that force the public education system to rely on high-stakes testing."[17] These authors find that high-stakes testing regimes do not achieve what they are designed to achieve. However, to think beyond efficacy to the underlying assumptions about "achievement," it is necessary to raise theoretical concerns. Theoretically, at the very least, the enforcement-oriented assumptions of NCLB fail to consider the limitations of defining "achievement" through high-stakes tests, fail to question what knowledge and whose knowledge constitute legitimate or official curricula that students are expected to master, fail to interrogate the problematic assumptions of learning modeled on digestion or commodity acquisition (as opposed to dialogic, constructivist or other approaches to learning), and such compartmentalized versions of knowledge and learning fail to comprehend how they relate to the broader social and political realities informing knowledge-making both in schools and in society generally.

Renaissance 2010

In Chicago, Renaissance 2010, essentially written by the Commercial Club of Chicago, is being implemented by Chicago Public Schools, a district with more than 85 percent of students who are poor and non-white. It will close 100 public schools and then reopen them as for-profit and nonprofit charter schools, contract schools, and magnet schools, and will bypass important district regulations. The right-wing Heartland Institution hailed the plan "Competition and (public private) Partnerships Are Key to Chicago Renaissance Plan," while the president of the Chicago Teachers Union described it as a plan to dismantle public education.[18] These closings are targeting neighborhoods that are being gentrified and taken over by richer and whiter people who are buying up newly developed condominiums and townhomes. Critics of the plan view it as "urban cleansing" that principally kicks out local residents.[19]

Like NCLB, Renaissance 2010 targets schools that have "failed" to meet Chicago accountability standards defined through high-stakes tests. By closing and reopening schools, Renaissance 2010 allows the newly privatized schools to circumvent NCLB AYP progress requirements, making the list of Chicago's "need improvement" schools shorter. This allows the city to claim improvement by simply redefining terms.

NCLB and Renaissance 2010 share a number of features including not only a high-pressure model, but also reliance on standardized testing as the ultimate measure of learning, threats to teacher job security and teachers' unions, and a push for experimentation with unproven models, including privatization and charter schools, as well as a series of business assumptions and guiding language. For example, speaking of Renaissance 2010, Mayor Daley stated, "This model will generate competition and allow for innovation. It will bring in outside partners who want to get into the business of education."[20]

Beyond its similarities to NCLB, Renaissance 2010 is being hailed as a national model in its own right across the political spectrum. The Bill and Melinda Gates Foundation is the most heavily endowed philanthropy in history, worth about $80 billion, with projects in health and education. Its focus on school reform is guided by the neoliberal Democratic Leadership Council's Progressive Policy Institute. Though it offers no substance, argument, or evidence for why Renaissance 2010 should be replicated, the economically unmatched Gates Foundation praises Renaissance 2010 as a "roadmap" for other cities to follow.[21] As Pauline Lipman, a progressive urban education scholar at the University of Illinois at Chicago, writes:

> If Chicago's accountability has laid the groundwork for privatization, Renaissance 2010 may signal what we can expect nationally as school districts fail to meet NCLB benchmarks. In fact, failure to make "adequate yearly progress" on these benchmarks, and the threat of a state takeover, is a major theme running through the Commercial Club's argument for school choice and charter schools. Business and political leaders seem to believe turning schools over to the market is a common sense solution to the problems in the schools. (Lipman, 2005)[22]

Both NCLB and Renaissance 2010 involve two stages of capitalizing on disaster. The first stage involves the historical underfunding and disinvestment in public schooling that has resulted in disastrous public school conditions. For those communities where these schools are located, it is the public and private sectors that have failed them. However, the corporate sector is usually represented not only in mass media but also much conservative and liberal educational policy literature as coming to rescue the incompetent public sector from itself. As Dorothy Shipps points out in her book *School Reform, Corporate Style: Chicago 1880–2000*, the corporate sector in Chicago and around the nation has long been deeply involved in school reform, agenda setting, and planning in conjunction with other civic planning. As she asks, "If corporate power was instrumental in creating the urban public schools and has had a strong hand in their reform for more than a century, then why have those schools failed urban children so badly?"[23]

Creative Associates International, Incorporated

In Iraq, Creative Associates International, Incorporated (CAII), a for-profit corporation, has made over a hundred million dollars from no-bid contracts with the U.S. Agency for International Development (USAID) to rebuild schools, develop curriculum, develop teacher training, and procure educational supplies. The company has avoided using local contractors and has spent the majority of funds on security while the majority of schools continue to languish in squalor. Educational privatization typifies the way the U.S. invasion has been used to sell off Iraq. Privatization and the development of U.S.-style charter schools are central to the plan (conservative consultants from the right-wing Heritage Foundation have been employed), despite the fact that these are foreign to Iraq's public education system; and members of right-wing think tanks have been engaged to enact what invasion and military destruction has made a lucrative opportunity financially and ideologically. Privatization of the Iraqi schools is part of a broader attempt to privatize and sell off the Iraqi nation while for-profit educational contractor CAII appears as the spearhead of U.S. foreign policy to "promote democracy."[24] As I discuss at length elsewhere[25] the claims for "democracy promotion" in Iraq appear to have more to do with using this human-made disaster for promoting the interests of corporations and transnational capital and nothing to do with expanding meaningful and participatory democracy.

Hurricane Katrina

Likewise, following the natural disaster of Hurricane Katrina in the U.S. Gulf Coast, a for-profit educational contractor from Alaska, named Akima, won a no-bid contract to build temporary portable classrooms in the Gulf Coast. But for-profit education's big haul in the Big Easy was the U.S. Department of Education imposing the largest-ever school voucher experiment for the region and nation. Right-wing think tanks had prepared papers advocating such an approach, describing public school privatization as a "silver lining" and a "golden opportunity."[26] Six months after Hurricane Katrina, the destroyed New Orleans public schools sat slime-coated in mold, debris, and human feces, partially flooded and littered with such detritus as a two-ton air conditioner that had been on the roof and the carcasses of dead dogs.

All 124 New Orleans Public Schools were damaged in some way and only 20 have reopened with more than 10,000 students registered. There were 62,227 students enrolled in NOPS before the storm. (Capchino, 2006)[27]

The devastation nearly defies description.

… Katrina roared in, severely damaging about a quarter of the schools: Roofs caved in. Fierce winds blew out walls and hurled desks through windows. Floodwaters drowned about 300 buses. Computers, furniture and books were buried in mud. Dead dogs and rotting food littered hallways.[28]

Yet days after the disaster *the Washington Times* quoted long-standing advocate of school vouchers Clint Bolick of the Alliance for School Choice. Bolick used the tragedy to propose wide-scale privatization of the New Orleans public schools in the form of a massive voucher scheme. He said, "If there could be a silver lining to this tragedy, it would be that children who previously had few prospects for a high-quality education, now would have expanded options. Even with the children scattered to the winds, that prospect can now be a reality—if the parents are given power over their children's education funds."[29] Calling for the privatization of public schools, Bolick's metaphor of the "silver lining" would be repeated over and over in the popular press immediately after the storm. Karla Dial in the *Heartland News* wrote, "Emergency vouchers could be the silver lining in the storm clouds that brought Hurricane Katrina to the Gulf Coast on August 29."[30] Reuters quoted Louisiana State Superintendent of Education Cecil Picard as saying, "We think this is a once-in-a-lifetime opportunity. I call it the silver lining in the storm cloud."[31] Jack Kemp, who served in the Reagan administration, a longtime proponent of business approaches to urban poverty, took poetic license but stayed with the theme of precious metal, "…with the effort to rebuild after Katrina just getting underway, the Right sees, in the words of Jack Kemp, a 'golden opportunity' to use a portion of the billions of federal reconstruction funds to implement a voucher experiment that, until now, it has been unable to get through Congress."[32] The governor of Louisiana saw gold too. Although, before the storm, the state legislature had rejected the governor's attempt to seize control of the public schools from the city, "legislation proposed by Governor Blanco in November allows the state to take over any New Orleans school that falls below the statewide average on test scores and place it into the state's Recovery School District. Under this low standard, management of 102 of the 115 Orleans Parish schools operating before Katrina would be transferred to the state. The governor sees it as an effort to grasp what she called a "golden opportunity for rebirth."[33]

Brian Riedlinger, the director of the Algiers Charter Schools Association that would control all but one of the reopened New Orleans schools six months after the tragedy, employed a creative variation on the theme, invoking the poetry of Coleridge and the discourse of hygiene, "I think the schools have been a real albatross. And so I think what we're giving parents is the possibility of hope, a possibility of wiping the slate clean and starting over."[34] Long-standing advocates of public school privatization Paul T. Hill and Jane Hannaway carried the hygienic metaphor a step further, writing in their Urban Institute report, "The Future of Public Education in New Orleans," that "[e]ducation could be one of the bright spots in New Orleans' recovery effort, which may even establish a new model for school districts nationally."[35] This "bright spot," according to Hill and Hannaway, which should be a national model, calls for refusing to rebuild the New Orleans public schools, firing the teachers and by extension dissolving the teachers' union, eradicating the central administration, and inviting for-profit corporations with sordid histories such as The Edison Schools[36] and other organizations to take over the running of schools.[37] Sajan George is a director of Alvarez & Marsal, a Bush administration–connected business-consulting firm that is making millions in its role subcontracting the rebuilding of schools. George, a "turnaround expert" contracted by the state, brought these metaphors together, stating, "This is the silver lining in the dark cloud of Katrina. We would not have been able to start with an almost clean slate if Katrina had not happened. So it really does represent an incredible opportunity."[38]

An incredible opportunity indeed.

Hurricane Katrina in New Orleans typifies the new form of educational privatization. The disaster has been used to enrich a predominantly white, tiny business and political elite while achieving educational privatization goals that the Right has been unable to achieve before: (1) implement the largest-ever experiment in school vouchers; (2) allow for enormous profits in education rebuilding by contracting firms with political connections; (3) allow the replacement of a system of universal public education with a charter school network designed to participate in the dispossession of poor and African American residents from their communities. Such documents as those by the Urban Institute and the Heritage Foundation discuss strategies to make the temporary voucher scheme permanent and even how to take advantage of future disasters.

Vouchers use public money to pay for private schools and thus stand as a potentially lucrative business opportunity. Right-wing think tanks and advocates of educational privatization have been calling for wide-scale voucher schemes for decades, alleging that the competition for consumers' money will drive up quality and drive down costs. For example, the Heritage Foundation has been lobbying for vouchers for decades and published a report immediately after the hurricane calling for vouchers, as did the Urban Institute.[39] Support for vouchers comes largely from the neoliberal ideological belief that applying business ideals to the necessary bureaucratic public sector guarantees efficiencies. Critics of vouchers have contended that (1) encouraging parents to "shop" for schools will take scarce federal resources away from those public schools most in need of them—schools that have historically been underfunded by having resource allocations pegged to local property taxes[40]; (2) vouchers have traditionally been used to maintain or worsen racial segregation in the face of desegregation policies[41]—particularly relevant legacy to the racial dispossession going on in New Orleans; (3) vouchers undermine universal public schooling by redefining a public good as a private commodity and stand to exacerbate already existing inequalities in funding; (4) vouchers undermine the public democratic purposes of public schooling by treating citizens as consumers; and (5) vouchers undermine the constitutional separation of church and state.

Not only was the voucher agenda being pushed unsuccessfully for years before the storm, but also until Katrina the only federally funded voucher scheme was implemented by the U.S. Congress in the District of Columbia.

> One that has been "marked by a failure to achieve legislatively determined priorities, an inability to evaluate the program in the manner required by Congress, and efforts by administrators to obscure information that might reflect poorly on the program. (People for the American Way, 2005)[42]

This voucher scheme was surreptitiously inserted into federal legislation by being rolled into a budget bill, and it was aggressively supported by one of the richest people on the planet, Wal-Mart inheritor John Walton of the Walton Family Foundation, one of the largest spenders pushing privatization of public education.[43]

Not only did New Orleans not have a voucher scheme prior to Katrina, but a K-12 voucher bill had just been defeated in the Louisiana state legislature just before the hurricane.[44] The bill would have allowed for public tax money to fund private or religious schooling.

Despite public democratic deliberation on the issue concluding against vouchers, conservative privatization advocates moved quickly to take advantage of the disaster. Within two weeks after the hurricane struck, the Heritage Foundation released a "special report" refashioning their long-standing agenda as "principled solutions" for rebuilding. "Heritage has been pushing school vouchers since 1975 and so it is no surprise that the organization now strongly believes that a voucher proposal that would fund private schools constitutes a successful response to the crisis."[45]

The Bush administration, so slow to provide federal emergency aid to residents, was nonetheless quick to respond to extensive media criticism by following the privatization proposals of such right-wing think tanks. The administration proposed $1.9 billion in aid to K-12 students with $488 million designated for school vouchers. The editors of *Rethinking Schools* accurately wrote, "This smells like a back-door approach to get public funding for private schools and would essentially create the first national school voucher plan."[46]

Privatization advocates were quite explicit in their desire to undermine local control over educational decision-making and to create a situation in which it would be very difficult to reverse the implementation of vouchers. For example, Karla Dial reporting in the right-wing Heartland Institute *School Reform News*, quotes Chris Kinnan of Freedom Works, a D.C. organization fighting for "smaller government" and more "personal freedom."

> "Having those vouchers for a couple of years would change the way parents and students and even educators think about them," Kinnan said. "The impact would be so powerful that if you did it right, [school] systems would be competing to attract these [kids with vouchers]. It's all about changing the incentive. Once you have that freedom it would be very difficult to go back to the community control system."[47]

For Kinnan and his ilk, "freedom" means privatizing public control over public resources so that fewer people with more wealth and power have more political control over said resources. The genius of framing the amassing of political and economic control over public resources as individual consumer choice is that it takes on the deceptive appearance of increasing individual control while it actually removes individuals from collective control. Privatizers aim to treat the use of public resources as "shopping" by "consumers," thereby naturalizing the public sector as a market—as a natural, politically neutral entity ruled by the laws of supply and demand rather than as a matter of public priority, political deliberation, and competing values and visions. Such metaphors of consumer culture not only conceal the ways that public goods and services are different from markets (public services aim to serve public interest and collective goals not the amassing of private profit), but such appeals also fail to admit that markets themselves are hardly neutral and natural but are, on the contrary, hierarchical, human-made political configurations unequally distributing power and control over material resources and cultural value.

Clint Bolick of the Alliance for School Choice was also scheming to get a foot in the door. Hopeful that the initial one-year period for vouchers in the Bush proposal could be extended indefinitely, he said, "I think that if emergency school vouchers are passed this time they will be a routine part of future emergency relief. I'm also hopeful that when the No Child Left Behind Act is modified that it will be easier for Congress to add vouchers to the remedies available under that law."[48]

The Heritage Foundation, the Alliance for School Choice, and the Heartland Institute were hardly alone, as a large number of right-wing groups committed to vouchers praised the president's plan. Gary Bauer, of the group American Values, hailed the "rebuilding challenge as an opportunity to implement conservative ideas such as school vouchers and tax free zones."[49] The Bush plan was praised by the Family Research Council, Rich Lowry of the *National Review*, Gary McCaleb of the Alliance Defense Fund, Marvin Olasky of *World Magazine*, and William Donohue of the Catholic League, among others.[50]

The Yankee Institute took a full page color advertisement in Heartland's *School Reform News* with a letter from its executive director, Lewis Andrews, who admonishes readers that when the real estate bubble bursts and public education "cost soars relative to home values" in rich communities, "savvy reformers will be prepared to make the case for school vouchers in all communities."[51] The ad begins with the expression, "Every cloud has a silver lining."

Implicit in Andrews' statements is the fact that privatizers have already been taking advantage of the historical failure to fund education properly in poor and working-class communities. Before Katrina, per pupil spending in New Orleans stood at about $5,000 ($4,986 in 1998). To put this in perspective, per pupil spending in suburban public school districts in wealthy suburbs around the nation reaches as high as roughly quadruple this amount despite the fact that they face far fewer obstacles. As the Right clearly grasps, the question of privatization is inextricably linked to matters of public funding. Vouchers, charters, and EMOs cannot make headway with well-financed public schools in richer communities. Crisis and emergency benefit privatization advocates can seize upon a situation with preformulated plans to commodify this public service. To put it differently, privatizers target those who have been denied adequate public investment in the first place. As the United Federation of Teachers' Joe Derose insists, the policy emphasis in rebuilding should be on the chronic underfunding plaguing the New Orleans public schools rather than on the schemes to privatize them.[52] As the above quotes from Bolick, Kinnan, and Andrews illustrate, the Right is eager to take advantage of crisis to subvert democratic oversight over policy matters of great public importance.

The Bush administration has long aimed to expand vouchers. In 2002 vouchers were removed from the No Child Left Behind bill at the last moment as part of an effort to secure bipartisan support.[53] Not only do the Katrina federal vouchers cover far beyond the Gulf Coast region, but they take advantage of the crisis to promote the idea of vouchers and privatization generally. For example, while select counties and parishes in Alabama, Mississippi, Louisiana, and Florida are included in the Emergency Impact Aid, the entire state of Texas is included in the voucher scheme. While emergency funds do not permit public school rebuilding, they nonetheless give funding to schools in 49 states. What is more, the vouchers can be given to charter schools without charter schools meeting section 5210 (1) of ESEA No Child Left Behind that requires charter schools to be developed with public charter agencies. In other words, the vouchers allow public funding for charter schools that do not need to be held accountable to public oversight institutions that regulate charter schools. As a result, the Aid favors not merely the public funding of private schools but even encourages the development of charter schools unregulated by the public sector by funding them when they would otherwise be ineligible to receive federal funding for having failed to meet basic requirements.[54]

The Emergency Impact Aid is also being used to promote and publicize vouchers as a legitimate school reform. Secretary of Education Margaret Spellings made this goal of proselytizing vouchers quite explicit in her speech of April 5, 2006, in a New York church, saying that, in addition to expanding charter schools and the voucher scheme in D.C., "most importantly, we've armed the parents of 48 million public school students nationwide with the information to be smart educational consumers and become real advocates for their children."[55] Spellings notably embraces the neoliberal description of education as a business with consumers rather than as a public good crucial for the making of citizens capable of developing skills and dispositions of self-governance. In this speech Spellings explains that No Child Left Behind's provision allowing students to attend other schools and its designation of schools as "failed" are designed to expand "choice." This is how she describes both vouchers and the NCLB provision allowing students to go to any school—a measure implemented to set the stage for vouchers. And as Spellings explains, the voucher scheme in New Orleans is part of an aggressive broader attempt to use federal power to privatize public schooling:

> More than 1,700 schools around the country have failed to meet state standards for five or six years in a row. And many of these schools are in districts where public school choice isn't a real option. We're proposing a new $100 million Opportunity Scholarship Fund to help thousands of low-income students in these schools attend the private school of their choice or receive intensive one-on-one tutoring after school or during the summer. (Press release, Secretary Spellings, 2006)[56]

Immediately after Katrina, Secretary Spellings even sought to waive a federal law that bans educational segregation for homeless children with the obvious purpose of using public funding for private schooling even in explicitly segregated schooling.[57] What is crucial to recognize here is that disasters are being taken advantage of and produced to set the stage for educational privatization. Whether public schools are being systematically underfunded, as were the New Orleans Public Schools before Katrina and then declared "failed" (as NCLB is designed to do nationwide), or whether a storm blows them to smithereens does not matter to the privatizers—though the aftermath of Katrina indicates the Right has found just what can be accomplished through sudden massive destruction.

What goes undisclosed in the Department of Education's mandated notification is a comparison of how much money a student received in her prior public school relative to the federal funding for the private school. In fact, the vouchers give significantly less money per pupil than New Orleans students received. New Orleans students received an already very low per pupil funding of roughly $5,000 while Bush's voucher scheme pays only $750 per pupil. Clint Bolick argues that a prime reason for vouchers is to save money. Cutting funding for education certainly saves money, but it does not explain how educational services are paid for. The numbers do not appear to add up. Congress approved $645 million in the Hurricane Education Recovery Act that applies to 49 states and $496 million to the states most severely damaged to reopen schools under the Immediate Aid to Restart School Operations Program. In September 2005, Spellings stated that there were 372,000 schoolchildren displaced from Louisiana and Mississippi. Yet in March 2006, she gave a figure of 157,743 students nationwide who are eligible for a portion of the HERA money as of the first quarter of the year. That would mean HERA should pay about $4,088 per pupil, but schools will receive only

$750 per pupil and $937.50 for students with disabilities. Where is the money going? Instead of going to rebuild aggressively the destroyed schools in the regions hardest hit needing the full amount, the money is being dispersed throughout 49 states and D.C.:

> States and the District of Columbia will receive funding under this emergency, onetime program. Funds may be used to hire teachers; provide books and other classroom supplies; offer in-school or outside supplemental services such as tutoring, mentoring and counseling; and cover transportation and health costs.[58]

It would be myopic to think that this funding is merely about paying for the new burden of educating hurricane evacuees. This shifting of educational resources around the nation under the guise of emergency needs to be understood in relation to the failure of the Bush administration to pay states' federal funds as part of NCLB. As Monty Neil points out,

> Not only has the federal government failed to meet the social, economic, and healthrelated needs of many children, but NCLB itself does not authorize nearly enough funding to meet its new requirements. The Bush administration has sought almost no increase in ESEA expenditures for FY2005 and the coming year. The funds Congress has appropriated are about $8 billion per year less than Congress authorized. Meanwhile, states are still suffering from their worst budget crises since World War II, cutting education as well as social programs needed by low-income people. (Neil, 2004)[59]

It appears that "emergency" is being used to cover failed promises that have nothing to do with emergency other than the emergencies created by an administration hostile to supporting public education in the first place. But such coverage is taking the form of privatization. Failures of a conservative executive and legislature to support public education need to be understood in relation to a conservative judicial branch that in 2002 ruled vouchers constitutional. The political Right is waging war on public education while doing all it can to force through privatization initiatives that are unpopular and difficult to win politically.

Neoliberalism and the Uses of Disaster in Public Schooling

Contemporary initiatives to privatize public schools through the use of disaster can only be understood in relation to neoliberal ideology that presently dominates politics.[60] As David Harvey elucidates, neoliberalism, also described as "neoclassical economics" or "market fundamentalism," brings together economic, political, and cultural policy doctrine. Neoliberalism, which originates with Frederic Von Hayek, Milton Friedman, and the "Chicago boys" at the University of Chicago in the 1950s, expresses individual and social ideals through market ideals. Within this view, individual and social values and aspirations can best be reached through the unfettered market. In its ideal forms (as opposed to how it is practically implemented) neoliberalism demands privatization of public goods and services, removal of regulation on trade, loosening of capital and labor controls by the state, and the allowance of foreign direct investment. For neoliberalism, public control over public resources should be taken from the "necessarily bureaucratic" state and placed with the "necessarily efficient" private sector. The implosion of the Soviet Union and the fall of the Berlin Wall were used by neoliberals to declare that there could be no alternative to global capitalism—Thatcher famously called this the TINA thesis, There Is No Alternative to the Market. Within the logic of capitalist triumphalism, the only thing to do would be to put into effect the dictates of the market and spread the market to places previously inaccessible.

The financial past performance of neoliberalism, as Harvey explains, is not one of accomplishment but rather one of failure having caused crises, instability, and unreconciled contradictions regarding state power.[61] However, as he shows, neoliberalism has been extremely accomplished at upwardly redistributing economic wealth and political power. Consequently, Harvey suggests understanding neoliberalism as a long-standing project of class warfare waged by the rich on everyone else. Neoliberalism has damaged welfare state protections and undermined government authority to act in the public interest. As well, these policies have brought on wide-scale disaster around the globe, including a number of countries in Latin America and the Pacific rim. Such disasters have compelled governments to reevaluate neoliberalism as it has been enjoined by the so-called "Washington consensus." In fact, recent elections throughout Latin America with Left victories have largely been a reaction to the neoliberal "Washington consensus" that imposes neoliberal globalization through institutional mechanisms such as the IMF and World Bank.

Initially seen as a wacky doctrine, neoliberalism was not brought into the mainstream of policy and government circles until the late 1970s and early 1980s in Thatcher's U.K. and in Reagan's U.S. As Harvey details, Chile, under brutal dictator Pinochet, was a crucial test field for the ideology, resulting in increased commercial investments in Chile alongside 30,000 citizen disappearances. The widening reception to neoliberalism had to do with the steady lobbying of Right-wing think tanks and electoral victories but also with the right conditions, including economic crises that challenged the Keynesian model and Fordist modes of economic production and social formation in the late 1970s.[62] Neoliberalism has a distinct hostility to democracy. As Harvey writes,

> Neoliberal theorists are, however, profoundly suspicious of democracy. Governance by majority rule is seen as a potential threat to individual rights and constitutional liberties. Democracy is viewed as a luxury, only possible under conditions of relative affluence coupled with a strong middle-class presence to guarantee political stability. Neoliberals therefore tend to favour governance by experts and elites. A strong preference exists for government by executive order and by judicial decision rather than democratic and parliamentary decision-making.[63]

Such opposition to democracy and preference for elite governance is ceaselessly expressed by such neoliberal education writers as those of the Koret Task Force of the Hoover Institution such as John Chubb, Terry Moe, Eric Hanuschek and company.[64] For progressive and critical educators principally concerned with the possibilities for public schooling to expand a democratic ethos and engaged critical citizenry, neoliberalism's antidemocratic tendencies appear as particularly bad.

In education, neoliberalism has pervasively infiltrated with radical implications, remaking educational practical judgment and forwarding the privatization and deregulation program. The steady rise of privatization and the shift to business language and logic can be understood through the extent to which neoliberal ideals have succeeded in taking over educational debates. Neoliberalism appears in the now commonsense framing of education through presumed ideals of upward individual economic mobility (the promise of cashing in knowledge for jobs) and the social ideals of global economic competition. In this view national survival hinges upon educational preparation for international economic supremacy. The preposterousness of this assumption comes as school kids rather than corporate executives are being blamed for the global economic race to the bottom. The "TINA" thesis (There Is No Alternative to the Market) that has come to dominate politics throughout much of the world has infected educational thought as omnipresent market terms such as "accountability," "choice," "efficiency," "competition," "monopoly," and "performance" frame educational debates. Nebulous terms borrowed from the business world such as "achievement," "excellence," and "best practices" conceal ongoing struggles over competing values, visions, and ideological perspectives. (Achieve what? Excel at what? Best practices for whom? And says who?) The only questions left on reform agendas appear to be how to best enforce knowledge and curriculum conducive to individual upward mobility within the economy and national economic interest as it contributes to a corporately managed model of globalization as perceived from the perspective of business. This is a dominant and now commonplace view of education propagated by such influential writers as Thomas Friedman in his books and *New York Times* columns, and such influential grant-givers as the Bill and Melinda Gates Foundation.

This neoliberal view of education dangerously eradicates the role of democratic participation and the role of public schools in preparing public democratic citizens with the intellectual and critical tools for meaningful and participatory self-governance. By reducing the politics of education to its economic functions, neoliberal educational thinking has deeply authoritarian tendencies that are incompatible with democracy. Democracy is under siege by the tendency of market fundamentalism to collapse politics with economics, thereby translating all social problems into business concerns with the possibilities for continued profit making. Yet, democracy is also under siege by a rising authoritarianism in the U.S. that eviscerates civil liberties and attacks human rights domestically and internationally through the USA Patriot Act, "extraordinary rendition" (state-sanctioned kidnapping, torture, and murder), spying on the public, and other measures that treacherously expand executive power. Internationally, this appears as what Harvey has termed "The New Imperialism" and others have called "militarized globalization" that includes the so-called "war on terror," the U.S. military presence in more than 140 countries, the encirclement of the world's oil resources with the world's most powerful military, etc. This is on top of a continued culture of militarism that educates citizens to identify with militarized solutions to social problems. In education, I have called this militarism "education as enforcement" that aims to enforce global neoliberal imperatives through a number of educational means.[65]

David Harvey offers a compelling economic argument for the rise of repression and militarization, explaining the shift from neoliberalism to neoconservatism. Neoliberal policy was coming into dire crisis already in the late 1990s as deregulation of capital was resulting in a threat to the U.S. as it lost its manufacturing base and increasingly lost service sector and financial industry to Asia.[66] For Harvey, the new militarism in foreign policy is partly about a desperate attempt to seize control of the world's oil spigot as lone superpower parity is endangered by the rise of a fast growing Asia and a unified Europe with a strong currency. Threats to the U.S. economy are posed by not only the potential loss of control over the fuel for the U.S. economy and military but also the power conferred by the dollar remaining the world currency and the increasing indebtedness of the U.S. to China and Japan as they prop up the value of the dollar for the continued export of consumer goods. For Harvey, the structural problems behind global capitalism remain the financialization of the global economy and what Marx called "the crisis of overproduction" driving down prices and wages while glutting the market and threatening profits. Capitalists and states representing capitalist interests respond to these crises through Harvey's version of what Marx called primitive accumulation, "accumulation by dispossession."

Privatization is one of the most powerful tools of accumulation by dispossession, transforming publicly owned and controlled goods and services into private and restricted ones—the continuation of "enclosing the commons" begun in Tudor England. If neoliberalism came into crisis due to the excesses of capitalism (deregulation and liberalization yielding capital flight, deindustrialization, etc.), then the neoconservative response—emphasizing control and order and reinvigorated overt state power—makes a lot of sense. As Harvey explains in *A Brief History of Neoliberalism,* central to the crisis of neoliberalism are the contradictions of neoliberalism's antipathy to the nation and reliance on the state. Neoconservatives have responded to the neoliberal crisis by using national power to push economic competition, to pillage productive forces for continued economic growth, and also to control populations through repression as inequalities of wealth and income are radically exacerbated, resulting in the expansion of a dual society of mobile professionals on the one side and everyone else on the other.[67] The surging culture of religious right-wing populism, irrational new age mysticism, and endless conspiracy theorizing appear to symptomatize a cultural climate in which neoliberal market fundamentalism has come into crisis as both economic doctrine and ideology. Within this climate, private for-profit knowledge-making institutions, including schools and media, are institutionally incapable of providing a language and criticism that would enable rational interpretation necessary for political intervention. Irrationalism is the consequence. Not too distant history suggests that this can lead in systematically deadly directions.[68]

At the present moment there is a crucial tension between two fundamental functions of public education for the capitalist state. The first involves reproducing the conditions of production—teaching skills and know-how in ways that are ideologically compatible with the social relations of capital accumulation. Public education remains an important and necessary tool for capital to make political and economic leaders or docile workers and marginalized citizens or even for participating in sorting and sifting out those to be excluded from economy and politics completely. The second function that appears to be relatively new and growing involves the capitalist possibilities of pillaging public education for profit, in the U.S., Iraq, or elsewhere. Drawing on Harvey's explanation of accumulation by dispossession, we see that in the U.S. the numerous strategies for privatizing public education—from voucher schemes, to for-profit charter schools, to forced for-profit remediation schemes, to dissolving public schools in poor communities and replacing them with a mix of private, charter, and experimental schools—all follow a pattern of destroying and commodifying schools where the students are redundant to reproduction processes, while maintaining public investment in the schools that have the largest reproductive role of turning out managers and leaders.

Strategies of capitalist accumulation, dispossession, and reproduction, appear to be at odds. After all, if public schooling is being pillaged and sold off, then how can it reproduce the social order for capital? Yet privatization is targeting those most marginal to capitalist reproduction, thereby making the most economically excluded into commodities for corporations. Hence, EMOs target the poor, making economically marginalized people into opportunities for capital the way that for-profit prisons do. Reproduction and dispossession feed each other in several ways: in an ideological apparatus such as education or media, privatization and decentralization exacerbate class inequality by weakening universal provision, weakening the public role of a service, putting in place reliance upon expensive equipment supplied from outside, and justifying further privatization and decentralization to remedy the deepened economic differentiation and hierarchization that has been introduced or worsened through privatization and decentralization. The obvious U.S. example is the failure of the state to properly fund public schools in poor communities and then privatizing those schools to be run by corporations.[69] Rather than addressing the funding inequalities and the intertwined dynamics at work in making poor schools or working to expand the democratic potential of public schools, the remedy is commodification.

It is crucial to emphasize that what Klein terms "disaster capitalism" and Harvey terms "accumulation by dispossession" are not just an economic project but also a cultural project and that these need to be comprehended together. What Henry Giroux has termed the "cultural pedagogy of neoliberalism"[70] is typified not merely by the language of "silver linings" and "golden opportunities" but by the turn to business language and models in thinking about the social world, including public school reform and policy. Not only have public school debates been overrun by the aforementioned neo-liberal language, but as we see in New Orleans, business "turnaround specialists" such as Alvarez and Marsal are brought in to dictate school rebuilding while residents are dispossessed of their communities through economic rationales. The state and Alvarez and Marsal invoked "supply and demand" to justify not rebuilding the New Orleans public schools (residents do not return because the schools have not been rebuilt and then the planners declare that there is no demand for school rebuilding). The idealization of choice, markets, business, deregulation, and anti-unionism is propagated in a number of ways through the cultural pedagogy of neoliberalism. It is essential to remember what Pierre Bourdieu emphasized about neoliberalism.

> Neoliberal economics ...owes a certain number of its allegedly universal characteristics to the fact that it is immersed or embedded in a particular society, that is to say, rooted in a system of beliefs and values, an ethos and a moral view of the world, in short, an *economic common sense*, linked as such to the social and cognitive structures of a particular social order. It is from this particular economy [that of the United States] that neoclassical economic theory borrows its fundamental assumptions, which it formalizes and rationalizes, thereby establishing them as the foundations of a universal model. That model rests on two postulates (which their advocates regard as proven propositions): the economy is a separate domain governed by natural and universal laws with which governments must not interfere by inappropriate intervention; the market is the optimum means for organizing production and trade efficiently and equitably in democratic societies. (Bourdieu, 2005)[71]

A number of educational forces in addition to schools are required to keep such premises appearing natural and hence unquestionable. Mass media is one of the most powerful pedagogical forces ongoingly educating the public to understand "the economy" as natural and inevitable whether through news programs that report stock prices like the weather or through sports that align capitalist values of numerically quantifiable progress and growth with the possibilities of the human body, or through police shows (nearly half of U.S. TV content) that replace the primary role of the police (protecting private property) with the drama of seldom-committed spectacular murders, or the social Darwinist game shows that make contestants compete for scarce resources, including money, cut-throat corporate jobs, trophy spouses, and cut-face plastic surgery to compete all the better, or through the advertising behind it all that sells the fantasies that comprise a particular kind of radically individualized, cynical consumer view of the self and the social world. Such media products function pedagogically to define what is possible to think and what is impossible to imagine for the future.

Yet, as powerful as mass media is as a pedagogical force, the traditions of critical pedagogy, critical theory, cultural studies, feminism, progressive education, and critical cultural production offer powerful tools to produce different kinds of visions—hopeful, democratic visions that articulate with growing democracy movements around the world. The neoliberal postulates that Bourdieu denaturalizes appear increasingly dubious at best as wealth and income are radically redistributed upwards in the U.S. while nation after nation in Latin America rejects the neoliberal "Washington consensus" in favor of another path that coheres generally much more with the democratic ideals of the global justice movement.[72]

The Assault on Teacher Education

Alongside the current attempts of business and the political Right to capitalize on disaster, these same forces have taken aim at teacher education in the U.S. The Carnegie Corporation through its Teachers for a New Era initiative has invoked its ominous warning from the 1983 *A Nation at Risk* report, suggesting that the present state of teacher education is akin to an act of war by a foreign power.[73] That is, teacher education in the U.S. is being described of late as, if not a disaster, then as culpable for the oft-alleged disastrous state of public education in the U.S. In the summer of 2006, the *New York Times,* which had been writing mostly favorably of charter schools for years, published an editorial that strongly criticized charter schools yet concluded the editorial by suggesting that the one big problem with public education is teacher education.[74] The World Economic Forum, in the fall of 2006, issued a press release that the United States had fallen in one year from first to sixth in rankings of global competitiveness. Of central blame for this alleged disaster: the education system. And in the fall of 2006, Arthur Levine, former president of Teachers College of Columbia University, issued a widely publicized report, "Educating School Teachers" (available at www.edschools.org), denouncing the current state of teacher education and calling for many baccalaureate- and master's-level programs to be simply closed. Levine's proposals have been criticized by the AACTE and NCATE as being "elitist" for wanting to close all but the elite teacher education programs. Levine's perspective shared with those of Carnegie, the World Economic Forum, and the *Times* both a view of teacher education as a problem and a primary responsibility of teacher education being to prepare teachers to prepare future workers for global economic competition. Levine serves on the board of DePaul University in Chicago (where I teach). DePaul signed a deal with the newly created for-profit company American College of Education (ACE) for DePaul to sell teacher education accreditation from its closed branch campus to ACE.[75] ACE had no physical site or programs when it bought the accreditation that allows it to sell teacher education online courses paired with in-school practica in the Chicago Public Schools. Faculty in the School of Education at DePaul were not consulted. The decision sets up the for-profit ACE to compete with DePaul's own teacher education programs. The university justified the move on the basis of income generated by the sale of the accreditation. ACE's model is being developed by Reid Lyon, a Bush insider formerly of the National Institutes of Heath. Lyon's vision typifies the broad movement to remake teacher education. He advocates the end of educational theorizing, derides "philosophy" as worthless to teacher education, and calls for teacher candidates to learn "scientifically effective" instructional methods that have been empirically confirmed with hard data. ACE board members include former Secretary of Education Rod Paige (the one who described the National Education Association as a terrorist organization) whose Texas miracle of high test scores has been revealed to be based in the fabrication of hard data. Paige, Lyon, Levine, as well as Carnegie, the World Economic Forum and many other prominent institutions and policy makers ultimately understand the role of teacher education programs through neoliberalism. That is, they view teacher education as principally preparing teachers to make competent workers who can contribute to global economic competition and whose opportunities are understood as individual capacity to negotiate an economy controlled by others. In these reports teachers and teacher educators are framed as responsible for the well-being of the economy in that the primary responsibility of schools is preparing competent workers and future consumers. Oddly, such reports and institutions do not lay a heavy onus on business schools, though business schools do prepare future managers of the economy with disproportionate power to shape economic decisions. Such a belief about business schools would expect far too much from a course of study while neglecting the ways multiple forces, structures, and institutions impact on individual and collective decision-making. Yet teacher education is being held responsible for the fate of the U.S. economy. At the same time, the neoliberal view fails to admit the democratic roles of public education in preparing students to govern themselves and others in a just and egalitarian manner by developing their capacities for engaged political interpretation and individual and collective action.

Thoroughly at odds with critical pedagogical approaches, these neoliberal views of teacher education have an accommodationist bent that views the social order as fundamentally just and do not make central the role that teachers can play in preparing democratic citizens. Perhaps most ominously, a number of these individuals and institutions advocate measuring the value of teacher education instruction by the numerical test scores of the students of teaching candidates. Such a positivist approach to knowledge both separates claims to truth from animating underlying assumptions and insists on understanding learning as a product and knowledge as a commodity to be deposited into students so that they can "make achievement gains." Such thinking removes from consideration crucial questions about whose knowledge is worth learning and why, how knowledge relates to authority, and who designed the tests that supposedly neutrally and objectively measure knowledge that is alleged to be of universal value. These concerns are in addition to questions of who is profiting financially from test publishing, textbook sales, and the vast resources that go into such dubious "performance-based" reforms that are increasingly being extended from their destructive presence in K-12 to teacher education.

The neoliberal assault on teacher education participates in how the Right is capitalizing on disaster by producing forms of teacher education that restrict from the curriculum matters central to the making of a democratic culture. For teacher educators the most crucial matter at stake in debates over privatization and school reform generally is the possibilities for public schooling to expand a democratic ethos and foster democratic practices and social relations with regard to politics, culture, and economy. What is being done for profit and ideology in New Orleans and Iraq, in Chicago and throughout the U.S. with NCLB and the assault on teacher education does just the opposite by political dispossession, economic pillage, and cultural symbolic violence. It is incumbent upon teacher educators to develop pedagogical and material strategies to expand democratic struggles for the public to take back schools, re-sources, and cultural power as part of a broader democratic alternative to the antidemocratic neoliberal approaches that capitalize on disaster and imperil the public.

This chapter originally appeared in Deron Boyles (ed.), *The Corporate Assault on Youth: Commercialism, Exploitation, and the End of Innocence* (New York: Peter Lang, 2008).

Notes

1. Naomi Klein, "The Rise of Disaster Capitalism," *The Nation* (May 2005).
2. For the most recent update on the state of educational privatization see the research provided by the Educational Policy Studies Laboratory at Arizona State University available at www.schoolcommercialism.org.
3. "Reading, Writing, and Enrichment: Private Money Is Pouring into American Education—And Transforming It," *The Economist* (January 16, 1999): 55. I detail a number of business publications that were salivating over privatizing public schooling in "Junk King Education," chapter one of Robin Truth Goodman and Kenneth J. Saltman, *Strange Love, Or How We Learn to Stop Worrying and Love the Market* (Lanham, MD: Rowman and Littlefield, 2002). In academic circles Paul Hill was striving to make education an investment opportunity. Paul Thomas Hill, Lawrence C. Pierce, James W. Guthrie. *Reinventing Public Education: How Contracting Can Transform America's Schools* (Chicago: University of Chicago Press, 1997). Hill appears at the forefront of calls for Katrina profiteering in 2005.
4. See, for example, William C. Symonds, "Edison: An 'F' in Finance," *Business Week*, 3806 (November 4, 2002): 2, and Julia Boorstin, "Why Edison Doesn't Work," *Fortune*, 146 (December 9, 2002): 12. For a detailed discussion of Edison's financial problems and the media coverage of them, see Kenneth J. Saltman, *The Edison Schools: Corporate Schooling and the Assault on Public Education* (New York: Routledge, 2005).
5. See "Junk King Education" in Robin Truth Goodman and Kenneth J. Saltman, *Strange Love, Or How We Learn to Stop Worrying and Love the Market* (Lanham, MD: Rowman and Littlefield, 2002).
6. See Richard J. Bernstein's important discussion of the need for a democratic ethos based on Dewey's notion of Creative Democracy in *The Abuse of Evil* (New York: Verso, 2005).
7. See William I. Robinson, *Critical Globalization Studies* (New York: Routledge, 2003).
8. The editors of *Rethinking Schools* describe the federal voucher scheme after Hurricane Katrina as "back door privatization." "Katrina's Lesson's," *Rethinking Schools* (Fall 2005): 4–5.
9. David Hursh offers an important discussion of how neoliberal educational policies destroy democratic public educational ideals in "Undermining Democratic Education in the USA: The Consequences of Global Capitalism and Neo-liberal Policies for Education Policies at the Local, State, and Federal Levels." *Policy Futures in Education* 2, nos. 3 and 4 (2004): 607–620.
10. For an excellent collection of criticisms of No Child Left Behind see Deborah Meier and George Wood (eds.), *Many Children Left Behind* (Boston: Beacon, 2004). In relation to what Henry Giroux has called the "war on youth" being waged in the U.S., see his important chapter on NCLB in Henry A. Giroux, *Abandoned Generation* (New York: Palgrave, 2003). See also the collection of writings on NCLB on the rethinkingschools.org website.
11. School rewards professional and ruling class knowledge and dispositions and disaffirms and punishes the knowledge and dispositions of working class, poor, and culturally non-dominant groups. See, for example, the work of Antonio Gramsci, Pierre Bourdieu and Jean Passeron, Louis Althusser, Raymond Williams, Michael Apple, Henry Giroux, Peter McLaren, Stephen Ball, Sonia Nieto, Jean Anyon, Gloria Ladson-Billings, Michelle Fine, Lois Weis, to name just a few.
12. See Edward W. Wiley, William J. Mathis, David R. Garcia, "The Impact of Adequate Yearly Progress Requirement of the Federal 'No Child Left Behind' Act on Schools in the Great Lakes Region," *Education Policy Studies Laboratory*, September 2005, available at <edpolicylab.org>.
13. Ibid., "Executive Summary," 3.
14. Ibid.
15. See, for example, the contributors in Meier and Wood, *Many Children Left Behind.* Also see, for example, the writing of Stan Karp and Gerald Bracey on NCLB. A number of excellent resources on privatization and

commercialism implications of NCLB can be found at the site of the Educational Policy Studies Laboratory at www.schoolcommercialism.org.

16. Alfie Kohn, "NCLB and the Effort to Privatize Public Education" in Many *Children Left Behind*, Deborah Meier and George Wood (eds.), (Boston: Beacon, 2004), 79–100.

17. Sharon L. Nichols, Gene V. Glass, David C. Berliner, "High-Stakes Testing and Student Achievement: Problems for the No Child Left Behind Act," *Educational Policy Studies Laboratory* available at http://edpolicylab.org, "Executive Summary," 3.

18. For an important scholarly analysis, see Pauline Lipman, *High Stakes Education* (New York: Routledge, 2004).

19. Activist groups include: Parents United for Responsible Education, Teachers for Social Justice, and Chicago Coalition for the Homeless, among others.

20. Deb Moore, "A New Approach in Chicago," *School Planning and Management* (July 2004): 8.

21. "Snapshot: Chicago Renaissance 2010," Possibilities: An Education Update, page 2, The Bill and Melinda Gates Foundation, available at http://www.gatesfoundation.org/Education/ RelatedInfo/Possibilities/Possibilities2004.

22. Pauline Lipman, "'We're Not Blind. Just Follow the Dollar Sign,'" *Rethinking Schools Online19*, no. 4 (Summer 2005). available at www.rethinkingschools.org.

23. Dorothy Shipps, *School Reform, Corporate Style: Chicago 1880–2000* (Lawrence: The University of Kansas Press), x.

24. Pratap Chaterjee, *Iraq, Inc.: A Profitable Occupation* (New York: Seven Stories Press 2004).

25. Kenneth J. Saltman, "Creative Associates International, Inc.: Corporate Education and Democracy Promotion in Iraq," *Review of Education Pedagogy Cultural Studies 28* (2006): 25–65.

26. For example, Clint Bolick of the Alliance for School Choice described privatization as the "silver lining" of the cloud that was Hurricane Katrina. His op-ed or quote was then carried by countless publications, including the neoconservative *National Review* and *The Heartland Institute* and the *Washington Times, USA Today*, etc. The quote was picked up and repeated by others advocating the same.

27. April Capchino, "More than 100 N.O. Schools Still Closed," *New Orleans City Business* (February 27, 2006).

28. Sharon Cohen, "New Orleans' Troubled Schools Get Overhaul," Associated Press, March 4, 2006. YahooNews, news.yahoo.com.

29. Clint Bolick, "Katrina's Displaced Students," *Washington Times*, September 15, 2005.

30. Karla Dial, "Emergency School Vouchers Likely for Katrina Victims," *Heartland Institute School Reform News* (November 2005). available at www.heartland.org.

31. Sharon Cohen, "New Orleans' Troubled Schools Get Overhaul" Associated Press, March 4, 2006. YahooNews, news.yahoo.com.

32. People for the American Way, "Hurricane Katrina: A 'Golden Opportunity' for the Right-Wing to Undermine Public Education" 11/14/05, available at www.pfaw.org.

33. Paul Hill and Jane Hannaway, "The Future of Public Education in New Orleans," *After Katrina: Rebuilding Opportunity and Equity into the New New Orleans* (The Urban Institute, January 2006).

34. Online NewsHour, "Rebuilding New Orleans Schools" December 19, 2005, available at www.pbs.org/newshour/bb/education.

35. Hill and Hannaway, "The Future of Public Education in New Orleans."

36. See Kenneth J. Saltman, *The Edison Schools: Corporate Schooling and the Assault on Public Education* (New York: Routledge, 2005).

37. Hill and Hannaway, "The Future of Public Education in New Orleans."

38. Cohen, "New Orleans' Troubled Schools Get Overhaul."

39. People for the American Way, "Hurricane Katrina: A 'Golden Opportunity' for the Right-Wing to Undermine Public Education," November 14, 2005. available at www.pfaw.org.

40. Linda Baker makes this important point about the embedded funding implications of "choice" in the context of how No Child Left Behind allows students to choose any school, "All for One, None for All," *In These Times*, October 24, 2005.

41. For an excellent discussion of the history of voucher debates see Jeffrey Henig, *Rethinking School Choice* (Princeton: Princeton University Press, 1994).

42. People for the American Way, "Hurricane Katrina: A 'Golden Opportunity' for the Right-Wing to Undermine Public Education" 11/14/05, available at www.pfaw.org.

43. See the eulogy for Walton, who died in a private airplane crash, in the right-wing Hoover Institution in the Fall 2005 issue of Education Next magazine, p. 5. It is important to mention that Walton's multi-billion dollar inheritance was the result of Wal-Mart's spectacular growth that came not only from the entrepreneurial savvy of Sam Walton but also his commitment to union-busting, displacing the cost of health care onto public coffers by refusing to offer adequate health insurance to employees, the destruction of small businesses throughout the U.S. through monopolistic practices, and of course being a significant contributor to the vast loss of manufacturing sector work to China. See the excellent documentary film Wal-mart: The High Cost of Low Prices.

44. Bolick, "Katrina's Displaced Students."

45. People for the American Way, "Hurricane Katrina: A 'Golden Opportunity' for the Right-Wing to Undermine Public Education," 11/14/05. available at www.pfaw.org.

46. The Editors, "Katrina's Lessons," *Rethinking Schools*, Fall 2005, p. 5.

47. Karla Dial, "Emergency School Vouchers Likely for Katrina Victims" *Heartland Institute School Reform News*, November 2005, available at www.heartland.org.

48. Ibid.

49. People for the American Way, "Hurricane Katrina: A 'Golden Opportunity' for the Right-Wing to Undermine Public Education," 11/14/05. available at www.pfaw.org.

50. Ibid.

51. *Heartland Institute School Reform News*, November 2005, p. 9, available at www.heartland.org.

52. Cohen, "New Orleans' Troubled Schools Get Overhaul."

53. George Wood, "Introduction," Many Children Left Behind, edited by Deborah Meier and George Wood (Boston: Beacon, 2004), ix.

54. See U.S. Department of Education, Volume I, Frequently Asked Questions, Emergency Impact Aid for Displaced Students, January 12, 2006.

55. Press Release, "Secretary Spellings Delivers Remarks on School Choice," For Release April 5, 2006, available at www.ed.gov/news/pressreleases/2006/04/04052006.html.

56. Ibid.

57. Judd Legum, Faiz Shakir, Nico Pitney, Amanda Terkel, Payson Schwin, and Christy Harvey, "Katrina: Ideology over People," ThinkProgress.Org, September 15, 2005, available online at www.americanprogressaction.org.

58. Press Release, "Secretary Spellings, Gulf Coast Rebuilding Coordinator Powell Announce $1.1 Billion for Hurricane-Affected Students and Schools," March 2, 2006.

59. Monty Neil, "Leaving No Child Behind: Overhauling NCLB," in *Many Children Left Behind*, edited by Deborah Meier and George Wood (Boston: Beacon, 2004), 102-103.

60. Henry Giroux's *The Terror of Neoliberalism* (Boulder: Paradigm Press, 2004) offers a crucial analysis of the cultural pedagogy of neoliberalism. For discussion of neoliberal pedagogy in relation to school curriculum, film, and literary corporate cultural production see also Robin Truth Goodman and Kenneth J. Saltman, *Strange Love, Or How We Learn to Stop Worrying and Love the Market* (Lanham, MD: Rowman & Littlefield, 2002). An excellent mapping and analysis of these conservatisms and others can be found in Michael Apple's *Educating the Right Way* (New York: Routledge, 2001).

61. David Harvey, *A Brief History of Neoliberalism* (Oxford: Oxford University Press, 2005).

62. For an excellent succinct discussion of the shift from Fordism to post-Fordism with the rise of neoliberal globalization and the concomitant shifts in social organization as well as implications for cultural theory see Nancy Fraser, "From Discipline to Flexibilization? Rereading Foucault in the Shadow of Globalization" Constellations 10, no. 2 (2003): 160-171.

63. Harvey, *A Brief History of Neoliberalism*, 66-67.

64. See, for example, Chubb and Moe's neoliberal education bible, *Politics, Markets, and America's Schools*. See also the several Koret edited collections, including *A Primer on America's Schools*.

65. See Kenneth J. Saltman and David Gabbard (eds.), *Education as Enforcement: The Militarization and Corporatization of Schools* (New York: Routledge, 2003).

66. Harvey offers important tools for comprehending neoliberalism and neoconservatism in both *A Brief History of Neoliberalism* and *The New Imperialism*. For a discussion of Harvey's recent work and the implications for public school privatization and theoretical limitations of this work see Kenneth J. Saltman, "Review of a Brief History of Neoliberalism," *Policy Futures in Education*, 2007.
67. The expansion of the dual society as a result of neoliberal globalization has been importantly theorized by Zygmunt Bauman, *Globalization: The Human Consequences* (New York: Polity, 1998) and Nancy Fraser, "From Discipline to Flexibilization? Rereading Foucault in the Shadow of Globalization," *Constellations 10*, no. 2 (2003): 160-171.
68. See Theodore Adorno, *The Stars Down to Earth and Other Essays on the Irrational Culture* (New York: Routledge, 2001).
69. See Kenneth J. Saltman, *Collateral Damage: Corporatizing Public Schools—A Threat to Democracy*, (Lanham, MD: Rowman & Littlefield Publishers, 2000).
70. Henry A. Giroux, *The Terror of Neoliberalism* (Boulder: Paradigm, 2004).
71. Pierre Bourdieu, *The Social Structures of the Economy* (Malden, MA: Polity, 2005), 10-11.
72. A valuable source for entry into the literature on the global justice movement is Z Net available at zmag.org.
73. See www.teachersforanewera.org.
74. Editorial Desk, "Exploding the Charter School Myth," *New York Times* (August 27, 2006): Section 4, page 9.
75. Joshua Benton, "Tactics Spur Accreditation Debate," *The Dallas Morning News*, May 28, 2006, available at www.dallasnews.com.

Bibliography

Benton, Joshua. 2006. "Tactics Spur Accreditation Debate," *The Dallas Morning News*. May 28. available at www.dallasnews.com.

Bolick, Clint. 2005. "Katrina's Displaced Students," *The Washington Times*. September 15.

Bourdieu, Pierre. 2005. *The Social Structures of the Economy*. Malden, MA: Polity.

Capchino, April. 2006. "More than 100 N.O. Schools Still Closed," New Orleans City Business February 27.

Chaterjee, Pratap. 2004. *Iraq, Inc.: A Profitable Occupation*. New York: Seven Stories Press.

Cohen, Sharon. 2006. "New Orleans' Troubled Schools Get Overhaul," Associated Press. March 4.

Dial, Karla. 2005. "Emergency School Vouchers Likely for Katrina Victims," *Heartland Institute School Reform News*. November. available at www.heartland.org.

Economist, The. 1999. "Reading, Writing, and Enrichment: Private Money Is Pouring into American Education—And Transforming It.," *The Economist*. January 16: 55.

Editorial Desk. 2006. "Exploding the Charter School Myth," *New York Times*. August 27: Section 4, page 9.

Editors, The. 2005. "Katrina's Lesson," *Rethinking Schools*. Fall: 4-5.

Gates Foundation, The. 2004. "Snapshot: Chicago Renaissance 2010," *Possibilities: An Education Update*, The Bill and Melinda Gates Foundation, available at http://www.gatesfoundation.org/Education/RelatedInfo/Possibilities/Possibilities2004.

Giroux, Henry A. 2004. *The Terror of Neoliberalism* Boulder: Paradigm.

Harvey, David. *A Brief History of Neoliberalism*. 2005. Oxford: Oxford University Press

Hill, Paul and Jane Hannaway. 2006. "The Future of Public Education in New Orleans," After Katrina: Rebuilding Opportunity and Equity into the New New Orleans. The Urban Institute, January.

Klein, Naomi. 2005. "The Rise of Disaster Capitalism," *The Nation*. May.

Kohn, Alfie. 2004. "NCLB and the Effort to Privatize Public Education" in *Many Children Left Behind*, Deborah Meier and George Wood (eds.), Boston: Beacon, 79-100.

Legum, Judd, Faiz Shakir, Nico Pitney, Amanda Terkel, Payson Schwin, and Christy Harvey. 2005. "Katrina: Ideology over People," ThinkProgress.Org. September 15. available online at www.americanprogressaction.org.

Lipman, Pauline. 2005. "'We're Not Blind. Just Follow the Dollar Sign,'" *Rethinking Schools Online* 19, no. 4, Summer. available at www.rethinkingschools.org.

Moore, Deb. 2004. "A New Approach in Chicago," School Planning and Management. July: 8.

Neil, Monty. 2004. "Leaving No Child Behind: Overhauling NCLB" in *Many Children Left Behind*, Deborah Meier and George Wood (eds.), Boston: Beacon. 102–103.

Nichols, Sharon L., Gene V. Glass, David C. Berliner. "High-Stakes Testing and Student Achievement: Problems for the No Child Left Behind Act," Educational Policy Studies Laboratory, available at http://edpolicylab.org, "Executive Summary," 3.

Online NewsHour. 2005. "Rebuilding New Orleans Schools," December 19. available at www.pbs.org/newshour/bb/education.

People for the American Way. 2005. "Hurricane Katrina: A 'Golden Opportunity' for the Right-Wing to Undermine Public Education." November 14. available at www.pfaw.org.

Press Release. 2006. "Secretary Spellings Delivers Remarks on School Choice." April 5. available at www.ed.gov/news/pressreleases/2006/04/04052006.html.

Press Release. 2006. "Secretary Spellings, Gulf Coast Rebuilding Coordinator Powell Announce $1.1 Billion for Hurricane-Affected Students and Schools." March 2.

Saltman, Kenneth J. 2006. "Creative Associates International, Inc.: Corporate Education and Democracy Promotion in Iraq," *Review of Education Pedagogy Cultural Studies* 28: 25–65.

Shipps, Dorothy. *School Reform, Corporate Style: Chicago 1880–2000*. Lawrence: The University of Kansas Press. x.

Wiley, Edward W., William J. Mathis, David R. Garcia. 2005. "The Impact of Adequate Yearly Progress Requirement of the Federal 'No Child Left Behind' Act on Schools in the Great Lakes Region," *Education Policy Studies Laboratory*. September. available at edpolicylab.org.

Wood, George. 2005. "Introduction," *Many Children Left Behind*, Deborah Meier and George Wood (eds.). Boston: Beacon.

PART THREE

Teachers and Teacher Education

"If all U.S. schools could function as well as the most advantaged do, there would be no need for systemic change. It is not that the U.S. teachers and students cannot succeed when they are well supported. It is that the system fails to support so many of them. This is the real crisis of American education."
    —Linda Darling-Hammond

"For me the school is a social and historical institution, and in being a social and historical institution, the school can be changed. But the school can be changed not exclusively by a decree, but by a new generation of teachers, of educators who must be prepared, trained, and formed."
    —Paulo Freire

"Your knowledge, my knowledge, everybody's knowledge should be made use of. I think people who refuse to use other people's knowledge are making a big mistake. Those who refuse to share their knowledge with other people are making a great mistake, because we need it all."
    —Myles Horton

CHAPTER SEVEN

Teacher Education Reform in Volatile Times

Forward to the Basics

KENNETH TEITELBAUM

There may be fields about which relatively little is written and that generate sparse commentary, but that is surely not the case for Teacher Education. In scholarly books and articles, technical reports and op-eds, and speeches and interviews, there is virtually a tsunami of words written and spoken by those in and out of the field, in praise or criticism. At the same time, as is the case for teachers, not everyone (who thinks they do) understands the purposes, possibilities and limitations for those who work in university-based programs that strive to prepare outstanding professionals for K-12 educational settings. To say this is not to declare the field immune or off limits from the valid critiques and recommendations of those who can perhaps provide the fresh perspective of an outsider, so to speak. It is to suggest how crucial it is for those who have such involvement to speak clearly, substantively and publicly in stating the case for high-quality teacher education that does not simply embrace the latest and loudest arguments being made. Perhaps, in a curious way, we need to go forward to "the basics" of teaching and teacher education to clarify what those in the field can (and should) actually do.

One hesitates to use a phrase such as "the basics," as it can too easily be viewed as something unexamined, literal-minded, overly fragmented, or even reactionary (Jardine, Clifford & Friesen, 2008). Certainly those who advocated for more progressive or critical educational change during the last several decades expressed serious concerns with proposals that harkened "back to the basics" of more traditional (teacher-directed, didactic, test-based, monocultural, etc.) approaches to schooling. But a more generous sense of the basics can perhaps still be useful to describe how teachers and teacher educators actually live in the world, and how teaching and learning can possibly best take place. Perhaps amidst the clamor for "reform," there are basic claims (understandings), if not truths, that deserve our attention as we seem to rush headlong down the path of change. This chapter, then, seeks to address our current challenges and move the dialogue forward in a way that (re)considers basic assumptions that still may represent powerful, constituent elements of what it means to be and to prepare highly competent K-12 teachers.

The Challenge Facing University-Based Teacher Education

We are living in turbulent times, with innovations in technology and communication occurring rapidly, globalization creating dramatic socio-economic changes, clashes between modernizing and traditional cultures taking place in many parts of the world, climate change increasingly a planetary concern, and worries about national and global security becoming prominent. The sometimes anxious questioning being engendered by these transformations has resulted in a deep problematizing of long-standing social institutions and authority relations, which can certainly be viewed as a welcome development. But these are not conversations on a level playing field, with each of the multiple sides enjoying similar resources and political power to gain access to the public discourse. Much of what is put forth by even seemingly nonpartisan groups and individuals is generously funded by those with an ax to grind. Sometimes there is primarily an ideological perspective to push; at other (and possibly the same) times, there is a real, significant financial stake in the outcome of educational debates, with the possibility of millions or even billions in profits from one of the last remaining public sectors not overly privatized. The dizzying pace with which changes are being proposed and implemented makes it all the more difficult for many to make good sense of the arguments.

In recent years the debates have been about not only the effectiveness of public education but its value as a common good, a social value that resulted from historical struggles to, as Chomsky (2013) simply puts it, promote the basic perception that "we should care about other people." Accompanying such questioning are sometimes vitriolic claims made against the teaching profession and related challenges to the legitimacy of "traditional" programs that prepare teachers. Indeed, those complaining about the quality of schooling and classroom teachers are increasingly laying a good dose of the blame at the doorstep of teacher education.

Of course the alarms regarding public schooling have been going off fairly regularly for a long time. For example, at the turn of the 20th century, Joseph Mayer Rice lambasted the lifeless system of schooling provided to children, eventually embracing a social efficiency approach that advocated "a scientific system of pedagogical management [that] would demand fundamentally the measurement of results in the light of fixed standards" (Kliebard, 2004, p. 20). At the same time, John Dewey lamented the dominance of teacher authority and student passivity and advocated for the democratic ideal in the classroom. A half-century later, a host of popular books harshly criticized teachers and schooling, with such titles as *Quackery in the Public Schools*, *Let's Talk Sense about Our Schools* and *Educational Wastelands*, and, after the launching of Sputnik in October 1957, *Life* magazine headlined our "Crisis in Education." Several decades later, with Japan presumably gaining on us economically, the National Commission on Excellence in Education (1983), convened by President Reagan's Secretary of Education, Terrell Bell, issued *A Nation at Risk: The Imperative for Educational Reform*, a report that famously claimed that "the educational foundations of our society are presently being eroded by a rising tide of mediocrity that threatens our very future as a Nation and a people." And there have been many similar publications and reports (and films) during the last century about the failings of our public schools and blaming teachers. Some have been based on solid evidence; some on anecdotal information; all emanating from particular ideas, often inadequately explained, about schooling, curriculum, instruction, learning, students and society.

Tensions between tradition and change have been prominent throughout our educational history (Reese, 2005) and some of our goals have surely not been met. Particularly troubling is the continued achievement gap between the wealthy and the poor and between black/Hispanic and white students. Too many teachers have been unable to create an optimal learning environment for all students and too many children cannot read, write and do math appropriately. In the last 40 years the United States has gone from having the world's highest rate of high school and college graduation to number 15 in college completion and number 21 in high school completion, with only seven of ten ninth graders receiving a high school diploma (55 percent of blacks and Hispanics) (Levin & Rouse, 2012). At the same time, too many students do not feel sufficiently challenged in school and do not have enough opportunities to actively engage with critical and creative thinking. It is probably still the case that the atmosphere in too many classrooms is "emotionally flat" (Goodlad, 1984). Watkins (2012b) reminds us that schools have long been dominated by "abhorrent…models of funding, over-reliance on testing, the use of Fordist/Taylorist models, and the embrace of Perrenialist curriculum theorizing" (p. 190). As Jonathan Franzen (2010) writes in his novel *Freedom,* it can become too easy to feel that "a public school sucked too much to bother trying to fix it" (p. 4).

Of course, schools do not function in a vacuum and many of our educational problems are a direct result of factors in the larger society, a point I will return to later. Moreover, it is at least questionable whether talk of a "crisis" in education is wholly warranted (Berliner & Biddle, 1995). For example, the results of the Trends in International Mathematics and Science Study (TIMSS) conducted every four years indicate that scores have gone up since the tests began in 1995. In addition, Carnoy and Rothstein (2013) suggest that conclusions "are often drawn from international test comparisons [that] are oversimplified, frequently exaggerated, and misleading" (p. 2). Claims about poor performance "ignore the complexity of test results and may lead policymakers to pursue inappropriate and even harmful reforms" (p. 2). Moreover, apparently a student at a "high-needs" school in San Francisco needs to point out what should be obvious: "Our English scores are bad, but that doesn't mean our school is bad" (Rizga, 2012).

Public schools have long been major battlegrounds for competing values and priorities, with teachers usually caught in the crossfire (Apple, 2006; Kliebard, 2004; Mathison & Ross, 2008), and teacher education certainly has not been immune from similar pressures. For example, a prominent observer wrote that "a professional educator would have had to restrict his reading almost entirely to children's literature in order to escape notice of the recurrent criticisms of American teacher education appearing in popular and professional publications during recent years." He referred to "today's heated discussions of the adequacy of teacher education programs," words that were shared more than a half-century ago (Popham & Greenberg, 1958, p. 118). Published several decades later were *Tomorrow's Teachers* (Holmes Group, 1986) and *A Nation Prepared: Teachers for the 21st Century* (Carnegie Forum on Education and the Economy, 1986), which "set an ambitious agenda for the reform of teacher education and the professionalization of teaching" (Drury & Baer, 2011, p. 8). John Goodlad (1999) commented that colleges of education "were born with a congenital malaise, into an inhospitable surround, or both,…[and] brought into academe the often-unappreciated baggage of connections with the low-status occupation of teaching in the lower schools" (p. 325). Indeed, as David Labaree (2004) points out, schools of education have been dealing with their low status for a very long time, often not very successfully, and in fact continue to be "the objects of attack from all quarters" (p. 170). They are "an obvious and easy target for anyone who wants to place blame for problems with American education" (p. 193). And yet, if they are at fault at all, it is because in large part they "did what was demanded of them." That is, "They provided mass programs of teacher preparation that did not cost much money or require much time. They put teachers in empty classrooms and drew students into the university. They tried to serve the needs of practitioners in the field. And for all this, they have been soundly punished—by academics and educators and the public alike" (pp. 205–6). These issues continue today, perhaps felt even more intensely as university colleagues, politicians, media pundits, and others take out their frustrations regarding other social problems (financial crises, culture wars, etc.) on the traditional scapegoat (and salvation) of society, our public schools, and increasingly teacher educators.

One recent challenge came from Arthur Levine (2006) in his influential study *Educating School Teachers*. While recognizing the "extraordinary" diversity in the field, Levine nevertheless made sweeping claims about the majority of traditional university programs being "characterized by curricular confusion, a faculty disconnected from practice, low admission and graduation standards…and weak quality control enforcement" (pp. 7 and 21). Many ensuing critiques adopted Levine's conclusion, ignoring questions about his data analysis and providing little additional evidence of their own. Most noteworthy has been Secretary of Education Arne Duncan, who in a speech in October 2009 charged that "by almost any standard, many if not most of the nation's 1,450 schools, colleges, and departments of education are doing a mediocre job of preparing teachers for the realities of the 21st century classroom" (Kumashiro, 2012, p. 56). Two years later, in announcing a new governmental initiative on teacher preparation, Secretary Duncan softened his language somewhat but still emphasized that "too few teacher preparation programs offer the type of rigorous, clinical experience that prepares future teachers for the realities of today's diverse classrooms" and that superintendents "who hire large numbers of new teachers…have been frustrated at having to retrain new teachers" (U.S. Department of Education, 2011, p. 1). In August 2009, *The New York Times* reported that the director of teacher education at Harvard University told participants at a conference that only about 100 teacher education programs are doing a competent job and "the others could be shut down tomorrow." Three years later, Nancy Zimpher, Chancellor of the State University of New York, initiated a major effort to improve teacher preparation in her state, referring to it as at a "crisis point"; E.D. Hirsch, Jr. claimed that education schools "are currently the origins of our problems, not their solution"; and the education dean at Boston University estimated that there were only a few dozen, 50 at most, schools of education that were of justifiable quality and spoke of "an entrenched training system that almost guarantees mediocrity in the classroom" (Innerst, 2012). Even James Cibulka, president of the National Council for Accreditation of Teacher Education, quoted in support of the 2011 U.S. Department of Education report referenced above, stated that "teacher preparation must…be 'turned upside down.'"

Such claims surely should be taken seriously, but in fact there seems to be relatively little research data to suggest the situation has changed markedly since Berliner and Biddle (1995) concluded that "despite the enormous size of the teaching force, evidence suggests that the average teacher in America is talented, high achieving, and well educated…. [W]e know of *no* persuasive evidence that would confirm the charge that America's teachers are particularly incompetent, untalented, or poorly trained by comparison with other professions" (p. 108).

And yet the drumbeat for reform persists, in part guided by a neoliberalist agenda that seeks to limit government (and public funding) and privatize virtually every sector of society. (Apple [2013] briefly describes neoliberalism as "a vision that sees every sector of society as subject to the logics of commodification, marketization, competition, and cost-benefit analysis" [p. 6]). That is, what is often proposed, especially by those outside the field, seems to have more to do with ideology, politics and money, and perhaps misplaced frustrations regarding other social issues, than research on educational quality (e.g., Kumashiro, 2012; Watkins, 2012a).

Much of today's language regarding "failing schools" and "ineffective teachers" comes from the No Child Left Behind (NCLB) legislation of 2001, but many observers have jumped on that bandwagon during the last decade to make essentially the same claims and to paint university-based teacher education with the same brush. Reinforced by the federal Race to the Top (RTTT) legislation of 2009, whereby financial incentives are provided to states to identify and shut down low-performing teacher education programs and to provide additional competitive points for making available alternative routes to teacher education, state departments of education across the country are scrutinizing university-based teacher preparation programs and proposing more demanding requirements for admission and program completion. They are creating more rigorous state certification exams and the American Federation of Teachers has even recommended a new bar exam for all prospective teachers to gauge how well they have mastered a subject and demonstrated the ability to teach it. There are proposals to hold programs accountable not only for how well their graduates perform in K-12 classrooms, as indicated by the achievement scores of K-12 students, but also whether or not they are hired in their own state and how long they stay in the teaching field. But while preparing high-quality teachers is certainly a vital goal, and the need for accountability and being good stewards of taxpayer money is clear, are these measures realistic, valid, and supported by research evidence? Do we know that they will lead (and have led) to improved teacher quality? Should teacher education programs be held accountable for K-12 students' test scores and teacher retention, about which they have relatively little direct influence?

This is not to say that the critiques of teacher education are wholly without merit and should simply be ignored. As Whitcomb, Borko and Liston (2008) recommend, we would do well to develop "a more coherent, practically informed, and vision-enhanced plan of teacher preparation" (p. 12). A thoughtful soul searching (beyond accreditation reviews) is called for, regarding the qualifications of our students, the purposes, relevance and rigor of our teaching and field experiences, the evidence we collect to assess effectiveness and the improvements we make based on our data collection, and the relationships we have with partnership schools. As Zeichner (2009) puts it, we need to "take teacher education seriously or do not do it" (p. 151).

But the challenge for teacher educators is not just about the effectiveness and legitimacy of their efforts. It is also about the attacks on the teaching profession that only make more difficult the very thing with which almost everyone agrees, which is to recruit more highly qualified (and diverse) students into the teaching profession. Neoliberalist policies have encouraged a level of standardization and an auditing culture that have undermined teachers' sense of professionalism and resulted in an increased teacher morale problem. Condemning the actions of the many for the sins of the few, and basically focusing on trying to improve teaching (and teacher education) "by inducing fear into the hearts of the incompetent" (Tucker, 2012), breeds resentment among all teachers (and teacher educators). According to the MetLife Foundation (2012), we are witnessing the highest level of dissatisfaction since 1989, with only 44 percent of teachers feeling very satisfied with their work (down from 59 percent in 2009) and 29 percent likely to leave the profession in five years (up from 17 percent in 2009). Reinforced by unsatisfactory work conditions (Johnson, Kraft, & Papay, 2012), a lack of resources, decreased opportunities for professional development, and the continuing low salaries especially for beginning teachers, as well as the negative word of mouth created by the 46 percent of teachers who leave the classroom within five years, fewer young people and career changers are seeking to become teachers. The enrollment decline, along with the continued "revolving door" caused by teacher discontent, will likely exacerbate the teacher shortage that currently exists in critical areas (American Association of State Colleges and Universities, 2005).

The increased availability of alternative routes to licensure adds to this enrollment decline for university-based teacher education programs. In turn, especially given the generally difficult financial situation facing most colleges and universities, there is increased pressure for recruitment and retention efforts, including the development of new delivery formats. The intensity of this concern undermines what is also called for, that is, more careful study, deliberation and revision of policies and practices. It does start to seem like a vicious cycle, designed, perhaps deliberately, for failure. That is, No Child Left Behind, Race to the Top and related initiatives adopt a heavy-handed and punitive approach with a preference for alternative providers, which serves to "cut out the involvement of traditional education schools, which could mean a diversion of potential students and tuition money from the institutions that produce the majority of public K-12 educators" (Richards, 2012).

There is more to the challenge we face. For example, there are the very problematic ratings and rankings done by the National Council on Teacher Quality, which, according to long-time education scholar Diane Ravitch, was created by the Thomas B. Fordham Foundation "to break the power of the hated ed schools" (Cody, 2012); the prevalence of value-added measures even though there are numerous analyses, including by those involved in their initial development, that dispute their efficacy and argue that they distort assessments of individual teacher effectiveness (Amrein-Beardsley, 2012; Hawkins, 2012); proposals to have teacher licensure wholly monitored by state departments of instruction, with little university participation (Richards, 2012); well-funded fast-track programs such as Teach for America that admit and support highly academic achieving students but provide them with little time to prepare for classrooms in typically low-income communities (and who generally have dramatically low retention rates); public charter schools that are allowed to sidestep the requirement to hire licensed teachers; proposals to link K-12 students' test scores to evaluations of teacher performance for salary (merit) raises, which could lead to increasing numbers of classroom teachers being unwilling to work with student teachers; and proposals to evaluate teacher education programs based on the student test scores of their graduates, which could lead to programs discouraging students from teaching in low-performing low-income schools. Overall it is a rather disheartening picture for those who work in university-based teacher education and who know firsthand the many significant contributions they make to K-12 teaching and learning. What do teacher educators say to their own students when they read about high school teachers such as the one who, after working long days with large classes and many assignments to grade, and increasingly upset by the denial of support services to her neediest students, states, "To be frank, I never felt more defeated in my life," and then leaves teaching for a career that pays more and provides more free time to spend with her own family (Kohanim, 2012)? And when students view the film *American Teacher* (2011) and hear a school superintendent remark that his son makes considerably more money selling cell phones than being a teacher? Given the trends, similar questions may also need to be addressed with teacher educators themselves. That is, what do I say as a dean when one of our first-year faculty colleagues wonders aloud whether he should plan to stay in teacher education, that is, whether there is a "future" for him and for his program? No doubt there are some who would celebrate such a conversation. But knowing this smart, thoughtful, and passionate new faculty member as I do, and knowing how much he can offer to the preparation of new and current teachers, I worry.

Some "Basics" to Consider

Limited to a select few, and of necessity briefly described, some (related) basic understandings of teaching and teacher preparation, borne out of years of experience, reading and research, can perhaps help in moving us forward in our deliberations. One can agree or disagree with these (and other) "basics," marshaling whatever evidence seems appropriate, but we would be wise at least to consider their implications regarding current reform proposals.

Teaching is complex. Good teaching is much more difficult than many people realize, especially given the typical nature of classroom life in public schools today. This may be particularly the case now because of "the phenomenal increase in the diversity and inclusiveness of U.S. public schools and the growing emphasis on standards and accountability that has dominated education policy for the past two decades" (Drury & Baer 2011, p. 9). The search for simple solutions, whether it involves teacher merit pay, changes in tenure laws, vouchers, or whatever, belies the complicated and intense nature of everyday teaching.

There is so much that is necessary to know but not sufficient to be an exemplary teacher. As is often referred to, Albert Einstein had the content knowledge to be a world famous theoretical physicist, but it is very doubtful that he would have been a competent middle school teacher. One also needs an incisive understanding of and adept skills in child/adolescent development, diverse cultures, learning theory, lesson and unit planning, curriculum organization and development, classroom management, instructional and assessment strategies, communication with youth and families, and so on. Anyone who thinks it is a straightforward matter to keep order in a classroom of 30 students, stay on topic, make adjustments on the spot, know all the students well enough to teach appropriately, and otherwise interact with them has never been a K-12 teacher (Farhi, 2012). Indeed, in order for teachers to teach children well, they must know them well. It takes time and careful reflection and study (and small classes) to build such relationships. Teachers need to attend to all the different learning moments that occur in schools, in and out of the classroom, and the complicated variability of how students learn, as well as school policies and laws, bureaucratic responsibilities, etc. It is truly "complex professional work" (Berry et al., 2011, p. 7), and teachers need to be prepared to address this complexity, including differing conceptions of the very purpose of schooling and nature of high-quality teaching.

Teacher education is necessarily limited I. Teacher education programs are significantly limited in what they can accomplish given the length of time students are enrolled, their students' lack of experience "on the other side of the desk," and their general lack of exposure to communities and cultures other than their own. Two or three years is simply not enough time for teacher education students to gain the knowledge, skills, dispositions and experiences to become the kind of outstanding teachers we seek for all classrooms. In a way, as Seymour Sarason (2002) suggested, all new teaching is "at best very trying or at worst a baptism of fire" (p. 36). What teacher education can do is prepare prospective students as much as possible for that "baptism," providing them with a rigorous foundation of knowledge and skills, and an awareness of the questions that need to be asked and the possible ways and resources for addressing them.

We should of course strive to prepare the best teachers possible for the realities of their first day, first week and first year of classroom teaching. But much of what they need to learn is done on the job during their first several years of teaching, and it is misguided, if not dishonest, for 25 school chiefs to issue a strong public vow "to take action to update their systems of teacher preparation and licensing, with an eye to ensuring teachers are ready the minute they take charge of their own classrooms" (Sawchuk, 2013). What exactly does "ready" mean here (and what specifically is not being done to get them ready)? First-year teachers have much to offer—their enthusiasm is typically infectious—but they also still have much to learn. Any new professional, in a hospital (where several years are spent as a resident) or in a courtroom (where several years will pass before handling a case alone), needs time and experience to truly be "ready" in any strong sense, no matter how much more we increase admission requirements, licensure standards, passing scores on certification exams, and the like. Teacher education can prepare them for as much as possible, but it cannot turn a wide-eyed novice (who often is 22 years old) into a wise veteran overnight.

Teacher education is necessarily limited II. It is unclear how much of what is taught and experienced in the university setting is adopted by graduates in K-12 classrooms. This may be because of a disconnect between the lessons of the teacher education program and the school setting, or because, while successfully learning the knowledge and skills that are the focus of teacher education programs, new (and veteran) teachers hold on to other views and follow paths that depart from the lessons taught at the university. Years ago questions were raised about the extent to which the university experience was in fact "washed out" by the K-12 school culture (Zeichner & Tabachnick, 1981). This should hardly be a startling observation and yet it seems to be one that is ignored by those who would hold teacher education programs accountable for, as an example, what a teacher can or chooses to do in a classroom years after their college graduation. As John Goodlad (1999) put it, John Dewey has been "universally acknowledged as his country's intellectual voice…and his views found their way didactically into the classrooms of teachers' education but were lost or distorted before reaching the schoolhouse" (p. 326.) Similarly, Fox and McNulty (2013) report on a "thoroughly prepared" graduate who started her career in "a small, urban school district with a diverse population of elementary students who had failed to meet annual yearly progress as defined by No Child Left Behind." This new teacher was "abruptly acculturated into a negative and cynical teaching environment," found herself "overwhelmed" in her first grade classroom, and was thinking about leaving the profession (p. 36). (She did stay at the school and is now in her third year, having moved to a kindergarten class.) Should her university-based teacher education necessarily be held responsible for this teacher's work in the classroom (apparently altered by an unsupportive school environment) and her almost leaving the teaching profession (discouraged by what she was experiencing)?

More nurturing school environments and effective staff development, not of a gimmicky "snake-oil" kind (Zeichner, 2009) but that allows teachers to learn and contribute to addressing genuine classroom and school-based issues and problems can surely help teachers such as the one described above be more successful in the classroom. These supports are crucial, particularly when, after a lengthy time of non-use, the understandings and skills learned at the university level and on the job essentially atrophy and have to be re-learned/re-practiced (Apple & Teitelbaum, 1986). Yet opportunities for such potentially constructive experiences are declining in the face of severe state budget cuts. As one education dean puts it: "Reaching and teaching every student is hard work. How long do these teachers have to do it on their own?" (Gillette, 2012). Moreover, at a time when rapid changes in information and globalization are taking place, we will no doubt expect K-12 students to learn more complex material and new analytical skills. New kinds of teaching and assessment will probably be needed (Murray, 2012). While teacher education programs themselves must develop coherent strategies to address such changes, other opportunities to assist classroom teachers need to be cultivated as well.

Good teaching means lifelong learning. As is the case for most professions, teaching is at its best a continuing lifelong learning experience. We need to encourage not discourage the exceptional teachers who are, as Perrone (1991) puts it, "passionate about learning." Such teachers "need opportunities to reflect on their learning, on how they first came to the interest they possess and how to revitalize those interests." Schools need to be settings "where teachers share their learning with each other, read together, and have opportunities for writing and further study." Each school needs to be "a center of inquiry, an intellectually oriented place" (p. 117), functioning as learning communities, or "teacher inquiry communities" (Zeichner, 2012), with a reflective culture and a generally inspiring environment. When staff development opportunities instead are eliminated, and when continuing education in the form of graduate degree programs no longer are required or accompanied by compensation, we are sending an opposite message about the necessity of keeping one's passion alive, staying current with the latest in one's content area and pedagogical knowledge, reflecting on and researching one's own practice, and collaborating with others to review policies and practices. Teachers need constructive feedback and professional development opportunities that are sustained over time, built in to their work hours, involving them in active learning and collaborative activities, and focused on decisions about purpose, methods, curriculum, assessment, classroom management, policy, and related issues that are germane to their own work context (Murray, 2012). They need as well to be exposed to excellent mentoring and induction programs from the start (Feiman-Nemser, 2003).

The point here is that university teacher educators generally understand that their work with prospective and current teachers is limited and that the only way that teachers can remain truly effective and vibrant in the classroom is for them to continuously build on their initial learning experiences on "how to be a teacher." We need a reculturing of the school environment to support such a view, with genuine teacher participation, and a more positive and respectful approach to the profession, rather than the mistrust, disrespect, discouragement and punitive measures that are represented by many current reform proposals. This is surely one lesson that we can draw from the recent successful educational experience in Finland (Sahlberg, 2011).

Disagreements are integral to the field. Alternative ideas and practices have always comprised the educational field, in large part because values and priorities are fundamental to teaching and curriculum (Kliebard, 2004; Teitelbaum, 2008). There has never been a kind of "golden age" of consensus regarding what and how to teach students, how to assess learning, what role administrators and teachers should play in the decision-making process, and so forth. Educators who are professionals should be aware of the history of their field and the alternative purposes and methods that have constituted it. Unless we strive to prepare automatons who will only be able to use others' pedagogical ideas and curriculum materials, unless we merely seek technicians to be able to primarily respond to instrumentalist demands, our teacher education programs should prepare individuals who can think for themselves (and on their feet) and who are knowledgeable about the many different possibilities of schooling, teaching, curriculum and assessment. This represents the "foundation" of being a teacher, though perhaps of most help to teachers when guided by a "place-conscious approach" (Bowman & Gottesman, 2013).

In other words, in the search for missing "coherence," which has been a concern at the forefront of the field at least since the initial Holmes Group report in 1986, we should be careful not to suppress long-standing differences. Spirited discussion over values and priorities, hopefully leading to a consensus and not enforced top-down conformity, is perhaps the hallmark of a democratic culture. It might even be argued that varied approaches to the preparation of teachers (differing teacher education programs), within certain broad parameters, allow students (prospective and current teachers) and K-12 schools to choose what fits them best among a host of defensible alternatives. High standards do not necessarily require standardization.

Teachers teach who they are. More powerful than lessons on the three R's or on proper behavior in the school corridor, teachers serve everyday as role models for the important and the unimportant, for the good and the bad, for the joyful and the sorrowful. While some would have us develop a profile of "the good teacher" based primarily on standardized test scores and the videotaping of individual lessons, a deeper, more nuanced perspective would take into account the multitude of ways in which teachers influence (and teach) children on a daily basis, which can perhaps only be ascertained by portfolios of materials and sustained observation by peers, supervisors, and others. Teacher educators must of necessity take this "whole person" into account. This is the case not simply for assessment purposes, and not only to address the appropriate dispositions for teaching, but in terms of impressing upon future and current teachers the profound effect they can have on their students. Maxine Greene (1995) gets at this when she suggests that "if I and other teachers truly want to provoke our students to break through the limits of the conventional and the taken for granted, we ourselves have to experience breaks with what has been established in our own lives, we have to keep arousing ourselves to begin again" (p. 109). Similarly, Sonia Nieto (2013) points out that "one cannot become a multicultural teacher without becoming a multicultural person." It follows that if we want children to adopt a lifelong passion for learning, critical and creative thinking, active engagement as a citizen, and the many other traits that most Americans presumably value, we can do no better than place in front of them in the classroom adults who themselves understand, appreciate, embrace and advocate for these traits in their own lives. It is the same for teacher educators, that is, "to model the same kind of caring and compassionate relationships [and, for example, culturally responsive teaching] with their teacher education students that they want their students to create with their pupils in elementary and secondary schools" (Zeichner, 2009, p. 30).

This suggests a teacher education experience that is more personal, reflective, caring and comprehensive than the common portrayal of teacher "training," which seems to assume that all we need to do is narrowly transmit basic competencies of knowledge and skills, perhaps in an intensive five-week program, maybe alongside an extended apprenticeship. But what do people really remember about the "good teachers" they have had? The most recent PhiDeltaKappan/Gallup Poll (2012) asked respondents to "think about the teacher who has had the most positive influence in your life" and provide three words or phrases that "best describe how that teacher made a difference." The three most common words/phrases submitted were "caring," "encouraging," and "attentive/believed in me" (p. 16). While content knowledge, classroom management, instructional and assessment strategies, curriculum development, etc. are of course of paramount importance to good teaching, these other characteristics that are so vividly remembered and appreciated need to be strongly encouraged as well. This takes time, focus, continuity, critical self-reflection, study, support, and deliberation. It is not something that can be addressed in one lesson, assessed on one test, or videotaped in one K-12 classroom hour. It needs to be in the forefront of teacher preparation and staff development.

An emphasis on the idea that fundamentally you "teach who you are" (Palmer, 2007) calls into question many current reform proposals. For example, as Fenstermacher and Richardson (2010) point out, high-stakes accountability forces teachers to look at their classes as an aggregate of individuals rather than as a community in which social relationships need to be nurtured, moral development needs to be fostered, and aesthetic sensibilities and democratic character need to be encouraged. It disconnects teachers from the interests and experiences of their students and "suck[s] the relational life out of the classroom." It makes it much less likely that teachers will feel encouraged and able to find the "space" to get to know their students, to engage in caring moments, and to do what they need to, especially for those students with exceptional needs. The emphasis on high-stakes accountability not only heightens the pressure on teachers to a dysfunctional level, it also makes it much less likely that children will enjoy their school experience and learn from all that their teachers can share with them. (Instead, as a *New Yorker* cartoon represents it, an elementary teacher says to two parents: "We've found by applying just the tiniest bit of an electric shock, test scores have soared.")

Context is crucial. In *The Handmaid's Tale*, Margaret Atwood (1985) returns several times to the phrase, "Context is all." This is of course an arguable point, especially in her adoption of the word "all," but it surely contains a great deal of truth. In order to properly assess schools in the United States, we need to give appropriate consideration to the nature and expectations of the social context in which they exist. While this context is not unchanging, at a moment in time it represents a set of parameters of what, generally speaking, public schools can and should do. To consider reforming schools, it becomes important not just to look inward at their policies and practices but "outward" toward the political, economic and cultural elements that are constituent parts of them. The same can be said for teachers and teacher educators, who can be viewed as functioning within myriad contexts that encourage certain practices and inhibit others. With the door closed and the blinds drawn, figuratively speaking, there is a sense of autonomy; much is within the teachers' control, and they can have a powerful influence on, for example, success and failure, engagement and alienation, pleasure and sorrow. But there remains much that is not entirely under their influence and to hold them wholly accountable for results is naïve and simplistic. The faulty equation of some reform proposals, based on the skimpiest of evidence, is K-12 student achievement scores = poor teacher performance = ineffective teacher preparation, with little or no consideration to the political, economic, and cultural contexts in which individual teachers and teacher educators work.

Unfortunately, many current reformers make "the fundamental attribution error," ignoring context and attributing an individual's success or failure solely to inherent qualities (Surowiecki, 2013). Teachers' work environments can be strikingly different, with regard to administrative support, available resources, policy mandates, professional autonomy, etc., which clearly will affect what teachers do in the classroom, how they view their role, how much of what they learned in their teacher education program they are able to adopt, etc. (Johnson, Kraft, & Papay, 2012). A teacher experiencing success in one environment might very well not in another. Likewise, a teacher teaching one grade level might have more difficulty teaching another, and obviously many other similar examples can be provided. It would seem to make little sense to hold individual teachers strictly accountable at a single point in time based on student standardized tests, as NCLB does, when highly differentiated (and in a sense unequal) work environments can be found across schools. And it would seem to make even less sense to hold teacher education programs accountable for those same K-12 student exams. (Consider perhaps the school district in Minnesota that switched to a later daily schedule and found that the average S.A.T. scores for the top 10 percent of the class rose by more than two hundred points, a result that the head of the College Board called "truly flabbergasting" [Kolbert, 2013, p. 26])

Of course community and student demographics are critical contextual factors as well. As Anyon (1997) points out, "100 years of federal, corporate, and state policies [have] starved and isolated the nation's cities" (p. 148), resulting in continued, substantial inequalities between wealthy suburban school districts and low-income urban (and rural) ones. Where one teaches can make a significant difference. Places where resources are scarce, the prospects for employment are deflated, and there exists a kind pervasive hopelessness among youth, or when community and parental interest and involvement are exceedingly low, create sometimes overwhelming challenges for teachers. Schools serving poor children must deal with significant social needs that can directly affect the possibilities for teaching and learning (Berliner, 2014). While we want to be very careful not to ignore or misrepresent the intra-group differences that exist, and to avoid stereotyping that presents populations of color as necessarily in deficit and "at risk," teachers (and teacher educators) do need to address the uneven proportion of people of color living in poverty when addressing issues of student success. As Milner (2013) suggests, among the relevant out-of-school factors are family structure, security of students, kinds of learning opportunities available outside the home, and parents' involvement with schoolwork. There are times when such factors (linked to "savage inequalities") will surely play a role in the "achievement" of students. As such, teachers need to be as prepared as possible to develop learning strategies and tools that speak to the needs of all students as well as ways to advocate for expanded school and community resources and services for their students. Perhaps if there is one critical issue that showcases complexity, limitations, lifelong learning, disagreements, teaching who you are, and context in teacher education, it is this one.

During his 2010 State of the Union address, President Obama stated that "in the 21st century, one of the best anti-poverty programs is a world-class education." I would suggest instead that one of the best ways to achieve a world-class education system is to have the best possible anti-poverty programs. Context is not destiny, but it is crucial.

Conclusion

One strives to hold on to the hope that seems inherent in teaching. As Perrone (1991) suggests, the teaching profession is challenging but "with many wonderful aspects. It provides a way to stay young at heart, to maintain a lifetime of active learning, to be a special part of the world of the present *and* the future while having opportunities to delve into the past. It is in every respect a profession of hope" (p. 131). Good veteran teachers know that every year represents a new beginning and that teaching is a rewarding profession not despite of but because of the complications and uncertainties that, as part of the human condition, are experienced in classrooms every day (Peterson, 2005).

Still, it is difficult during the current period not to feel that we are experiencing what West (2008) refers to as "hope on a tightrope." As Apple (2013) notes, "We are facing the possibility that any critical impulses within the education of teachers will be seen as 'deviant' and where teaching is seen as being simply a set of technical and procedural skills that can be measured on easily scored standardized tests." We will continue to have teachers committed to education but "missing many of the critical skills and dispositions that make teaching such a complex craft and who may only stay in the classroom for a few years before moving on" (p. 162). We will continue to have university scholars engage with important research on teacher education but increasingly the work of preparing teachers will be done by others who do not view such efforts as their responsibility. We will increasingly hear (and use) the language of accountability, efficiency, standardization, core knowledge, regulation, competition, and choice, but we will not have as much opportunity to talk about the common good, democracy, social justice, caring, critical questioning, imagination, collaboration, inspiration, and joy, all of which can enhance the school and classroom experience and foster academic achievement.

In support of democratic schooling, we would do well to keep in mind considerations of who No Child Left Behind and other similar legislation actually "leave behind" (Apple, 2006). Who benefits most from these reforms and who will be disadvantaged by their implementation? It seems clear that among the potential "losers" right now is university-based teacher education. Does the evidence exist to warrant such a frontal attack on these programs? Is it in the best interests of educational quality to develop an expanded marketplace of licensure paths? Does the compliance-and-control regulatory approach work well in the long run to support educational settings that function as vibrant professional learning communities? Do current reform proposals take into account the "basics" of what teacher educators (and teachers) need to do to foster high-quality school environments and classroom teaching?

To be sure, we need to embrace a fair-minded review of reform proposals and learn from those that seem promising to our efforts to improve the education of all children. But there are good proposals and discussions taking place among teacher educators and teachers as well and they should not be downplayed or ignored in the rush to follow privatized and marketized initiatives that sometimes seem more concerned with control, conformity and profit than educational excellence for the 21st century. Indeed, there is now compelling empirical evidence that, at least in three large urban school districts (Chicago, New York City, and Washington, D.C.), "market-oriented education reforms" (test-based teacher evaluations, school closures, and increased charter school access) have not helped to increase students' test scores and lessen achievement (or opportunity) gaps; have not led to success for "targeted students" as reformers first claimed; have led to an exodus of experienced teachers from the profession, but not necessarily bad ones; and have distracted from initiatives with greater promise and from attending to the important relationship between poverty and education (Weiss & Long, 2013).

Writing chapters like this one can perhaps make a small contribution to efforts to question the corporate business model that, admittedly during a time of great economic insecurity, has become so much a part of educational life. But it is clear that activism is needed as well, including in collaboration with grassroots teacher, parent and community groups and social and political movements (Ritchie, 2012; Apple, 2013). The comments of adult educator Myles Horton might be helpful to guide this work: "You can't just look at the problems of this world and wring your hands. You can talk yourself into a state of utter pessimism in which you believe all is lost and there's no way out. You have to *act* instead of talking. Act your way out of pessimism" (Wigginton, 1985, p. 318). That is the only approach that can truly sustain democratic life.

Note

Many thanks to Nancy Steinkraus and Robert Smith for their careful reading and helpful comments on an earlier draft of this chapter.

References

American Association of State Colleges and Universities (2005). *Policy matters: The facts—and fictions—about teacher shortage*. Washington, DC: American Association of State Colleges and Universities

Amrein-Beardsley, A. (2012). Value-added measures in education: The best of the alternatives is simply not good enough. *Teachers College Record*, January 12, retrieved from: http://www.tcrecord.org/content.asp?contentid=16648

Anyon, J. (1997). *Ghetto schooling: A political economy of urban educational reform*. New York: Teachers College Press.

Apple, M. W. (2006). *Education the "right" way: Markets, standards, god, and inequality*. New York: Routledge.

Apple, M. W. (2013). *Can education change society?* New York: Routledge.

Apple, M. W., & Teitelbaum, K. (1986). Are teachers losing control of their skills and curriculum? *Journal of Curriculum Studies*, 18: 177–184.

Atwood, M. (1985). *The Handmaid's Tale*. New York: Fawcett Crest.

Berliner, D. C. (2014). Effects of inequality and poverty vs. teachers and schooling on America's youth. *Teachers College Record*, retrieved from: http://www.tcrecord.org/Content.asp?ContentID=16889

Berliner, D. C., & Biddle, B. J. (1995). *The manufactured crisis: Myths, frauds, and the attack on public schools*. Reading, MA: Addison-Wesley.

Berry, B., et al. (2011). *Teaching 2030: What we must do for our students and our public schools—now and in the future*. New York: Teachers College Press.

Bowman, M. & Gottesman, I. (2013). Why practice-centered teacher education programs need social foundations. *Teachers College Record*, March 22, retrieved from: http://www.tcrecord.org/Content.asp?ContentID=17066

Carnegie Forum for Education and the Economy (1986). *A nation prepared: Teachers for the 21st century*. New York: Carnegie Forum for Education and the Economy

Carnoy, M., & Rothstein, R. (2013). *What do international tests really show about U.S. student performance?* Washington, DC: Economic Policy Institute.

Chomsky, N. (2013). Public education and the common good. Presentation at East Stroudsburg University, East Stroudsburg, PA, February 2, retrieved from: http://www.youtube.com/watch?v=7TLZN92-dZo

Cody, A. (2012). Payola policy: NCTQ prepares its hit on schools of education. *Education Week*, May 25, retrieved from: http://blogs.edweek.org/teachers/living-in-dialogue/2012/05/payola_policy_nctq_prepares_it.html

Drury, D., & Baer, J. (2011). *The American public school teacher*. Cambridge, MA: Harvard University Press.

Farhi, P. (2012). Flunking the test. *American Journalism Review*, April/May, retrieved from: http://www.ajr.org/Article.asp?id=5280

Feiman-Nemser, S. (2003). What new teachers need to learn. *Educational Leadership*, 60: 25–29.

Fenstermacher, G. D., & Richardson, V. (2010). What's wrong with accountability? *Teachers College Record*, May 26, retrieved from: http://www.tcrecord.org/Content.asp?ContentID=15996

Fox, K. R., & McNulty, C. P. (2013). Redefining first-year teacher support. *School Administrator*, 70: 36–42.

Franzen, J. (2010). *Freedom*. New York: Picador.

Gillette, J. (2012). Closing the teacher-development gap. *Education Week*, November 7: 24–26.

Goodlad, J. I. (1984). *A place called school: Prospects for the future*. New York: McGraw-Hill.

Goodlad, J. I. (1999). Whither schools of education? *Journal of Teacher Education*, 50: 325–338.

Greene, M. (1995). *Releasing the imagination: Essays on education, the arts, and social change*. San Francisco, CA: Jossey-Bass.

Hawkins, B. (2012). Student-testing pioneer Angermeyr is skeptical about high-stakes trends. *MINNPOST*, June 15, retrieved from: http://www.minnpost.com/learning-curve/2012/06/student-testing-pioneer-angermeyr-skeptical-about-high-stakes-trends

Holmes Group (1986). *Tomorrow's teachers*. East Lansing, MI: Holmes Group.

Innerst, C. (2012). Teacher education blamed for public schools' decline. *Nevada Journal*, November 13, retrieved from: http://nj.npri.org/nj98/07/teachers_ed.htm

Jardine, D. W., Clifford, P., & Friesen, S. (2008). *Back to the basics of teaching and learning*, 2nd ed. New York: Routledge.

Johnson, S. M., Kraft, M. A., & Papay, J. P. (2012). How context matters in high-need schools: The effects of teachers' working conditions on their professional satisfaction and their students' achievement. *Teachers College Record*, retrieved from: http://www.tcrecord.org/content.asp?contentid=16685

Kliebard, H. (2004). *The struggle for the American curriculum, 1893–1958*, third edition. New York: Routledge-Falmer.

Kohanim, J. (2012). "Why I left teaching." *Education Week*, August 22: 31.

Kolbert, E. (2013). Up all night. *The New Yorker*, March 8: 24–27.

Kumashiro, K. K. (2012). *Bad teacher! How blaming teachers distorts the bigger picture*. New York: Teachers College Press.

Labaree, D. F. (2004). *The trouble with ed schools*. New Haven, CT: Yale University Press.

Levin, H. M., & Rouse, C. E. (2012). The true cost of high school dropouts. *New York Times*, January 25, retrieved from: http://www.nytimes.com/2012/01/26/opinion/the-true-cost-of-high-school-dropouts.html?_r=0

Levine, A. (2006). *Educating school teachers*. Washington, DC: The Education Schools Project.

Marshall, T. H. (1950), *Citizenship and social class and other essays*. Cambridge: Cambridge University Press.

Mathison, S., & Ross, E. W. (Eds.) (2008). *Battleground schools*. Westport, CT: Greenwood Press.

MetLife Foundation. (2012). *The MetLife survey of the American teacher: Teachers, parents and the economy*. New York: Metropolitan Life Insurance Company.

Milner, H. R., IV (2013). Analyzing poverty, learning, and teaching through a critical race theory lens. *Review of Research in Education*, 37: 1–53.

Murray, J. (2012). Supporting effective teacher learning in American schools. *Teachers College Record*, April 13, retrieved from: http://www.tcrecord.org/Content.asp?ContentID=16751

National Commission on Excellence in Education (1983). *A nation at risk: The imperative for educational reform*. Washington, D.C.: U.S. Department of Education.

Nieto, S. (2013). *Finding joy in teaching students of diverse backgrounds*. Presentation for the Watson College of Education Public Speaker Series, University of North Carolina, Wilmington, Wilmington, NC, March 13.

Palmer, P. J. (2007). *The Courage to teach: Exploring the inner landscape of a teacher's life, 10th Anniversary Edition*. San Francisco, CA: Jossey-Bass.

Perrone, V. (1991). *A letter to teachers: Reflections on Schooling and the art of teaching*. San Francisco, CA: Jossey-Bass.

Peterson, S. (2005). Always another beginning. In Sonia Nieto (Ed.), *Why we teach*, pp. 156–166. New York: Teachers College Press.

Phi Delta Kappan/Gallup Poll (2012). Public's attitudes toward the public schools. Retrieved from: http://pdkintl. org/wp-content/blogs.dir/5/files/2012-Gallup-poll-full-report.pdf.

Popham, W. J., & Greenberg, S. W (1958). Teacher education: A decade of criticism. *Phi Delta Kappan*, 40: 118–120.

Reese, W. J. (2005). *America's public schools: From the common good to "No Child Left Behind."* Baltimore, MD: Johns Hopkins University Press.

Richards, E. (2012). State creates new path to teaching license. *JSO Online*, August 20, retrieved from: http://www. jsonline.com/news/education/state-creates-new-path-to-teacher-license-j96igd3-166831206.html

Ritchie, S. (2012). Incubating and sustaining: How teacher networks enable and support social justice education. *Journal of Teacher Education*, 63: 120–131.

Rizga, K. (2012). Everything you've heard about failing schools is wrong. *Mother Jones*, September/October, retrieved from: http://www.motherjones.com/media/2012/08/mission-high-false-low-performing-school

Sahlberg, P. (2011). *Finnish lessons: What can the world learn from educational change in Finland?* New York: Teachers College Press.

Sarason, S. (2002). *Educational reform: A self-scrutinizing memoir.* New York: Teachers College Press.

Sawchuk, S. (2013). State chiefs to examine teacher prep, licensing. *Education Week*, January 9: 11.

Surowiecki, J. (2013). The financial page: The turnaround trap. *The New Yorker*, March 25: 44.

Teitelbaum, K. (2008). Curriculum. In Sandra Mathison & Ross, E. Wayne (Eds.), *Battleground schools*, pp. 168–177. Westport, CT: Greenwood Press.

Tucker, M. (2012). Teacher quality and teacher accountability. *Education Week*, May 8, retrieved from: http://blogs. edweek.org/edweek/top_performers/2012/05/teacher_quality_and_teacher_accountability.html

U.S. Department of Education (2011). *Our future, our teachers: The Obama Administration's plan for teacher education reform and improvement.* Washington, D.C.: U.S. Department of Education.

Watkins, W. H. (Ed.) (2012a). *The assault on public education: Confronting the politics of corporate school reform.* New York: Teachers College Press.

Watkins, W. H. (2012b). Re-imagining public education. In W. Watkins (Ed.), *The assault on public education: Confronting the politics of corporate school reform*, pp. 189–192. New York: Teachers College Press.

Weiss, E., & Long, D. (2013). Market-oriented education reforms' rhetoric trumps reality. Washington, DC: Broader, Bolder Approach to Education. Retrieved from: http://www.epi.org/files/2013/bba-rhetoric-trumps-reality.pdf.

West, C. (2008). *Hope on a tightrope: Words and wisdom.* Carlsbad, CA: Hay House.

Whitcomb, J., Borko, H., & Liston, D. (2008). Stranger than fiction: Arthur Levine's *Educating school teachers*— The basis for a proposal. *Journal of Teacher Education*, 58: 195–201.

Wigginton, E. (1985). *Sometimes a shining moment: The Foxfire experience.* Garden City, NY: Anchor Press.

Zeichner, K. M. (2009). *Teacher education and the struggle for social justice.* New York: Routledge.

Zeichner, K. M. (2012). The turn once again toward practice-based teacher education. *Journal of Teacher Education*, 63: 376–382.

Zeichner, K. M., & Tabachnick, B. R. (1981). Are the effects of university teacher education "washed out" by school experience? *Journal of Teacher Education*, 32: 7–11.

CHAPTER EIGHT

A Critical Examination of Today's (Un)Democratic Reform Agenda for Teachers, Administrators, and Teacher Education

CAROLYN M. SHIELDS

The idea that the market should be allowed to make major social and political decisions; the idea that the State should voluntarily reduce its role in the economy, or that corporations should be given total freedom, that trade unions should be curbed and citizens given much less rather than more social protection- such ideas were utterly foreign to the spirit of the [1950s] time. (Giroux, 2005, p. 1)

Much has been written about today's neoliberal education reform context in education, both in the United States and in other developed countries. The above quotation by Henry Giroux acknowledges the radical neoliberal changes in ideology that have swept industrialized nations and dramatically affected social and political institutions, including both higher education and K-12 schooling, in the last half century.

It is well known that the playing field in K-12 public education is still far from even; hence, students from impoverished or non-majority families often struggle to complete high school in the same time frame and with the same academic outcomes as their peers from more advantaged families. In fact, the phrase "achievement gap" has passed into common parlance; and its accuracy and implications are rarely questioned. At the same time, critics (Ladson-Billings, 2006; Milner, 2013) argue that the notion of an achievement gap is misplaced and misnamed and that we should, instead, focus on the ways in which educational institutions offer inequitable opportunities to students. Indeed, although it is frequently believed that, in developed countries at least, access to education is equitable and open to all students, it is also well known that other aspects of equity (Farrell, 1999)—survivability, equity of outputs, and equity of outcomes—are far from being achieved. Thus, students from minoritized groups (lower income, non-dominant languages and cultures) are less likely to enter advanced, international baccalaureate, or gifted programs; and when they are placed in these higher level courses are less likely to survive than their dominant culture peers. Further, regardless of their high school program, minoritized students, in general, experience lower graduation rates and grades, and have fewer career opportunities open to them. Because none of these differential outcomes can accurately be attributed to the students' abilities, but instead, and more accurately to the beliefs, values, programs, and policies of most educational institutions, it would be more accurate to speak of an "education gap," an "opportunity gap," or an "institutional performance gap."

What may be less well known is that the playing field in higher education mirrors that of K-12 education, and continues, in many ways, to exacerbate the challenges for minoritized[1] students. Hence, even at its best, public education in most countries is far from democratic. In today's climate of increased accountability and emphases on free market and neoliberal policies and practices, most reform initiatives exacerbate current inequities and fail to democratize education. For example, business analyst Tim Laseter (2013) has suggested that the only thing higher education (worldwide) is doing correctly is reaching more students than ever before. His critique includes soaring costs, low graduation rates, and failure to meet the needs of employers. Thus, even the possibility that more people are involved in some way in higher education falls far short of being a deeply democratic reform.

This current context of augmented accountability, corporatization, and privatization at the university level has resulted in institutions of higher education paying increased attention to ratings by organizations such as the *US News and World Report* or Shanghai's *Academic Ranking of World Universities* in order to attract both students and funding agencies. Universities have become more entrepreneurial, rely more on donations, and streamline both admissions policies and programs to ensure a prominent position in today's highly publicized ratings. Almost unnoticed are the concomitant ways in which the press for increased standards, higher and more rapid completion and graduation rates, and more "cutting edge" research has simultaneously resulted in new and more demanding admissions standards with more students from impoverished or non-mainstream backgrounds being diverted to community colleges. A recent report sponsored by the Spencer Foundation (King, Douglass, & Feller, 2007) identified nine challenges facing public universities that its findings claim to be common internationally. These challenges include "the need to maintain access and improve graduation rates, increasing expectations by governments and the public to serve the broad social needs of society, disinvestment by state governments and the need for new financial models" (p. 4).

Karram (2013), critiquing the current state of affairs, argues that the "investment metaphor" often associated with entrepreneurialism is not working and that "it is essential that the three components—students, instructors and programmes—be viewed as part of a valuable social contract that embeds higher education in society, rather than as competing investment opportunities." In fact, this mission to advance democratic community, civil society, and the public good that has long been at the center of higher education is being eroded, undermined, neglected, and indeed destroyed, by current neoliberal approaches. Moreover, at this point, few educators have examined the ways in which recent strategies for reforming one segment of the system (for example K-12 education) serve to compromise the whole system, hence having an adverse impact on higher education as well. Giroux (2011) has explained the impact on higher education in this way:

> With the corporatization and privatization of higher education, it is increasingly more difficult for colleges and universities to expand and deepen democratic public life, produce engaged critical citizens, and operate as democratic public spheres. Moreover, higher educating is defaulting on its obligations to offer young people a quality and broad-based education. (As quoted in Johannsen, 2011, p. 16)

While attempting to hold education more accountable, state legislatures are also promoting increasingly undemocratic reform, in part by legislation that privatizes education in the guise of offering choice (without attention to quality) and in part by showing a marked lack of understanding of the ways in which education contributes to the overall quality of democratic life.

Purpose and Overview

The state of Michigan provides an excellent exemplar of the ways in which education reforms are playing out within an increasingly undemocratic context of legislative bills and rules, emergency managers, for-profit providers, school takeovers, and other strategies whose overall impact is to maintain the disparities in the status quo in the name of educational improvement and reform. Through its recent legislative and organizational initiatives to approve "alternative pathways" to both teacher and administrator certification, Michigan has opened the doors to an unlimited number of charter and on-line schools, privatized K-12 education services within public districts, permitted certification and even master's degrees to be offered by alternative providers, and defunded and de-emphasized the role of higher education in educator preparation. What must be emphasized is how these and similar legislative responses to current challenges simultaneously and paradoxically undermine the very basis for democratic education.

This chapter will first situate educational reform in a brief discussion of democracy and democratic education and offer ways of thinking about school reform as either technical or equity-oriented. Then I will provide an overview of some recent Michigan reforms and discuss and critique them, in order to demonstrate the negative impact of these and similar reforms on the democratization of education. More specifically, I will also argue that it is precisely in institutions located in, and striving to serve, historically marginalized and underserved communities where the negative impact is, and will be, greatest.

Some Theoretical Perspectives

Frequently we think of democracy simply as a form of governance with "one person, one vote" as the dominant concept. If we go beyond this thin notion of democracy, we might draw on the categorization of Marshall (1950), who identified *civil* citizenship (the right to individual freedoms), *political* citizenship (the right to be involved in the exercise of power), and *social* citizenship (the right to a degree of economic security, health services, and educational provision) (see Torres, 1998, p. 106). Although Marshall's work has more recently been critiqued for not including analyses related to gender, race, or socio-economic status, his categories help us to move beyond a very simplistic notion of democracy.

One historic and salient example of the problem associated with one person, one vote may be found in the civil rights movement of the United States and in the numerous legislative initiatives (even current attempts) to prevent African Americans from being accepted as fully participating citizens. As long as the majority can override the rights of a minority, the notion of voting as central to democracy is inadequate. Only a cursory reflection on the repression of indigenous peoples, the existence of slavery, the treatment of Asian railway workers, or the belief in "manifest destiny" with respect to early Native American and Mexican American conflicts reminds us of the ways in which a powerful majority may override the rights of other legitimate citizens.

As various individuals have been denied access to housing, to holding land or office, to education, or to voting, it is clear that civil citizenship has not always reflected democratic ideals. Similarly, almost two and a half centuries since the promulgation in 1776 of the Declaration of Independence, the "representation" of elected officials in the United States Senate and House of Representatives is far from representative of the general population. Indeed, November 2012 heralded a sea change in electoral power because, for the first time in U.S. history, women had been elected to hold 20% of the Senate seats (Geiger, 2012). The fact that, at least in the Democratic Party, the majority of members of the House would no longer be white and male was also touted as a victory. Similarly, in addition to the misnamed achievement gap mentioned earlier, data demonstrate repeatedly that African Americans and other minorities drop out (or stop out) of school, are homeless, incarcerated, and un- and underemployed at higher rates than their Caucasian counterparts. Even by Marshall's (1950) measures, democracy is far from being achieved in America.

Yet, a more useful way of thinking about democracy and democratic education comes from scholars such as Judith Green (1999), who advances a concept of *deep democracy* in which she presents the "experience-based possibility of more equal, respectful, and mutually beneficial ways of community life" (p. vi). This concept, she posits, is, at its core, a *"realistic, historically grounded ideal, a desired and desirable future possibility that is yet to be"* (p. ix, italics in the original). I ground this discussion of educational reform in a belief in this concept of democracy as a form of governance and civil society within which reform efforts should be directed at promoting this kind of mutually beneficial vision of life lived in common with all others in a society.

To accomplish this vision, it is also useful to take note of the research of Oakes and Rogers (2006), who examined numerous school reform initiatives and concluded that current strategies focused on technical reforms do not have the potential to promote equitable outcomes. Moreover, they argue that "merely documenting inequality will not, in and of itself, lead to more adequate and equitable schooling" (p. 13). Instead, it will be necessary for legislators, politicians, and the general public to find the political will and the moral courage to make difficult decisions, to ensure that the history of inequity and inequality in this country is disrupted. Moreover, they claim that current norms are intractable and cannot

> be understood, let alone altered, absent consideration of the larger social, economic, and political milieu
> in which current inequalities between and within schools seem so sensible to so many of those who are
> privileged currently. (p. 14)

It is with these concepts in mind—the need for a robust concept of democracy and for school reform to take into account current inequalities—that we proceed now to examine some of the myriad of reforms enacted in Michigan in the last two years.

The Reforms

On April 27, 2011, Governor Rick Snyder stated, "Michigan's future is absolutely dependent on making our education system a success for our students, our teachers, our parents, and our economy." He added, "Change does not have to create adversaries; it can create partners committed to a better future." To create this desired future, Snyder advanced a concept of education he described as occurring "any time, any place, any way and at any pace," based on a brief prepared by the private Oxford Foundation (a non-profit organization founded to focus on projects that "lessen the burdens of government;" Oxford Foundation, n.d.). The Oxford Foundation has no relationship to Oxford University nor is it really a foundation; rather it represents a collection of individuals also associated with the Mackinac Center, a Michigan think tank that advocates "free market" principles. In other words, it does not represent public opinion, nor does it purport to. Thus, both the limited network of interactions and influence and the policies themselves demonstrate how the dominance of neoliberal ideologies undermines democratic education in Michigan. Moreover, several pieces of legislation appear to be in direct opposition to the governor's lofty goal of creating a more successful education system for all.

As Governor Synder rolled out his reform agenda, Michigan school superintendents almost unanimously expressed concern, even dismay, at approaches they perceived would dismantle the democratically elected and autonomous school system in place in the state and replace it with a statewide system accountable only to the governor. Others expressed similar concerns, with such comments as: "This is a radical experiment, untried, unproven, and dangerous" or "I would like to believe that Gov. Snyder is interested in improving learning for students but I find that hard to believe when his plan is to entrust our children to any 'fly by night' for-profit organization without any accountability or transparency to our parents or taxpayers" or "I want to believe that Gov. Snyder has our students' best interest at heart, but I am beginning to believe he just wants to dismantle public education." Others, outside of Michigan, joined the outcry. Diane Ravitch wrote (in an article entitled "Michigan is on its way to ending public education"): "Governor Rick Snyder must hate public education. Certainly his advisors do" (Ravitch, 2012a). Two days later, she noted in her daily blog, "Governor Rick Snyder of Michigan is determined to break up public education and encourage privatization as rapidly as possible" (Ravitch, 2012b).

Additional criticism has been leveled at the undemocratic approach to the introduction of new policies in Michigan. For example, in order to revise the way in which education is financed and to revise a long-standing public finance act, Governor Rick Synder requested that conservative activist Richard McLellan "provide pro bono legal services to Eli Broad (http://www.broadfoundation.org) and the Snyder Administration in connection with the financial crisis facing the Detroit Public Schools ('DPS')" (McLellan, n.d.). McLellan was instrumental in the drafting of Michigan Charter School legislation, in the establishment of the Education Achievement Authority, and in the development of the Michigan Public Finance Act. Certainly, granting one person such extraordinary influence and power is antithetical to democratic process. The majority of this critique, however, is leveled at the ways in which the reforms and proposed finance act would dismantle public education in Michigan, weaken local control, fail to protect the poorest and least advantaged students in the system, and ultimately advance a neoliberal ideology aligned with the interests of for-profit providers.

Some Legislative Changes

Legislative initiatives in Michigan are not occurring in a vacuum but mirror, replicate, and only sometimes lead, similar efforts in other states. It is for this reason that examining the package of reforms, rather than focusing on one or two initiatives, gives a frightening impression of the undemocratic state of school reform nationwide.

Alternative Providers

Legislation passed in 2011 included bills to "lift the cap on the number of charter schools in Michigan" (SB618) and to lift all caps on cyber high schools (SB619)—both measures that purported to increase flexibility and choice and to ensure, through competition, that students are able to access education anywhere and anytime. In and of themselves, these changes are worrisome, given the dubious results of similar changes in other states. A study conducted by the Civil Rights Project at UCLA, entitled *Choice Without Equity* (Frankenberg, Siegel-Hawley, & Wang, 2010), focused on the increased stratification and inequality often brought about by a growth of charter schools. Studies of charter schools by Lubienski and Lubienski (2006) found that, when socio-economic status was taken into consideration, students in public schools outperformed their counterparts in charter schools. Moreover, as Apple (2006) and others have argued, choice is truly only choice when the playing field is level to begin with. Not everyone has the same opportunity or capacity to participate in alternative education programs.

Taken together, these findings suggest that authorizing unlimited alternative sites and formats for learning may well provide the democratic illusion of empowering parents with new and additional options for their children's education, but that they also disadvantage many students as well as the schools from which there may be a large exodus. A study in Canada of the unintended consequences of "choice" policies (Waithman, 2009) found that, unless supplemental policies were enacted to ensure the survival of schools in economically disadvantaged areas, those children whose parents, for one reason or another, could not avail themselves of a new opportunity were further disadvantaged as their current schools lost funding and other resources (e.g., special subject area teachers, librarians, and enrichment activities). Moreover, because schools of choice have the option of selective enrollment, they often do not enroll (or provide services for) students with various special needs.

Alternative Certification

In Michigan, however, the provision of alternative sites and formats for education may be less worrisome than the bills authorizing "alternative teacher preparation providers" (R. 390.1101), changes to teacher evaluation (HB 4627), and alternative administrator certification (R. 380.101). Each of these changes implies that quality is not the goal, but rather a diminution of the authority of established providers, including institutions of public higher education. One controversial change authorizes alternative providers to certify teacher candidates and permits for-profit entities (such as I-Teach) to prepare teachers in Michigan without holding them to the same conditions and standards as universities whose teacher education programs have been much scrutinized. Students with an undergraduate degree and a 3.0 GPA who can successfully pass the state competency tests are now able to become certified after 12 credit hours of preparation. Thus, teachers lacking adequate preparation in special education, diversity, or cultural competence will be able to obtain positions in schools with diverse and needy populations; and once again, it will likely be students from the least advantaged family circumstances who will be most disadvantaged by these underprepared teachers.

In addition to this reduction of standards, HB 4627, related to teacher evaluation, states that recommended changes in the requirements for a professional education teaching certificate "will assure that a teacher is not required to complete additional postsecondary credit hours beyond the credit hours required for a provisional teaching certificate" (section 5(e)). It is little wonder that colleges and universities in Michigan believe that their ability to promote the democratic purposes of education as foundational to an engaged civil society and caring global society is being undermined. Comparable issues are raised by R. 380.101, which permits similar modifications and a relaxing of requirements for administrator certification, again with a concomitant reduction in the practical and theoretical knowledge bases required to adequately perform leadership functions in education. One small, but further indication of a diminished focus on quality—and an emphasis on time, instead—is the change (in May 2012) from the use of the term "State Board Continuing Education Units" to 'State Continuing Education Clock Hour Units"—emphasizing time spent in an acceptable activity rather than on the nature and quality of the learning itself as acceptable for ongoing professional development (Michigan Department of Education, 2012).

Impact on Higher Education

There can be little doubt that these changes have a detrimental impact both on K-12 education and on institutions of higher education, on the quality of educator preparation, and ultimately on society at large. The provision for teachers to receive certification after completing a course of study involving 12 credits beyond their undergraduate degrees exacerbates the enrollment and funding challenges to higher education at a time when state contributions to higher education have been reduced from roughly 70% of operating funds to 30%, and when enrollments in education are declining due to changing demographics in many states. Legislation that states explicitly that students have no requirement to engage in further education beyond their initial certification sends a clear message that theoretical, scholarly, research-based preparation with carefully supervised field experiences is considered neither useful nor valid. Despite the fact that grants to assist less advantaged students with the costs of higher education have been preserved, there has also been a reduction in the number of semesters of student eligibility for these federal Pell grants. In turn, older students with family responsibilities and outside jobs are disadvantaged and deterred from returning for advanced certification or degrees. Once again, decisions seem to have been made independent of the careful examination of social conditions called for by researchers such as Oakes and Rogers (2006).

Although most educators and much of the general public perceive that quality preparation is being undermined by these reforms, there are also more subtle effects that will have a differential and negative impact on many students from challenged urban areas. In Detroit, for example ("ground zero for education in the country," according to Education Secretary Arne Duncan), where it is well known that public schools have struggled for some time, many students complete high school underprepared for higher education. In general, these (largely minoritized) students have a more difficult time than their suburban peers achieving the required 3.0 GPA in their undergraduate programs and hence are not eligible for the new, alternative preparation routes to higher education. In turn, if these students, who are already so underrepresented in education careers, wish to become teachers, they will be forced to complete the longer, traditional, and much more costly preparation programs, and hence, to graduate with considerably more debt.

In addition, given the need for institutions of higher education to demonstrate student achievement through metrics such as six-year completion rates, many universities that have traditionally been considered accessible to people from struggling urban communities have been forced to raise their admission standards (again reducing access for minoritized students). Hence, at a time when educators are trying to diversify the teaching and administrative workforce, students from minoritized groups have less access to preparation programs. At Wayne State University, for example, where the average age of the freshman class in education is 27, many students who will be the first in their families to participate in higher education already have family commitments and cannot complete the required programs in six years; neither are they eligible, for various reasons, to participate in such programs as Teach for America that require a two-year commitment, often far from these same family obligations.

Each of these changes, purporting to offer alternative routes to educator preparation, actually serves to further challenge students who have been traditionally excluded from careers in education, because the still uneven playing field in public education continues to put additional barriers and challenges in their way. Offering choice that redirects needed resources from accessible public schools or changing standards in ways that will ultimately impact even further the educational opportunities in disadvantaged communities is absolutely undemocratic.

The Education Achievement Authority

One major reform in Michigan that perhaps best typifies the ways in which school reform might negatively impact teachers, students, and administrators is the creation of the Education Achievement Authority (EAA). Supported and, to some extent, created by McLennan, the Mackinac Center, Broad Foundation and others, the EAA was unveiled as a "plan to dramatically redesign public education in Michigan's lowest-performing schools by including them into a new system that drives vastly more resources directly into their classrooms and offers greater autonomy to help ensure dramatic student achievement increases" (Education Achievement Authority, n.d.). I describe this plan in some detail to highlight some of the problems with school reform—not only in Michigan, but throughout the country.

This new system was announced as an innovative plan to "save" Michigan education by moving the lowest-performing 5% of schools in Michigan to a statewide system directly accountable to the governor. In the 2012–2013 school year, the EAA began with 15 "underperforming" schools in Detroit. When news of the possibility of Dr. Covington (former superintendent of school districts in Colorado, Alabama, and Kansas City) being appointed as Chancellor of the EAA reached Detroit, local newspapers published numerous articles begging for caution. One headline read, "Covington leaves a firestorm brewing in Kansas City" (Henderson, 2011a); a month later another suggested, "Covington needs to explain troubles in Kansas City schools" (Henderson, 2011b). The news circulated that Covington's previous district had been stripped of its state accreditation and that, although he had successfully "rightsized" the district by closing schools to balance the budget, student test scores had actually declined (Resmovits, 2011). Nevertheless, the EAA and the appointment of Covington were supported locally by Detroit Public Schools emergency manager Roy Roberts as well as nationally by Secretary of Education Arne Duncan, who "sang his praises," saying he was "deeply committed" (Resmovits, 2012).

Deeply committed, in his own words, to "student-centered instruction," Covington proceeded to give pink slips to all administrators and teachers in the schools that were to move elsewhere, to fill 25% of his teaching positions with Teach for America teachers, and to institute individualized, computer-based instruction. Of particular interest is the fact that, although the EAA is a distinctly separate authority from which students will graduate, the chair of the executive committee of the new authority is Roberts, whose position as DPS emergency manager seems to inherently put him in a conflict of interest. It is little wonder, perhaps, that he argues that the EAA is a "fair and effective reform measure" despite the lack of data regarding its performance.

As resources were moved from existing schools to schools (already poorly resourced) in the new authority, the latter struggled to maintain adequate programs and resources. This dilemma of the existing non-EAA schools is, of course, consistent with the earlier mentioned findings of Waithman and others. One educator, Detroit Federation of Teachers President Keith Johnson, expressed his apprehension in strong words: "Let us not go back to *Brown vs. Board of Ed* where we're willing to make an investment in one group of students and tell another group of students, 'Oh well, survive as you can.'" This restructuring again seemed to have occurred without careful examination of its impact on the whole system, and certainly without public dialogue about the equity issues involved.

In December 2012, less than four months after the opening of the first EAA schools, Governor Snyder introduced HB 6004 in the lame duck Michigan legislature, which would, among other things, provide for the oversight of

> a separate Michigan school district called the "reform district," whose leader, known as the chancellor, would have the powers of a school superintendent, and whose constituent schools would comprise those school buildings, statewide, where student achievement, as measured on state tests, fell within the lowest five percent of Michigan schools for three consecutive years. (HB 6004, 2012)

Again, this provoked an outcry related both to the content of the bill and the controversial nature of its related hearings. The House Education Committee heard hours of testimony from those in support of the bill, but frequently denied the opportunity to speak to the many parties opposed to the permanent inclusion of such an undemocratic approach to schooling in Michigan legislation. (Ultimately the bill was not taken to a vote in the 2012 legislative lame duck session, although it is being reintroduced in subsequent sessions.) Opponents raised concerns, including the authority's exclusion from participation in statewide testing, its ability to incur debts without being liable for them, and lack of transparency regarding funding (although the chancellor's initial $175,000 signing bonus and second year salary of $325,000 were widely publicized; Skubick, 2011). Aside from the fact that there will always be 5% of schools performing at the bottom of the pack (an intrinsic function of the concept of percent), there are no publicized mechanisms for moving schools away from the EAA and no provisions for limiting the extent of the takeover.

When opponents were finally permitted to testify, it became obvious that their concerns related to the wider issues of democracy and education and were not limited to critique of the EAA system per se. For example, Belant (2012), President of the Detroit Public Library Commission, wrote that "the most fundamental problem with House Bill 6004 is that it is grossly unconstitutional." Of particular concern was the fact that the bill contravened the Michigan Constitution's requirement that supervision of boards of education fall under the state board of education and not the governor, and that an additional provision of the bill would give the governor authority to strip assets from local boards and transfer them to the new "reform district." Many other concerns were raised about the curriculum, pedagogy, and timing of the proposed bilbefore any measures of success could be realized and prior to the accumulation of any data related to student performance.

On November 19, 2012, in testimony before the Michigan house standing committee on education, critics were vocal. The following quotations are taken from testimony documents provided to me by those making the testimony and hence, may be considered "personal communication" in that they are not part of a currently available public record.

State Board of Education Treasurer Marianne McGuire urged the legislature to proceed cautiously in that the curriculum that "essentially puts children in front of computers and asks them to proceed step by step on the computer's software" is a "mode of education that may work for some children but without necessary backup and support, students will not succeed." Thomas Pedroni, an associate professor at Wayne State University, extended the critique, explaining that true student-centered curriculum does not start with a computer-based program but with the child, and that "for a teacher to effectively teach children, the teacher must know her students.... [That children] have knowledge and identities that are rooted in particular historical and cultural experiences." To support the argument that time and data were needed before an appropriate assessment of progress could be made, Maiyoua Vang, an assistant professor at the University of Michigan-Dearborn, introduced data from the first year of Covington's similar experiment in Kansas City; it showed that, despite claims of student gains, student performance had actually declined in terms of students who exceeded expectations and increased in terms of students not achieving at grade level.

Dr. Rebecca Martusewicz, a professor at Eastern Michigan University, was particularly critical of the interlocal agreement that purported to establish a partnership between the EAA and her university, saying it had come as a surprise, and explaining that it quickly became apparent that "there was no intention of calling on [the] expertise" of faculty members, as originally discussed. Moreover, she argued that "the EAA concerns not the quality of public schooling for poor children and poor children of color and their academic achievement, but democracy." She then emphasized that "the EAA has been constructed, and is operating, in such a way to assault the basic premises of even a weak representative democracy," blaming the citizens of Detroit for the "economic, social and political deprivations they have suffered in the face of corporate outsourcing, racist housing policies, and radically underfunded schools in the last 50 years." These elements, she believed, were already reflective of "a weakened state of representative democracy."

When it was announced, in November 2012, that the EAA had achieved the short list to receive Race to the Top funding, an open letter to President Obama and Secretary Arne Duncan stated that

> the EAA receives public tax dollars but is not subject to oversight by Michigan's elected State Board of Education. This "new form" of school governance is particularly disturbing in its suppression of parent/community participation in the school decision-making process as there is no elected school board. Installing an appointed chancellor who only reports to the governor effectively disenfranchises the citizens of Michigan. (Strauss, 2012)

In other words, many experts, from various political and scholarly stances, critiqued Michigan's school reforms as being not only antidemocratic, but as undermining efforts already underway to improve educational services to Michigan's underserved and underperforming children.

Discussion

The foregoing description of some of the recent reforms in Michigan will sound familiar to readers from other jurisdictions both in the United States and elsewhere. Charter schools, cyber schools, an expansion of the cadre of educational providers, and enhancing opportunities for parental choice are frequent mantras of school reform in recent decades. At the same time, the potential of these reforms to undermine rather than enhance democracy, democratic education, and democratic citizenship must be carefully considered from a number of perspectives. The major areas of critique suggested by the above overview include:

The intended outcomes of the reforms

The impetus for reform

The processes of the reforms

The pedagogy and curriculum of school reform, and

The intended beneficiaries of the reform.

Each of these will be briefly addressed in the concluding section of this chapter.

The Intended Reform Outcomes

What is striking is that explicit goals of educational reforms are rarely stated. Governor Snyder, for example, indicated that he wanted the education system to be a "success" for Michigan's families, but did not suggest what might comprise that success. Would it mean that every student was engaged in a high-quality learning experience? Would every student develop critical or creative thinking skills? Might every student complete at least one college-level credit while in high school? Would it mean that the costs of public education would be transferred to the private sector? The goals are unknown.

Moreover, promoting a system of educational reform that offers education "any time, any place, any way, and at any pace" ensures neither equity nor quality. Interestingly, while there is no suggestion of content at all in the foregoing statement, there is also no implication that we have any knowledge about how children learn or any understanding of the strengths and weaknesses of various approaches. "Any way" implies that it just does not matter so long as students are receiving the mandated number of credits (or teachers are acquiring the appropriate number of clock hour credits); and "any pace" goes even further. It suggests that some students will learn more quickly or more slowly than others—and, although this is true, there is no end point that suggests that the goal is, ultimately, for all students to attain similar high standards or outcomes.

What is clear is that, as Oakes and Rogers (2006) argue, without an explicit emphasis on equity reforms and equity goals, educational reform is unlikely to reduce the "achievement gap" or correct the "opportunity gap" for those students who already are advantaged by the current system and those who are not. Moreover, a method that assumes that every student will learn at an appropriate pace by sitting in front of a computer denies almost everything that is known about the importance of social interaction and relationships in the process of learning.

"Any pace" does not imply that students who are behind will "catch up"; instead it signifies that each student will continue to move at whatever pace is deemed appropriate or, worse still, at whatever pace the student chooses. Thus, without explicit goals related to high-quality education and high standards and equity for everyone, there is no assurance that school reform will address the pressing needs of a democratic society.

The Impetus for Reform

It is clear from the description of many Michigan reforms that they are propelled by a strong neoliberal, market-driven ideology. From the involvement of the Mackinac Center with its explicit emphasis on "free market" reforms, to the certification of for-profit providers to offer teacher certification, to the unbridled opportunities for for-profit charter school operators to set up shop, much educational reform of the last several decades has clearly focused on providing opportunities for entrepreneurs whose underlying motive (sometimes despite elaborate protests to the contrary) is primarily financial rather than fundamentally educational. Here, Giroux's comment, cited earlier, should resonate strongly with those concerned about democratic education. If one is concerned about the ability of a democratic society to offer equal and equitable benefits to all members of its society, one needs to carefully consider the wisdom of permitting an increased role for markets in social and political life. It is well known that while inequality between the wealthiest and least prosperous segments of the population has risen in most developed countries, it is highest in the United States where, by 2007, the top 1% of the population accounted for 24% of all income (Noah, 2010)—a gap that is still widening rapidly. Given that growing disparity, only the most naïve would believe that underlying the profit-making motive is a desire to improve and equalize education.

The Process of Reform

If the impetus for school reform is, in general, to decrease the role of government and to increase the profitability of for-profit providers, then public participation becomes unnecessary and perhaps even undesirable. In fact, although in the United States education comes under the purview of the states, with an emphasis in many jurisdictions on local control, there is already little evidence that educational reform takes into consideration the perspectives or needs of the local population as a whole. In Michigan, when the governor considered it necessary to revise the public finance act, he turned not to a committee representative either of elected officials or of the public at large, but to one individual with a particular ideology—"to reduce the burden of government." Regardless of the ensuing recommendations (which would ultimately serve to further dismantle public education), the process itself was fundamentally undemocratic.

Moreover, one might want to consider what it might mean to "lessen the burden of government" for a service that is universally mandated and that aims to provide not only a level playing field but a means of social mobility for the least advantaged in our society. The goals of democracy will not be accomplished by lessening the role of government in education and permitting it to be replaced by neoliberal, for-profit institutions.

This is clearly evidenced in the efforts to bring a bill before the House to permanently formalize a school district that had no public accountability, but that reported directly to the governor. A bill that would arbitrarily and without supporting evidence, and without general consultation, redistribute taxpayers' money is, again, fundamentally undemocratic.

There have been numerous critiques of the low voter turnout for school board elections in general (Allen & Plank, 2005); however, providing emergency managers with unlimited powers, ignoring the decisions and directions of elected boards, and creating non-elected and non-accountable entities are not the ways to enhance public participation. Moreover, if we desire to promote Green's (1999) concept of deep democracy that offers mutual benefit and promotes a hopeful and promising future for all, then it is appropriate to expand opportunities for public input, rather than to narrow them.

The Pedagogy and Curriculum of School Reform

The same concepts might be applied to the pedagogies and curricula of public schooling. Half a century ago, as educators were encouraged to understand the role of social interaction in student learning, an approach referred to as "social constructivism" (Au, 1998) gained prominence. This concept undergirds Pedroni's notion that student-centered education must take into consideration students' prior lived experiences and their historical and cultural locations. This does not happen when all are confronted with the same software program. Students from Michigan's EAA have expressed their concern about the curriculum, saying, "Most of us feel that Buzz [the EAA's computer program] doesn't teach us anything. The videos sometimes have nothing to do with the questions that we need to answer and are sometimes pointless and childish cartoons" (Walker, 2013).

"Student-centered" pedagogies must take into account students' learning styles, vary the approach to build on current strengths and enhance alternative approaches. Most importantly, they must build on students' prior knowledge and lived experiences (Shields, Bishop, & Mazawi, 2005) to ensure that each student feels valued and appreciated as a respected member of the school community. Sitting in front of a canned program, regardless of how well it has been produced, can only work for some students at some times, and certainly not as the dominant instructional strategy. Indeed, that is exactly the knowledge that good teachers from high-quality preparation programs learn, and that has been disparaged by the introduction of so many fast-track teacher certification programs.

The Intended Beneficiaries of Reform

Always assumed, but often unstated, is that the goal of the intended reform initiative is to improve student learning in terms of enhancing the number of students who successfully master high-level concepts and proceed to the next level (college or university or beyond). Moreover, when reforms are implemented in order to provide increased choice to parents and families, one must repeatedly ask, "Choice by whom? Of what? For what?" The term "college readiness" (like so many educational reforms) seems desirable on the surface but has too often become synonymous with narrow, test score, and graduation-rate calculations.

As indicated earlier, choice is only choice on a level playing field. And, although the educational playing field in the U.S. and other developed countries is often assumed to be relatively level, the only area in which there may be some claim to equity is that of access. Yet if, as Farrell (1999) argued, equity requires equity of access, survivability, outputs and outcomes, then there is no equity in America's schools; for it is well known that students from less-advantaged backgrounds drop out at higher rates, are suspended at higher rates, and fail to acquire graduation credits at rates similar to their more advantaged classmates.

Current school reform initiatives do little to change these inequities. K-12 students whose parents cannot afford to pay transportation costs or to spend the time transporting their children to schools of choice have little opportunity to change the location of their education. Instead of moving students from school to school, from authority to authority, educators should take responsibility for educating all students. Students whose schools are closed or moved to a different authority such as the EAA find the experience disruptive and, more often than not, that it fails to enhance their learning. Students from Mumford High School, who call themselves the Social Justice League (SJL), for example, "believe students would be better served under the DPS system because the EAA has not delivered on its promise to educate them effectively" (Walker, 2013).

Constant educational change, frequent disruption and interruption of services, and inadequate, unproven, and unsuccessful reform are, in effect, at the heart of much of Detroit's declining school system and the repercussions are far-reaching. As schools lack resources, are mismanaged, and are taken over, population declines, more resources are lost, and the overall quality of education decreases. Students are disconnected from peers, from adult mentors and support systems, and from their communities. Ultimately, graduates have a more difficult time being accepted into a university program, and when they are accepted they often take longer to complete their program. The reputation of the system declines, an exodus ensues, and the process is repeated, with public education acquiring a worse and worse reputation.

The beneficiaries of such a system are not the institutions of public education, nor are they the students themselves, or even society at large. Instead, the real beneficiaries are the for-profit enterprises that have been encouraged to become alternate providers. Overall, under the majority of current school reform initiatives, those who lose are those who already lack the power or voice to influence the system. Those who gain are usually members of agencies such as the Broad Foundation or the charter school providers for whom neoliberal school reforms are ultimately financially beneficial.

Concluding Comment

We can and we must do better. But we must be careful and strategic. The foreword to a recently released report by the national Equity and Excellence Commission (2013) opened with this indictment of the current state of American education:

> This report summarizes how America's K-12 education system, taken as a whole, fails our nation and too many of our children. Our system does not distribute opportunity equitably. Our leaders decry but tolerate disparities in student outcomes that are not only unfair, but socially and economically dangerous. Our nation's stated commitments to academic excellence are often eloquent but, without more, an insufficient response to challenges at home and globally. (p. 9)

What is new in this report is the resounding recognition that "parity is not equity" (p. 10) and the acknowledgment that American education "must foster the nation's civic culture and sense of common purpose, and create the unified nation that *e pluribus unum* celebrates" (p. 12).

But we must be watchful. The report continues to advocate more "coordinated reform." Coordination may well be needed, but as the report outlines, and as this chapter has argued, it must be coordinated reform that enhances and undergirds *democratic* schooling and not the opposite. The recommendations of the commission contain a "five-part framework of tightly interrelated recommendations to guide policymaking," including equitable school finance; effective teachers, principals and curricula; academically focused early childhood education; mitigating the impact of poverty; and responsible accountability and governance systems (p. 9). These five areas are not new, and unless a radically different approach to reform is taken, the results will be one more iteration of reshuffling, redeveloping, renaming, and repackaging unproductive strategies.

Meaningful and democratic reform will require that every jurisdiction focus on equity reforms that truly have the potential to reduce inequities. An equitable finance reform could remove funding disparities and reallocate resources that are sufficient and efficiently used instead of increasing the profits of wealthy corporations. Requiring "a uniform entry 'bar' into the profession," instead of the current uneven playing field that privileges for-profit, non-governmental agencies could be a step in the right direction. Developing a policy infrastructure that would provide more services to underserved and less advantaged students could increase opportunities for equitable access.

To create democratic school reform, we must not only "decry" disparities in student outcomes, but redress inequities in the educational system itself—inequities that threaten the social and economic fabric of our country. To do so, we will have to take seriously the lessons one can learn from Michigan and reconsider how to provide educational opportunities that are flexible and far-reaching, but also democratic. We must take seriously the need for reforms to promote a "desired and desirable future" (Green, 1999) of mutual benefit for the well-being of our society as a whole. To do so will require commitment, courage, focus—and a great deal of hard work.

Notes

1. The term *minoritized* refers to a group of people who have been ascribed the characteristics of a minority (Shields, 2005) regardless of whether or not they are in the numerical minority. In other words, those groups that have traditionally held power may continue to exclude or marginalize others, regardless of shifting numbers, resulting in people who may actually comprise the numerical majority being treated as if their position and perspective are of little worth. Minoritized populations have less influence and their perspectives are often silenced by the voices of the powerful. For example, schools on the Navajo reservation whose student population is over 95% Navajo, still use a largely western and Caucasian-based curriculum; schools with majority Latino or African American populations may still use a Eurocentric curriculum that distorts or misrepresents history.

References

Allen, A., & Plank, D. N. (2005). School board election structure and democratic representation. *Educational Policy, 19*(3), 510–527.

Apple, M. (2006, January). *Embracing diversity: New challenges for school effectiveness and improvement in a global learning society*. Keynote address given at the Annual conference of the International Society for the Study of School Effectiveness and School Improvement, Fort-Lauderdale, FL.

Au, K. H. (1998). Social constructivism and the school literacy learning of students of diverse backgrounds. *Journal of Literacy Research, 30*(2), 297–319.

Belant, R. (2012). Testimony on HB6004 before the House Education Committee. *The Michigan Citizen*. Accessed February 2013 at http://michigancitizen.com/testimony-on-hb-6004-before-the-house-education-committee/

Education Achievement Authority. (n.d.). About the Education Achievement Authority (EAA). Accessed at http://www.michigan.gov/eaa

Equity and Excellence Commission. (2013). *For each and every child: A strategy for education equity and excellence* Washington, DC: Author. Accessed February 2013 at http://www2.ed.gov/about/bdscomm/list/eec/equity-excellence-commission-report.pdf

Farrell, J. P. (1999). Changing conceptions of equality in education. In R. F. Arnove & C. A. Torres (Eds.), *Comparative education: The dialectic of the global and the local* (pp. 149–177). Lanham, MD: Rowman & Littlefield.

Frankenberg, E., Siegel-Hawley, G., & Wang, J. (2010). *Choice without equity: Charter school segregation and the need for civil rights standards.* Los Angeles, CA: The Civil Rights Project/Proyecto Derechos Civiles at UCLA. Accessed February 2013 at http://civilrightsproject.ucla.edu/research/k-12-education/integration-and-diversity/choice-without-equity-2009-report

Geiger, K. (2012, November 8). Senate, house display growing electoral power of women and minorities. *Los Angeles Times.* Accessed February 2013 at http://articles.latimes.com/2012/nov/08/nation/la-na-congress-women-20121108

Giroux, H. A. (2005). The terror of neoliberalism: Rethinking the significance of cultural politics. *College Literature, 32*(1), 1–20.

Green, J. M. (1999). *Deep democracy: Diversity, community, and transformation.* Lanham, MD: Rowman & Littlefield.

H.B. 6004 (2012). House Bill 6004: A preliminary analysis. *Legislative analysis.* Accessed February 2013 at http://www.legislature.mi.gov/documents/2011-2012/billanalysis/House/pdf/2011-HLA-6004-1.pdf

Henderson, S. (2011a), Covington leaves a firestorm brewing in Kansas City, *Detroit Free Press*, August 26. Accessed July 2013 at http://www.freep.com/article/20110826/BLOG2503/110826040/Stephen-Henderson-Covington-leaves-firestorm-brewing-Kansas-City

Henderson, S. (2011b). Covington needs to explain troubles in Kansas City schools. *Detroit Free Press*, Sept. 21. Accessed July 2013 at http://www.freep.com/article/20110921/COL33/110921027

Johannsen, C. C. (2011, April 22). Higher education under attack: An interview with Henry A. Giroux. *Truthout.* Accessed January 25, 2013 at http://www.truth-out.org/higher-education-under-attack-interview-henry-giroux/1303196400

Karram, G. (2013). Education's investment metaphor misses the point. *University World News, 256.* Accessed February 2013 at http://www.universityworldnews.com/article.php?story=2013012215371593

King, C. J., Douglass, J. A., & Feller, I. (2007). *The crisis of the publics.* Berkeley, CA: Spencer Foundation, Center for Studies in Higher Education, University of California, Berkeley.

Ladson-Billings, G. (2006). From the achievement gap to the education debt: Understanding achievement in U.S. schools. *Educational Researcher, 35*(7), 3–12.

Laseter, T. (2013). A new model needed for higher education. *University World News, 256.* Accessed February 2013 at http://www.universityworldnews.com/article.php?story=20130125144645554

Lubienski, C., & Lubienski, S. T. (2006). *Charter, private, public schools and academic achievement: New evidence from NAEP mathematics data.* New York, NY: National Center for the Study of Privatization in Education Teachers College, Columbia University.

McLellan, R. (n.d.). McLellan Law Offices. Accessed February 2013 at http://richardmclellan.com/rdm/education_policy%20

Michigan Department of Education. (2012). State continuing education clock hours (SCECH)/secure central registry (SCR). Accessed February 2013 at http://www.michigan.gov/mde/0,1607,7-140-6530_5683-219674-,00.html

Milner, H. R., IV (2013). Rethinking achievement gap talk in urban education. *Urban Education,48*(1), 3–8.

Noah, T. (2010). The United States of Inequality. Slate. Accessed February 22, 2013 at http://www.slate.com/articles/news_and_politics/the_great_divergence/features/2010/the_united_states_of_inequality/introducing_the_great_divergence.html

Oakes, J., & Rogers, J. (with Lipton, M.). (2006). *Learning power.* New York: Teachers College Press.

Oxford Foundation Michigan. (n.d.) Oxford Foundation. Accessed at http://oxfordfoundationmi.com/oxford-foundation/

Ravitch, D. (2012a). Michigan is on its way to ending public education [Blog post]. *Diane Ravitch's Blog.* Accessed February 2013 at http://dianeravitch.net/2012/11/18/michigan-is-on-its-way-to-ending-public-education/

Ravitch, D. (2012b). Michigan plan to dissolve school districts [Blog post]. *Diane Ravitch's Blog.* Accessed February 2013 at http://dianeravitch.net/2012/11/20/michigan-plan-to-dissolve-school-districts/

Resmovits, J. (2011, September 1). John Covington faces questions from Kansas City residents as he heads to Detroit. *Huffington Post.* Accessed February 2013 at http://www.huffingtonpost.com/2011/09/01/john-covington-kansas-city-detroit_n_944802.html

Resmovits, J. (2012, September 8). Roy Roberts, Arne Duncan questioned about Detroit school reforms. *Huffington Post*. Accessed February 2013 at http://www.huffingtonpost.com/2011/09/08/roy-roberts-arne-duncan-detroit-reform_n_953875.html

Shields, C. M., Bishop, R., & Mazawi, A. (2005). *Pathologizing practices: The impact of deficit thinking on education*. New York, NY: Peter Lang.

Skubick, T. (2011). New school system chancellor John Covington's pay could hit $425K. MyFoxDetroit. Accessed February 2013 at http://www.myfoxdetroit.com/story/18457909/new-school-system-chancellor-john-covingtons-pay-could-hit-425k

Snyder, R. (2011). A special message from Governor Rick Snyder: Education Reform. Accessed February 2013 at http://www.michigan.gov/documents/snyder/SpecialMessageonEducationReform_351586_7.pdf

Strauss, V. (2012), Michigan coalition opposes Race to the Top finalist in letter to Obama, Duncan, The Answer Sheet, *The Washington Post*, accessed at http://www.washingtonpost.com/blogs/answer-sheet/wp/2012/11/30/michigan-coalition-opposes-race-to-top-finalist-in-letter-to-obama-duncan/

Torres, C. A. (1998). *Democracy, education, multiculturalism*. Lanham, MD: Rowman & Littlefield.

Waithman, M. (2009). The politics of redistribution and recognition: A retrospective case study of one inner-city school (Unpublished EdD dissertation). University of British Columbia, Vancouver, Canada.

Walker, V. L. (2013). Mumford students take a stand against inadequate education. *The Michigan Citizen*. Accessed February 2013 at http://michigancitizen.com/eaa-is-failing-us/

CHAPTER NINE

Teacher Education and Markets Matter[1]

DANIEL P. LISTON

Colorado voters and their state legislature have been busy. In fall, 2012, voters approved a recreational marijuana amendment to the state constitution making it legal to possess and purchase small amounts of the drug for non-medicinal purposes. A bit cautious, Governor Hickenlooper indicated that substantial regulatory procedures were still needed before anyone broke out the Cheetos and Goldfish to celebrate the state's newfound marijuana freedom.[2] The fall 2012 elections also changed the composition of the state legislature (now majority Democratic in what was a traditionally Republican state). With the altered party dominance, Representative Claire Levy proposed legislation that would rescind the "right" for college students to conceal and carry (C&C) handguns in university classrooms. Student proponents of C&C were not happy with new developments while University of Colorado-Boulder faculty appeared pleased with a return to the ban on concealed guns in the classroom. However, female C&C students convinced enough legislators that their safety concerns trumped faculty demands for gun-free classrooms.[3] Guns will stay in our university hallways and classrooms. And with the onset of 2013, State Senator Michael Johnston has been working diligently on a number of education bills. One would alter the state funding of K-12 public education to increase the available tax revenues and distribute those funds differentially—with more funds going to districts with fewer resources.[4] Another would drastically reduce the role of the state in the teacher certification process—deregulating teacher education and teacher licensure.[5] The Colorado legislative landscape is almost as varied as its geographic scenery. From decriminalizing and regulating marijuana sales, to regulating handgun use in a nominally cowboy state, to enhancing revenues for poorer school districts and deregulating teacher education, the Colorado legislative peaks have become quite high and the valleys low. Just how high and low depends on one's political perspective.

What concerns me here are the teacher education deregulation efforts as well as the varied educational responses. In effect, I want to place this proposed legislative effort within a larger political and historical context, noting the dilemmas and trade-offs, as well as suggest a democratic educational response. First, I describe the outline of Senator Johnston's proposed deregulation agenda.[6] Next, I place this reform within the context of current and past teacher education reform agendas. Third, I delineate a few of the likely outcomes if such deregulation were actually to occur. And finally, I suggest one democratic, educational agenda—a Great Books of sorts—for this and other pressing public school issues.

The Proposal

State Senator Mike Johnston is no stranger to the classroom or educational politics. He is a Teach for America graduate, former teacher in the Louisiana bayou, author of *In the Deep Heart's Core* (2003), past public school principal of an integrated arts high school in Mapleton Public Schools (serving a low-income community just north of Denver), founding organizer of New Leaders for New Schools (an alternative educational administrator preparation program),[7] and now Colorado state senator (from a predominantly African American section of Denver). Johnston's educational experiences are substantial and multi-faceted. He supports and has instigated numerous educational innovations at the classroom, school, and now statewide policy levels. He cannot and should not be dismissed by progressive-minded educationists as a "neoliberal" reformer—despite the fact that his teacher education proposals come straight from the pages of the deregulation reform proponents.

Johnston's legislative proposal has yet to be formally submitted but various drafts have been circulated. If it doesn't reach the legislative floor in 2013, it will likely appear in 2014. It stands a good chance of passing both houses and being signed by the Governor. Even if it doesn't become law in Colorado, it will surely make the rounds to other states. This deregulatory effort will not be peculiar to Colorado.[8] Colorado residents and political leaders, like those in many others in states, have expressed dissatisfaction with the highly regulated teacher preparation process. In many ways Johnston's bill represents a significant instance of a larger political movement from state-sponsored monopolization in teacher education to its market-oriented deregulation. It bears close inspection. One of the more recent drafts contains seven key proposals—four of which I will focus on here. (The bill addresses reform to both teacher and principal licensure. I focus on the proposed teacher reforms.) The four include:

1) Free teacher and principal preparation programs to innovate based on what they know works best.

Eliminate all state regulations that mandate certain course hours, program length or preparation route for teachers and principals, freeing higher education and alternative licensure programs to prepare teachers and school leaders the way that research and practice prove to be effective. Education is the only area of professional study—at either the undergraduate or graduate level—where the state mandates what coursework must be completed and for how long. On the back end, because of provisions put in place by SB10-36, we will be able to compare the effectiveness of educator preparation programs based on data collected through the educator identifier system. Educator preparation programs will continue to be accredited, with teacher candidates who complete those programs receiving an endorsement on their license that they have an institutional recommendation from an accredited preparation program.

2) Increase the pipeline of great teachers and principals by opening up the profession to qualified applicants from all professions and backgrounds.

To obtain a Transitional License (initially for three years), all applicants must:

1. Have a bachelor's degree;
2. Pass the appropriate state-approved content test; and
3. Pass a background check.

Everyone enters the teaching profession with a Transitional License, whether they've come through an alternative route program, a traditional teacher prep program, from out of state, or through a mid-career transition.

3) Allow strong teachers to earn a professional license based on their performance and ensure that teachers who need support get professional development linked to their area of need.

For teachers with Transitional Licenses:

• Three consecutive years of Effective/Highly Effective ratings and non-probationary status earns a five-year Professional License.

• After three years, if a teacher maintains a Transitional License, that teacher maintains a Transitional License on a two-year renewal cycle for as long as is necessary. At the end of two years, the teacher must submit to CDE proof of professional development that aligns with areas of deficiency in yearly evaluations along with their license renewal.

4) Educators on the ground know more about performance than a central department of education, so teachers who earn and keep tenure should have their license automatically renewed.

Professional License (lasts five years) conferred on those who demonstrate three consecutive years of Effective or Highly Effective teaching.

• Automatic renewal at five-year mark for teachers with non-probationary status under the state's evaluation framework. Evaluating principal must certify on teacher's evaluations that they are completing their professional development plan.

• Teachers renewing a license under probationary status after five years will be on a two-year renewal cycle (with proof of PD targeted at evaluation areas of deficiency) until they re-earn non-probationary status.

Johnston's proposal aims to deregulate Colorado's role in the certification and licensing of beginning and practicing teachers. Rather than have the state determine and enforce the content of teacher preparatory programs, Johnston aims to open the school doors so as to allow principals the responsibility for hiring, and training as needed, those individuals who meet their screening process criteria and job requirements.[9] The decision to hire someone prepared in a university teacher education program will be a district- or building-level decision, rather than a state requirement. In his revised scenario, principals, most likely in concert with district human resource departments, will have the flexibility to hire individuals whether they have been prepared in universities or not. University teacher preparations programs will no longer be the primary gate-keepers for teachers' first entry into schools. In effect, we would move from state and professional regulation of teacher preparation to more of a market-based approach. It is a huge game changer.

Recent Teacher Education Reform Efforts

During the last decade we have seen multiple reform efforts aimed at enhancing quality teacher education, including the professionalization model; the social justice approach; the practice-based teacher education reform efforts; and the deregulation proposals.[10] Briefly, the professional development model, as outlined by Linda Darling-Hammond and others, makes the case that the teaching profession has a body of professional knowledge and instructional practices that are supported by research and can be used to structure a more defined and well-delineated approach to initial teacher education and subsequent professional development (Darling-Hammond & Wei, 2009; NCTAF, 1996). Darling-Hammond and Wei (2009) warn that the field is vulnerable to external critiques because only a small number of programs have taken seriously the call to design quality programmatic preparatory routes utilizing that professional knowledge base. The social justice model describes the inequities of public schooling in our democratic society and proposes to prepare teachers attuned to and capable of remedying those injustices (Villegas, 2007; Cochran-Smith, 2009; Zeichner, 2009). Grounded firmly in, and extending, the traditional progressive ideology of many schools of education, this approach construes teachers as significant change agents—helping to alter the inequities of an unjust educational machine. The practice-based reform agenda maintains that learning teaching requires significant and nuanced instructional preparation and training (Ball & Forzani, 2009; Grossman et al., 2009). Proponents of this approach argue that, without concerted attention to the complexities of instructional interactions and the use of "high leverage practices," teacher candidates are ill-prepared for classroom demands.

These three reform agendas arise from the professional teacher education community. Contrary to popular and established academic opinions, the field of teacher education contains thoughtful and wise scholars and practitioners.[11] These reform proposals are substantial and rich. Unfortunately, the teacher education field also can be fairly characterized as ideologically narrow—adhering to progressive educational tenets with religious-like adherence and missionary zeal (Labaree, 2004, 2008). All three of the previously mentioned reform efforts abide by, for the most part, progressive understandings of teaching and learning. Many teacher educators view this child- (and sometimes culturally) sensitive approach as the necessary antidote to a traditional and misguided view of learning and schooling. Many others, especially outside of the academy, do not agree.

Johnston's proposal is clearly an effort within the deregulatory approach and, as such, represents an attempt to utilize market forces to remedy the perceived ills of teacher preparation. In the deregulatory reform effort's framing, our existing (and mostly university-based) teacher education programs have failed to provide the promised pipeline of quality teachers who are ready for the realities of today's schools. Seat-time in teacher preparation programs doesn't assure quality teachers. The deregulatory reformers also cite the cumbersome national and regional (state-sponsored) bureaucratic and regulatory constraints as barriers to recruiting talented individuals to choose teaching (Hess, 2009, 2010; Podgursky, 2004;). In further explaining the lack of readiness among many graduates of university-based preparation programs, most in the deregulatory camp criticize the overriding progressive framing of university-based teacher education as much too narrow, unduly theoretical, and practically unfeasible. So as to alter this dismal situation, deregulation proponents offer market competition as a solution. Podgursky (2004) argues for a "most efficient flexible regime of teacher preparation." For Podgursky, ineffective and inefficient university-based programs need to be replaced by a much more competitive market approach with the following public school and licensing features:

> 1) accountability for student learning through testing, sanctions, and parental choice; 2) state regulators who actively promote a competitive market in teacher quality and protect schools from anticompetitive practices on the part of the teachers unions, schools of education, or other education producer organizations; 3) minimal state licensing standards for teachers (criminal background check, bachelor's degree, test of general and content knowledge); 4) full information on teacher test results provided to school administrators; and 5) award of a permanent or full license on the basis of successful job performance. (Podgursky, 2004, pp. 270–271)

Johnston seems to have heard and embraced Podgursky's charge. In effect, his proposed teacher licensure legislation incorporates key elements of points two through five. Johnston's plan represents an attempt to reduce anti-competitive regulations; provide maximal access for minimally prepared individuals; create a structure of subsequent licensure-candidate testing, reporting and professional development; and award teachers permanent licenses on the basis of assessed teaching performance. It appears that the deregulation movement has grown in strength within the state and wants to alter significantly the teacher education landscape. What goes on in Colorado will not stay in Colorado. Once implemented, it will likely be exported. And if it doesn't pass, other state legislatures will certainly attempt it. The "market allure" will be too strong for many to ignore.

Potential Consequences of the Proposed Legislation

It helps to anticipate the likely consequences and developments if the proposed legislation were to become law. Democracy demands at least educated guesses informed, in part, by relevant social scientific findings. We need to ask ourselves if the current regulatory regime supports our desired educational goals. The deregulation proponents answer with a resounding "no." They maintain that what state and professional control have failed to provide, the market will rectify.

During the last seventy-five years the teaching profession has been organized and governed by a mix of state regulations, professional oversight, and organized labor demands. This admixture of labor, professional, and state control is now under fire. The deregulators would put in its place an overarching market framework and set of mechanisms to rectify the ills of "state" control. It appears that the deregulation reform movement would let the market reign. The question before us is whether or not the market could do a better job than our current regulatory system and if some other combinations of effective market and state controls can be envisioned and instituted.

In the deregulatory proponents' framing, the market will enhance the number of quality applicants within the teaching labor pool, reduce the number of bureaucratic impediments to teacher preparation and licensure, dismantle the narrow progressive ideological dominance within teacher education, provide principals and districts with greater influence and direction over their workforce, and, in effect, deliver more and better quality teachers for the students who need them. While there are those on the educational left who decry these efforts as sheer lunacy, further entrenching existing inequalities and enabling pernicious class, racial, and cultural dominance, I think it wise to show that each deregulation claim appears more plausible and reasonable than straightforwardly crazy and dangerous. If educationists committed to democratic deliberation and public education hope to stem what may become more insistent and vociferous calls for deregulation, these proposals can no longer be derided and dismissed. What follows are significant features of the deregulatory call for teacher education reform along with reminders of persistent and unresolved issues.

Increase the Number of Quality Applicants for Teaching

The deregulators maintain that the current pipeline to teaching is much too small and eliminates candidates who are talented but unwilling (or unable) to follow the more traditional routes to certification. Podgursky (2004) argues the following:

> ...Suppose that five uncertified applicants randomly drawn from...[a pool of adequately screened candidates] are allowed to apply for the job, along with five certified applicants. Even though the uncertified applicants are of lower average quality than the certified candidate, 39 percent of the time an uncertified applicant will be the best of the ten applicants. By expanding the applicant poof from five to ten candidates, the mean quality of the best teacher has increased as well. This illustrates the hidden cost of a licensing entry barrier: shrinking the applicant pool gives schools fewer choices and less freedom to pick out talent, and reduces the mean quality of the resulting hires.
>
> Intuitively, if there is a large dispersion in quality within the two groups, sometimes the best candidate will be from the uncertified group. The distributions overlap a great deal. This will also be true even if we make the average certified teacher better than 70 percent or 80 percent of uncertified teachers. Licensing barriers, if strictly enforced, tell a school district that they can never hire an uncertified candidate. This makes districts worse off. (pp. 261–262)

While additional presumptive conditions and background information are needed, common sense seems to indicate that a larger pool of adequately screened certified and uncertified candidates enhances the number of quality candidates. Determining the chances that these quality candidates will be competent teachers at entry and become quality teachers in the years ahead needs to be addressed. But Podgursky's point cannot simply be ignored.

Reduce Bureaucratic Impediments

The deregulatory proponents maintain that state licensure regulations, professional (i.e., National Council for Accreditation of Teacher Education accreditation processes, and organized labor demands have created a plethora of unnecessary and almost byzantine regulatory constraints. (See e.g., Ballou & Podgursky, 1999; Hess, 2001, 2009; Podgursky, 2004). While I can't list all of the complaints here, the neoconservative characterization of professional educators as "educrats" has been around for some time (e.g. Bennett, 1992; Finn, 1993). And for many citizens this educrat designation rings true. Parents, from all ideological stripes, complain about the dense public school bureaucracies and the quagmire of rules and regulations. The acclaimed "rubber rooms" (detailed in the 2010 documentary *Waiting for Superman)* used by school districts to house their "problematic" teachers fuels the populist sense that public education is hand and hog-tied by its own dense regulations. University teacher preparation is frequently considered a convoluted bureaucratic and ineffectual preparatory effort (Joncich-Clifford & Guthrie, 1990, Kramer, 1991; Labaree, 2004, 2008). Admittedly, many of these critiques of bureaucratic inefficiencies accompany other large-scale state regulatory efforts. Recall the last visit to your state's department of motor vehicles. However, it is an issue that cannot summarily be dismissed. Unfortunately, Johnston's bill moves too far toward the minimally regulated market approach. Some balance, some middle ground, between hyper regulation and little or no regulation would be preferable to Johnston's bare market approach.

Overcome the Narrow Progressive Blinders

In their development from normal schools to their place within universities, departments, schools, and colleges of education have been viewed as somewhat suspect members of higher education. From a university arts and sciences perspective, the certification effort may seem more craft-based than intellectually driven. From the public school practitioners' framing, university-based teacher education is theoretically driven and practically bereft. This troubling relationship between theory and practice has long accompanied teacher education. More recently, university-based teacher education and the units that house them have been depicted as ideologically narrow and exclusive in their orientation. David Labaree (2004), Stanford historian and scholar, has argued that schools of education and the scholars within embrace a progressive orientation toteaching and learning. It is a view that promotes meaningful connections between the child and the curriculum, a view that is opposed to many of the more traditional practices of public schooling. The deregulation proponents proclaim that this progressive ideology unduly limits the range and options available to teacher candidates and prepares them poorly for the realities of public schooling. Recently, Larry Cuban (2008) has argued that many elementary teachers actually "hug the middle" road between progressive and traditional educational practices in their daily instructional efforts. But they came to this integration with little help or scaffolding from their university mentors. Deregulating and uncoupling the tight linkage between progressively framed university-based teacher preparation and the certification/licensure process could promote greater variety among teacher preparatory programs. But inviting individuals with little or no professional training to lead children's learning seems more than questionable—it seems to represent bad judgment.

Put Districts and Principals in Control

The deregulatory framing asserts that if teacher preparation can be decoupled from university-based, progressively framed, and monopolistically controlled teacher educators, school districts are the proper location and building principals should be central players in guiding the teacher preparation process. The schools, where K-12 students are educated, are the suitable places for teacher preparation.[12] And principals should be key players in guiding their staff's development, further education, and training. For too long, the training reins have been in the wrong hands. But even these reformists have to wonder if, along with the heavy duties principals currently carry, we should expect them to manage their staffs' preparation and development as teachers.

And Then We Get More and Better Skilled Teachers.

In combining these four elements, the deregulatory reformers maintain, we will enhance the number and quality of our teaching corps. Increase the number of teaching applicants, reduce the unnecessary barriers to licensure, overcome the narrow progressive ideology, put principals and districts in charge—and we will have a deregulated market that will promote more numerous paths from which candidates and districts can choose. Those programs that work will survive and thrive. Those that don't work won't persist. That is, they say, the magic and power of the market.

An Interlude—or—What to Do Now?

Before outlining one of my preferred democratic responses to these recent deregulatory legislative efforts, a few comments are in order. For some time I have worried and warned that the state of American teacher education was unstable and wondered when a significant move to dismantle university-based teacher education might occur (Liston, 1995, 2012). Over time, I have come to find the intellectual (and progressive) framings prevalent in university schools of education to be discomfiting, narrow, and much too rigid. Too many university educationists see themselves as self-appointed change agents. These university educationists may have harmed, not helped, our democratic educational mission. It seems oddly self-serving and illicit to vilify public schools as indoctrinatory and then to justify and pursue narrow and ideologically framed teacher education programmatic efforts. One indoctrination does not justify another. Unfortunately, however, that is our current state of affairs. Educationally, I find that circumstance disconcerting, morally unjustified and politically misguided.[13]

Given the prominence of the market in our American culture, the general cultural distrust of, and dislike for, academic educationists, and the frustrations many experience with K-12 schooling and higher education, it is not surprising that these deregulation proposals are gaining popularity. Educationists and teacher educators need to wake up to the world around them. The public wants meaningful alternatives. Educationists would be wise to examine those alternatives. Among some of my professional colleagues, I may appear a bit too understanding, almost appreciative, of the deregulatory reform path. I have to admit that I have grown to admire the entrepreneurial spirit and the organizational pluck and determination that successful innovative efforts exhibit. Looking outside of the educational sphere, we can find numerous recent examples arising from biochemical research, software design and applications, as well as new and improved beer brewing techniques. Within the educational realm, Teach for America (TFA), with all its noted faults and serious frailties, has been quite successful in creating a refined corps-member selection process, a data-informed mentoring system, and an advertising narrative that entices (Foote, 2008). But all is not copacetic within TFA or in university-based teacher education. The bona fide argument that TFA ill prepares teachers for our most at-risk populations is one that many progressively oriented university-based educators have yet to acknowledge as a problem of their own programs as well. We all too easily vilify organizations like TFA and KIPP (Knowledge is Power Program) and don't critically reflect on our own efforts. It's time to recognize that both K-12 education and teacher preparation can be conceived in quite distinct and varied forms.

The world is a complicated place and, while claims of evil and sinister forces abound in the progressive and social justice lexicon, it is the banality of evil that we should attempt to recognize. But not here, not now. What I value in the deregulation proposals is a potential for distinct and varied paths to teaching—paths that are not available today in university-based teacher education programs. These paths could represent the different and legitimate ways we understand teaching, education, and schooling. A limited and regulated market approach could support wide-ranging and (over time) well-defined communities of teaching practice (e.g., teaching for cultural literacy, social justice transformation, progressive reform or spiritual sustenance). Preparing teachers for those distinct communities could be an engaging and lively affair (Liston, 2012).

In earlier essays I, along with others, have argued that education is an "essentially contested" concept and so it is unlikely that we will arrive at THE democratically sanctioned definition; university-based teacher education is unwilling to change in substantial and meaningful ways; and we need to embrace the fact of multiple definitions for what constitute justified and desirable approaches to education and teacher education (Liston, 2011, 2012; Liston, Whitcomb, & Borko, 2009; Whitcomb, Borko, & Liston, 2007, 2008a, 2008b; Zeichner & Liston, 1996, 2013). While I am fond of distinguishing among conservative, progressive, radical, and spiritual approaches to teaching, that is certainly not the only available and powerful framing. Within the realm of learning, Barbara Rogoff and colleagues have described multiple kinds of organized approaches to learning: assembly-line, intent-participation, Socratic, recitation, constructivist, and inquiry approaches (Rogoff, Paradise, Mejía Arauz, Correa-Chávez, & Angelillo, 2003). It would be wise to create opportunities to engage and educate students, parents, and teacher candidates to the varied options that exist—conceptually and institutionally.

What I fear is that the market framework will end up promoting mostly bare-bones teacher training efforts to serve a voracious and productive public education machine that all too often runs roughshod over its workers (our teachers) and, most importantly, their charges (our students and children). It is a reasonable fear and one that is grounded in the largely leftist moral and political critiques of capitalism, patriarchy, and racism. In these times, I find that the strongest route for social change comes not from some any sort of social justice movement in higher education but rather in the community organizing efforts of those oppressed. Myles Horton's Highlander Center[14] and his life-long community work (1997) and Bob Moses' Algebra Project (2002) are two shining examples of such community endeavors. But I know capable community organizers and the political skill required. I understand that community organizing is not the route for my or many educators' talents. And so I turn to educational conversations among people encouraged to listen, not as a charged political force with a set direction, but as a means to enable democratic deliberation, communication, discernment, and choice. We should be engaging in these conversations regardless of the deregulation debate. We are long past due creating serious, deliberative, attentive, and democratic dialogues about our educational and schooling options.

A (Kind of) Great Books Proposal for Teacher Education

Some five years ago, elbows deep in yet another *Journal of Teacher Education* editorial, my colleague and co-editor Jennie Whitcomb looked over at me and asked: "What would the list of top ten or one hundred books, articles, films, or video clips include? What constitutes the great books of education?" (Liston, Whitcomb, & Borko, 2009). We each gave some of our own suggestions. What struck me then, and stays with me now, is the idea that perhaps we should expand our educational audience to parents and students. For some time, Ken Zeichner and I have maintained that reflective teaching entails critical deliberation over the ends of education as well as the social conditions of schooling (Liston & Zeichner, 1991, and Zeichner & Liston 1996, 2013). Preparing teachers means, in part, engaging candidates in these deliberative discussions about the ends and means of education and schooling. Inviting candidates into schools as practicing teachers, as Johnston's bill does, without any intellectual or instructional preparation, is irresponsible. It now seems time to enlarge the deliberative circle to include citizens—parents, taxpayers, and students—those who have a stake in our educational and democratic futures. If citizens are to become educated "consumers" of schooling and teacher preparation, further education is required. The Great Books initiative, as well as Parker Palmer's (2011) recent call for democratic Action Circles, provide a possible framing for this public educational effort.

Mortimer Adler and Robert Hutchins, early and mid-20th century University of Chicago affiliated public intellectuals, were seminal in creating the Great Books program. Intended as an effort to democratize elite higher education (and some say impose the Western canon on the masses), they created the loose structure and content for community conversations around books that expressed the foundational ideas of Western society and culture. Works included were ones that had contemporary interest, could be read again and again with benefit, and addressed perennial issues facing humanity (Adler, 1992). Held in public libraries across the country, from the earlier part of the 20th century and continuing today, these groups encouraged the discussion of powerful ideas through examining the established and "great" works. While, in practice, the program undoubtedly did not always achieve its goals and has been criticized for a narrow and biased rendering of Western culture, it appears to have invited those who count not attend college to engage in rich conversations about suggestive ideas and things that mattered. As one facilitator remarked, the purpose of the Great Books program was simply to "get everyone talking and then find connections—person-to-person, person-to-book." (Paley, 1986, p. 122). Vivian Paley elaborates:

> Years ago, when I was a young woman in New Orleans, I led a Great Books discussion group that met at the public library. The participants came from many occupations and educational backgrounds, and they were all older and more experienced than I. What advantage I had was contained in the list of questions provided by the Great Books people, who also sent along the following directive: There are no right or wrong answers. Get everyone talking and then find connections—person-to-person, person-to-book.
>
> The advice was sound: do the required reading, ask most of the questions, and manage to connect a number of the ideas that arise at each meeting. Unfortunately, I did not fare too well; something was missing from my performance—a simple ingredient called curiosity. I was not truly interested in the people sitting around the table or curious about what they might think or say. Mainly I wanted to keep the discussion moving and to avoid awkward silences. (p. 122)

Paley is helpful here in at least three significant ways. She reminds us that in rich, interpretive discussions of great works we need to move away from the desire to ascertain "right or wrong answers"; find connections among people and texts; and be curious about the ideas and people before us. In effect, she encourages us to listen—really listen—to one another. The same advice could be given for discussions of education's great books.

This engagement in public, face-to-face discussions about distinct and varied educational options is needed today. Given the move toward charter schools and voucher options throughout the country[15] and the distinct possibility that greater choice in teacher education will follow, parents and prospective teachers should understand the educational options. Even without substantial changes in teacher education, public education about education is sorely lacking and needed. To the Great Books framing I would add another element—what Parker Palmer has recently depicted as educating the "heart" of democracy.[16]

Palmer (2011) maintains that our U.S. democratic society and its citizens are at risk of becoming systemically broken. We don't know how to keep alive and well our vibrant differences while attending to our commonalities and community. We divide our selves from each other and within our selves. Palmer calls on us to repair and maintain democracy's neglected infrastructure—the ways we can create and strengthen the connections in our public lives. He suggests that we should attend to "the invisible dynamics of the human heart and the visible venues of our lives in which those dynamics are formed" (p. 9). In order to perform this work, he asks us to pay more attention to what he terms the five "habits of the heart." Palmer construes the heart as referring not "merely to our emotions but to the core of the self, that center place where all of our ways of knowing converge—intellectual, emotional, sensory, intuitive, imaginative, experiential, relational, and bodily, among others. The heart is where we integrate what we know in our minds with what we know in our bones, the place where our knowledge can become more fully human" (p. 6). For Palmer, these five habits include the following basic tenets for all Americans:

> We must understand that we are all in this together.
> We must develop an appreciation of the value of "otherness."
> We must cultivate the ability to hold tension in life-giving ways.
> We must generate a sense of personal voice and agency.
> We must strengthen our capacity to create community. (pp. 44–45)

Combining what Palmer and the Center for Courage and Renewal[17] have coined as "Action Circles" with a Great Books approach would represent a new and renewed move toward public democratic education.

Conclusion

I don't relish or joyously anticipate the deregulation and market experiment in teacher education. And I certainly don't know—if and when it happens—what will transpire. My guess is that some principals and districts may rely on the tried but not always true method of university-based teacher preparation. Other districts may create their own systems of on-line programs. Some boutique programs may arise—and some strongly framed teacher-identity programs (teacher as social activist, or progressive reformer, or cultural literacy expert…) may develop. Whether state universities will continue to support teacher education or scholarly, educational inquiry may prove to be another intriguing crossroads. But educationists can no longer afford to ignore the deregulatory and market reforms knocking at the door. That much I know. An informed and attuned public would serve itself and our schools better than an uninformed one.

Notes

1. I'd like to thank Ian Renga, Michele Seipp, and Jennie Whitcomb for comments and suggestions on earlier drafts of this manuscript. I also want to thank Joe DeVitis and Ken Teitelbaum for their willingness to support another "border-line" essay—one that is neither fish nor fowl in its ideological stance.
2. http://blogs.westword.com/latestword/2012/11/john_hickenlooper_amendment_64_cheetos_goldfish.php
3. http://www.denverpost.com/breakingnews/ci_22746936/colorado-gun-bills-guns-campus-goes-before-senate

4. http://www.coloradostatesman.com/content/994072-legislators-learn-abc%3Fs-new-school-finance-act
5. http://coloradocitizen.com/rethinking-how-colorado-licenses-teachers/
6. I received the text of the draft legislation for a Skype discussion with Senator Johnston and the Research on Teaching and Teacher Education seminar in early February 2013 via Senator Johnston's office and Jennie Whitcomb—Associate Dean of Teacher Education at University of Colorado at Boulder.
7. http://www.newleaders.org/new-leaders-named-top-non-profit.
8. See Zeichner and Sandoval (In progress).Colorado has had two systems of accreditation for the past 10–15 years—one for University-Based Teacher Educationand one for district-based programs and other alternative certification routes. The Colorado Department of Education has recently tried to rein that in, making the district-based and alternative certification more responsive to state regulation and review.
9. See Zeichner 2009 where he identifies three reform agendas: professionalization; deregulation; and social justice agendas. In our Research on Teaching and Teacher Education Doctoral Seminar syllabus (2013), Jennie Whitcomb and I add a fourth reform agenda—the practice-based reform agenda.
10. Colorado has had two systems of accreditation for the past 10-15 years—one for UBTE and one for district-based programs and other alternative certification routes. The Colorado Department of Education has recently tried to rein that in, making the district-based and alternative certification more responsive to state regulation and review.
11. I mention these scholars because all too many educationists and their critics fail to recognize the strength of inquiry accomplished within the field of teacher education. I'll keep the list to a dozen. It could easily include many more names. But for those who would like to survey their arguments, I would include Deborah Ball, Hilda Borko, Margret Buchmann, Linda Darling-Hammond, Mary Diez, Sharon Feimen-Nemser, Pam Grossman, Rick Hess, Mary Kennedy, Maggie Lampert, Ana Maria Villegas, and Ken Zeichner.
12. In the UK the "de-evolution" of teacher education moved from university-based to more school-based approaches. See Liston, 1995.
13. See my earlier sympathetic critiques in *Capitalist Schools: Explanation and Ethics in Radical Studies of Schooling* (1988).
14. http://highlandercenter.org/
15. http://www.nytimes.com/2013/03/28/education/states-shifting-aid-for-schools-to-the-families.html?hp&_r=0
16. In *Reflective Teaching: An Introduction* (2013; 2nd ed.), Ken Zeichner and I have elaborated more fully on how Palmer's recent insights can be brought to schools and teaching.
17. Center for Courage and Renewal, http://www.couragerenewal.org/

References

Adler, M. (1992). *A second look in the rearview mirror.* New York: Macmillan.

Ball, D., & Forzani, F. (2009). The work of teaching and the challenge for teacher education. *Journal of Teacher Education, 60*(5), 497–511.

Ballou, D., & Podgursky, M. (1999). Teacher training and licensing: A layman's guide. In C. Finn & M. Kanstoroom (Eds.), *Better teachers, better schools* (pp. 31–82). Washington, DC: Fordham Foundation.

Bennett, W. (1992). *The devaluing of America.* New York: Simon and Schuster.

Cochran-Smith, M. (2009). Toward a theory of teacher education for social justice. In M. Fullan, A. Hargreaves, D. Hopkins, & A. Lieberman (Eds.), *The international handbook of educational change* (2nd ed., pp. 445–468). New York: Springer.

Cuban, L. (2008). *Hugging the middle.* New York: Teachers College Press.

Darling-Hammond, L., & Wei, R. C. (with Johnson, C. M.). (2009). Teacher preparation and teacher learning: A changing policy landscape. In G. Sykes, B. L. Schneider, & D. N. Plank (Eds.), *Handbook of education policy research* (pp. 613–631). New York: Routledge & Washington, DC: American Educational Research Association.

Finn, C. (1993). *We must take charge: Our schools and our future.* New York: Free Press.

Foote, D. (2008). *Relentless pursuit.* New York: Vintage Books.

Grossman, P., Compton, C., Igra, D., Ronfeldt, A., Shahan, E., & Williamsen, P. (2009). Teaching practice: A cross-professional perspective. *Teachers College Record, 111*(9), 2055–2100.

Hess, F. M. (2001). *Tear down this wall: The case for a radical overhaul of teacher certification.* Washington, DC: Brookings Institution Press.

Hess, F. M. (2009). Revitalizing teacher education by revisiting our assumptions about teaching. *Journal of Teacher Education, 60*(5), 450–457.

Hess, F. M. (2010). Not yet sold on NCATE's 'Transformative' Clinical Vision. Retrieved from http://www.aei.org/article/education/k-12/not-yet-sold-on-ncates-transformative-clinical-vision/.

Horton, M. (1997). *The long haul.* New York: Teachers College Press.

Johnston, M. (2003). *In the deep heart's core.* New York: Grove Press.

Joncich-Clifford, G., & Guthrie, J. (1990). *Ed schools.* Chicago: University of Chicago Press.

Kramer, R. (1991). *Ed school follies.* New York: Free Press.

Labaree, D. (2004). *The trouble with ed schools.* New Haven, CT: Yale University Press.

Labaree, D. (2008). An uneasy relationship: The history of teacher education in the university. In M. Cochran-Smith, S. Feiman-Nemser, & J. McIntyre (Eds.), *Handbook of research on teacher education* (3rd ed., pp. 290–306). New York: Routledge.

Liston, D. P. (1995). Work in teacher education: A current assessment of U.S. teacher education. In N. Shimahara & I. Holowinsky (Eds.), *Teacher education in industrialized nations* (pp. 87–123. New York: Garland.

Liston, D. P. (1998). *Capitalist schools.* New York: Routledge.

Liston, D. P. (2011). The futility of ideological conflict in teacher education. In J. Devitis (Ed.), *Critical civic literacy* (pp. 446–458). New York, Peter Lang.

Liston, D. P. (2012). Reconsidering university-based teacher education. *Curriculum and Teaching Dialogue, 14*(1&2), 15–30.

Liston, D., Whitcomb, J., & Borko, H. (2009). The end of education in teacher education: Thoughts on reclaiming the role of social foundations in teacher education [Editorial]. *Journal of Teacher Education, 60*(2), 107–111.

Liston, D., & Zeichner, K. (1991). *Teacher education and the social conditions of schooling.* New York: Routledge.

Moses, R. (2002). *Radical equations.* Boston: Beacon Press.

National Commission on Teaching and America's Future (NCTAF). (1996). *What matters most: Teaching for America's future.* Washington, DC: Author.

Paley, V. (1986). On listening to what the children say. *Harvard Educational Review. 56*(2), 122–131.

Palmer, P. (2011). *Healing the heart of democracy.* San Francisco: Jossey-Bass.

Podgursky, M. (2004). Model 4. Improving academic performance in US public schools: Why teacher licensing is (almost) irrelevant. In F. M. Hess (Ed.), *A qualified teacher in every classroom? Appraising old answers and new ideas* (pp. 255–277). Boston: Harvard Education Press.

Rogoff, B., Paradise, R., Mejía Arauz, R., Correa-Chávez, M., & Angelillo, C. (2003). Firsthand learning through intent participation. *Annual Review of Psychology, 54,* 175–203.

Villegas, A. M. (2007). Dispositions in teacher education: A look at social justice. *Journal of Teacher Education, 58*(4), 370–380.

Whitcomb, J., Borko, H., & Liston, D. (2007) Stranger than fiction: Arthur Levine's *Educating school teachers*—The basis for a proposal. [Editorial], *Journal of Teacher Education, 58*(3), 195–201.

Whitcomb, J., Borko, H., & Liston, D. (2008a). Why teach? [Editorial]. *Journal of Teacher Education, 59*(1), 3–9.

Whitcomb, J., Borko, H., and Liston, D. (2008b). Why teach?: Part II [Editorial]. *Journal of Teacher Education, 59*(4), 267–272.

Zeichner, K. M. (2009). *Teacher education and the struggle for social justice.* New York City: Routledge.

Zeichner, K., & Liston, D. (1996). *Reflective teaching.* Mahwah, NJ: Lawrence Erlbaum.

Zeichner, K. and Liston, D. (2013). *Reflective teaching,* 2nd ed. New York: Routledge.

Zeichner, K. & Sandoval, C. (In progress). Venture philanthropy and teacher education policy in the U.S.: The role of the New Schools Venture Fund.

PART FOUR

Diversity and Social Justice

"Learning to look through multiple perspectives, young people may be helped to build bridges among themselves; attending to a range of human stories, they may be provoked to heal and to transform.... [T]he community many of us hope for now is not to be identified with conformity. As in Whitman's way of saying, it is a community attentive to difference, open to the idea of plurality."
 —Maxine Greene

"No person is your friend [or kin] who demands your silence, or denies your right to grow and be perceived as fully blossomed as you were intended."
 —Alice Walker

"In the end, if teachers believe that students cannot achieve at high levels, that their backgrounds are riddled with deficiencies, and that multicultural education is a frill that cannot help them to learn, the result will be school reform strategies that have little hope for success."
 —Sonia Nieto

CHAPTER TEN

Diversity, Social Justice, and Resistance to Disempowerment

CHRISTINE E. SLEETER

Diversity, Social Justice, and Resistance to Disempowerment

In 2011, journalist Benjamin Herold asked: "Why aren't African-centered charters running turnarounds?" He pointed out that one of Philadelphia's most successful charter schools is the African-centered Imhotep Institute Charter High School, which serves students who are 99% African American and almost 90% from low-income families. Its track record is exemplary: over two-thirds of its students test at the proficient or above levels in reading and math, and about two-thirds go on to college. African-centered education, based on the intellectual knowledge, spiritual, and cultural ethos of people of African descent, grounds the programs of several schools that have substantially improved the academic achievement and well-being of African American students (Durdin, 2007). Yet, as Herold (2011) noted with frustration, when selecting reform models or operators to run charter schools, superintendents and school boards do not choose culturally centered models, instead turning to large charter school management companies, most headed by Whites. He argued that part of the problem is a deep reluctance of school boards to affirm culturally relevant education.

Since the early 1990s, standards, tests, and semi-privatized arrangements such as charter schools have dominated school reforms. But despite claims to the contrary, evidence indicates that they have not substantially improved student learning, especially among African American and Latino students (for studies of charter schools, see Davis & Raymond, 2012; Kelly & Lovelace, 2012). The National Assessment of Education Progress (NAEP) is a useful indicator of the impact of reform trends on students because it has been administered periodically since the early 1970s. When viewed since the early 1990s, NAEP data suggest that standards-based and semi-privatized school reforms are having a positive impact. For example, between 1992 and 2007, reading scores of White eighth graders rose from 267 to 274, and of Black eighth graders, from 237 to 249, narrowing the racial achievement gap by 5 points.

However, NAEP scores from the early 1970s offer a different picture. For fourth graders, the racial achievement gap had narrowed through the 1970s and 1980s, widened for about ten years when standards-based reforms began, then resumed narrowing. For eighth graders, the gap was narrowest in 1988, then it widened; scores of Black and Latino students did not inch back up to their 1988 level until 2004. For twelfth graders, the pattern is even more striking: racial achievement gaps were narrowest around 1988 and 1990. After dropping when standards-based reforms were initiated in the 1990s, scores for African American and Latino students only partially rebounded, then virtually flattened out and are still below where they had been earlier. In mathematics, the pattern is similar, although less striking (National Center for Education Statistics, 2011). But rather than questioning the reform paradigm itself, dominant discussions of schooling now blame teachers for the fairly flat test scores (Kumashiro, 2012).

In this chapter, I argue that the current reform paradigm was never designed primarily to serve the intellectual and cultural needs of America's diverse students, or to empower them for democratic participation. The fact that achievement gaps had been narrowing considerably before the reform movement commenced in the early 1990s is rarely acknowledged or discussed. I will argue that standards-based, semi-privatized reforms are part of a larger set of policies designed to further empower the most advantaged segments of society. While the structural arrangements are problematic, as other chapters in this volume show, what affects children and youth directly is what happens in the classroom. I will focus specifically on classroom curriculum, that which disengages and disempowers young people of color, then that which has the potential to empower.

Diversity, Social Justice, and School Reform under Neoliberalism

Today's school reforms centering on standards, tests, and semi-privatization are a product of a long-term elite assault on the ideals of democracy and social equality. Looking back to the end of World War I, we find that between 5% and 10% of the national income of the U.S. was going to the wealthiest 0.1% of the population. Their share declined sharply during the Great Depression as President Roosevelt pushed for the New Deal, which included emergency job relief, public works programs, public protections (e.g., social security), progressive and inheritance taxation to help fund public services, and regulations on corporations. The National Labor Relations Act, passed during that time, guaranteed workers the right to unionize, and established a framework for unions to negotiate wage agreements and other conditions of employment. By the early 1940s the top 0.1%'s proportion of the national income had dropped and plateaued at about 2% (Harvey, 2005; Saez, 2010).

Pushback against the New Deal began immediately. In 1947, a group led by Austrian political philosopher Friedrich von Hayak established neoliberal principles, derived from classical liberal philosophy: individual liberty, private property, and market competition. That group, subsequently joined by wealthy corporate leaders, believed that a society built on these principles flourishes, and worried that the state intervention policies of the New Deal undermined prosperity by favoring those presumed to be "takers" rather than "makers" of wealth. Beginning around 1970, in a linkage between business and conservative intellectuals, wealthy business people established lobbies to oppose government regulations, PACs to help elect corporation-friendly candidates, and think tanks such as the Heritage Foundation to shape public opinion. Globally, neoliberalism was presented as the solution to economic stagnation, first in Chile during the 1970s under Pinochet, then later in Mexico and other Third World countries (Harvey, 2005; Klein, 2008).

In the meantime, prompted by desegregation of the military during World War II and the U.S. Supreme Court decision *Brown v. Board of Education* in 1954, African Americans (with some White allies) organized massively to challenge racism. The Black Civil Rights movement spawned movements of other historically marginalized groups, including Mexican Americans, American Indians, women, and people with disabilities. As some victories were won, many Whites felt threatened, especially in the context of growing racial and ethnic diversity. So, rather than joining across lines of class to retain gains wrought by the New Deal and unionization, Americans fractured along lines of race and gender, enabling reassertion of the power of the top 0.1%.

In 1978, despite Democratic control of Congress and the Presidency, Congress passed deep capital gains tax cuts and raised the payroll tax rate. President Reagan, elected in 1981, immediately slashed capital gains taxes and rewrote tax codes to benefit corporations (Hacker & Pierson, 2010). By 1988, the share of national income of the wealthiest 0.1% had jumped from around 2% to about 5% (Harvey, 2005). At the same time, a barrage of critiques of multiculturalism, many funded by conservative think tanks, began to appear. They charged multiculturalism with creating divisiveness, weakening the school curriculum, and addressing minority student achievement by appealing to self-esteem rather than hard work.

Standards- and test-driven education reforms emerged in this context. In their discussion of four "ways" of reforming schools, Hargreaves and Shirley (2009) explain that the "first way," which captures my experience as a classroom teacher in Seattle during the 1970s, emphasizes innovation and freedom, but also inconsistency. Bottom-up community- and school-based reforms were encouraged during the 1970s and early 1980s, such as ethnic studies, women's studies, multicultural curriculum, and teacher power, which existed alongside mediocrity, poorly conceptualized innovations, and in many schools, no reform at all.

The "second way," designed to address limitations of "first way" reform and rooted in neoliberalism, emphasizes standardization, regulation, and competition among schools. In 1983, the National Commission on Excellence and Education's *A Nation at Risk* depicted schools, and U.S. society generally, as in a state of crisis. This report, along with additional reports, framed the main purpose of schools as regaining U.S. international economic competitive advantage. The business community offered its recommendations: standards, assessment, and accountability (Business Roundtable, 1999, p. 1). In response to the Business Roundtable's systematic pressure, states began to construct disciplinary content standards and testing programs; at the same time conservative think tanks were proclaiming the failures of multiculturalism, yielding standards that largely folded "diversity" into constructions of a common culture (Apple, 1993; Sleeter, 2002).

By the early 2000s, the dominant national school reform agenda, including The No Child Left Behind Act of 2001, promoted not only standards, tests, accountability, and market competition among schools, but also partially privatized structures such as charter schools and vouchers. Failing schools, located disproportionately in impoverished communities, began to be converted into charter schools, many run by private management companies (Berliner, 2006; Saltman, 2007). Education itself became an arena for profit-making. The linkage of standards, textbooks, and tests became highly lucrative, the main beneficiaries being the largest textbook publishing corporations: CTB-McGraw-Hill, Harcourt, Pearson, and Houghton Mifflin (Bracey, 2005). While testing, now a multibillion-dollar-per-year industry, consumed sizable chunks of school budgets, public education suffered severe funding cuts. By 2012, per-pupil funding for schools had fallen to below 2008 levels in 35 states—in many cases, far below (Oliff, Mai & Leachman, 2012).

Corporate-controlled neoliberal economic reforms had succeeded in restoring elite power and wealth. By 2009, the share of national income of the wealthiest 0.1% of the U.S. population had risen to 7.8% (Logan, 2011). Neoliberal school reforms had become firmly entrenched, with Common Core standards now the latest attempt to bolster lackluster student achievement. In this context, it is important to ask whose worldviews are reflected in standards- and text-based curriculum, and why that matters.

Curriculum That Disempowers

I argue that standards and tests institutionalize a curriculum that disempowers a huge proportion of students, being based in the worldview of the ruling elite and constructed to confer legitimacy on the existing social order. This is true regardless of whether the curriculum is delivered in a traditional public school or a partially privatized setting. Hickman and Porfilio (2012) point out that while each wave of curriculum reform is usually touted as being in the best interests of all, a look below that rhetoric reveals institutionalization of knowledge designed to confer legitimacy on existing power relationships.

Textbooks have long served as the U.S. tacit national curriculum (Apple, 1993), since a relatively small (and shrinking) number of companies produce texts written largely to adoption policies of large states (especially California and Texas). The resulting texts—ubiquitous in U.S. schools and classrooms, and the foundation for what most teachers teach—are much more similar to each other than different (Jobrack, 2012). The latest curriculum reform is the Common Core standards; at the time of this writing, teachers are being told that they are to create their own new curriculum around the Common Core. However, at least one major company (Houghton Mifflin Harcourt) has already rolled out texts aligned with the Common Core and one can expect others to rapidly follow, given the large potential market awaiting them. Reactions of multicultural educators range from suggestions for how to build diversity into Common Core–based curriculum to skepticism about the Common Core itself.

Apple's (1993) conception of "the selective tradition in official knowledge" (p. 237) helps us understand why Common Core is unlikely to change the experiences of minoritized students. While historically patterns in the selective tradition were blatant, today they are masked with a light sprinkling of "diversity." From the late 1960s until the early 1980s, communities of color and women pressured publishers to address the most glaring racial and gender omissions and stereotypes. But as national concern shifted toward establishing and aligning standards, texts and tests, these efforts subsided, leaving the deeper narratives that had traditionally structured texts—particularly in history and social studies—intact (cf. Hickman & Porfilio, 2012; Loewen, 1995; Sleeter & Grant, 1991). Although state curriculum standards have not been analyzed as widely as textbooks, analyses that exist find them to replicate the selective tradition of textbooks (Heilig, Brown & Brown, 2012; Sleeter, 2002).

Essentially, texts tacitly teach White supremacy by giving Whites the most attention and dominance in narratives and points of view. African Americans appear in a more limited range of roles and usually receive only a sketchy account historically, mainly in relationship to slavery. Asian Americans, Latinos, and Arab Americans appear as isolated figures with virtually no history or contemporary ethnic experience, and Native Americans are located mainly in the past. Immigration is represented as a distinct historical period in the Northeast, rather than as an ongoing phenomenon (Vecchio, 2004). Those texts that say anything about contemporary race relations or racism disconnect past from present, frame perpetrators of racism as a few bad individuals rather than a system of oppression, and portray challenges to racism as actions of heroic individuals rather than organized struggle (Alridge, 2006; Brown & Brown, 2010). Colonization is similarly glossed over in various ways, such as passive sentence construction that does not state who colonized whom, location of colonization in the past only, and sanitation of events (Stanton, 2012).

Women are still marginalized and shown in a more limited range of roles than men, particularly in history that establishes a national narrative, and in the sciences (Pienta & Smith, 2012). Texts take for granted heterosexuality as the norm, and ignore LGBT identities and experiences (Hickman, 2012). Texts similarly ignore disability, although some feature the occasional individual with a disability. Texts ignore contemporary poverty, instead teaching that the U.S. opportunity structure is based on principles of capitalism in which the promise of success goes to all who work hard (Jaeger, 2012). Texts also implicitly teach subtractive bilingualism by ignoring the cultures and languages of immigrants and their families (Montaño & Quintanar-Sarellana, 2012).

The main way students react to this curriculum—especially students of color—is boredom and disengagement. Many students of color also reject school knowledge as they mature and realize that it conflicts with what they have experienced and learned in their homes and communities (Epstein, 2009). Students' disengagement from and rejection of "official knowledge" is, I would argue, highly important to attend to.

Curriculum That Empowers

A curriculum that empowers engages students by speaking to their lived realities, treating them as intellectuals, explicitly linking their cultural identities with academic learning, and cultivating their ability to use participatory democratic processes to address problems in their communities. A significant body of research finds a positive relationship between academic achievement of Black and Latino students, high level of awareness of race and racism, and positive identification with their own racial group (Altschul, Oyserman & Bybee, 2008; Carter, 2008; Miller & MacIntosh, 1999; O'Connor, 1997; Sellers, Chavous & Cooke, 1998). While students usually develop ethnic/racial identities, political awareness, and knowledge of racism outside of school, curriculum that links academic learning, students' community-based culture and identity, and a deep analysis of racism and power prompts powerful learning. What follows are three examples. While all three are standards-based so they will be used and recognized as legitimate, they all use knowledge and intellectual frameworks from marginalized communities.

Mexican American Studies in Tucson

Established about forty years ago, ethnic studies challenges the cultural irrelevance of most curricula, serving as a foundation for situating curriculum and pedagogy within the experiences and intellectual frames of reference of communities of color in order to "reclaim the political space that silences [students'] voices" (Cammarota & Romero, 2011, p. 489). In Tucson, an outstanding Mexican American Studies program that demonstrates how ethnic studies empowers minoritized students academically, personally, and politically was taught for several years.

In 1996, a group of concerned Mexican American citizens petitioned the Tucson Unified School District for a Mexican American Studies curriculum. Two years later, the board approved funding for it, and Mexican American/Raza Studies was launched. I became acquainted with the program when I was invited to address the 2005 annual Raza Studies Summer Institute. What caught my attention was its unwavering vision of education reform and its powerful impact on students. The Mexican American/Raza Studies Department worked with schools to strengthen teaching and learning, developing a rich array of standards-aligned curriculum resources centered within Chicano studies intellectual frameworks for classroom use, from kindergarten through high school. Best known was the Social Justice Education Project (SJEP), a four-semester high school curriculum based on a model of "critically conscious intellectualism" for strengthening teaching and learning of Chicano students (Cammarota & Romero, 2009; Romero, Arce & Cammarota, 2007). The model has three components: 1) an academically rigorous curriculum that is standards-aligned, culturally and historically relevant to students, and focused on social justice issues; 2) critical pedagogy in which students develop critical thinking and critical consciousness, creating rather than consuming knowledge; and 3) authentic caring in which teachers demonstrate deep respect for students as intellectual and full human beings. The curriculum immersed students in university-level theoretical readings, and included a community-based research project in which students gathered data about manifestations of racism in their school and community, using social science theory to analyze patterns in their data and propose solutions to problems. Students gave formal presentations of their research results to the community, as well as to academic and youth conferences.

The impact of the program on students was closely scrutinized, initially to document its success in improving student achievement, then later to defend its existence. Arizona's Superintendent of Education commissioned Cambium Learning and National Academic Educational Partners (2011) to audit the program. The auditors found that students enrolled in the high school courses "graduate in the very least at a range of 5% more than their counterparts in 2005, and at the most, at a rate of 11% in 2010" (p. 47). On the state's academic achievement tests, students who had failed the reading and writing portions earlier, then completed a Mexican American Studies class, were more likely to pass by the end of their junior year than students who did not take the class. Importantly, in interviews students consistently credited the program for their academic success. A subsequent analysis commissioned by the district's desegregation Special Master found similar results (Cabrera, Milem & Marx, 2012). Cammarota (2007) noted that in addition to improving achievement and graduation rates, many students credited the Raza Studies project with saving their lives, and showing them how to stand up and fight racism for themselves.

Nonetheless, because of their own fear that the program was teaching sedition and despite its indisputable positive impact on student academic learning, several White leaders at the state level succeed in pushing through a law banning ethnic studies (see Palos, McGinnis, Fifer, Bricca & Amor, 2011). In January 2012, Tucson Unified School District shut down the program and reassigned the teachers to other courses. However, being under court order to desegregate its schools, Tucson's school board has been forced to recognize the powerful impact

Mexican American Studies has had on its students. At the time of this writing, ethnic studies is in the process of being reconstituted in Tucson.

Math in a Cultural Context in Alaska

Other ethnic studies programs for which data on student impact were gathered have also demonstrated a positive impact (Sleeter, 2011). Math in a Cultural Context (MCC) is a particularly interesting example because of its thoughtful curriculum planning, its ongoing use in serving indigenous Yup'ik students, and the large amount of data documenting the program. MCC is one of several projects created through collaboration between the University of Alaska Fairbanks and local indigenous communities, known as the Alaska Native Knowledge Network (www.ankn.uaf.edu/). Rather than rejecting the idea of standards, the Network created a very well-conceptualized set of Cultural Standards for Curriculum; MCC reflects a melding of those standards with those of the National Council of Teachers of Mathematics.

MCC is a 10-module supplementary mathematics curriculum for grades 1–7, developed collaboratively by Yup'ik Native elders, math teachers, and anthropologists. Beginning with Yup'ik everyday practices, the modules—such as "Parkas and Patterns," which teaches geometry, and "Salmon Fishing," which teaches probability—link practices based in indigenous cosmology and epistemology with specific mathematical concepts (Lipka, Andrew-Ihrke & Yanez, 2011). The highly contextualized curriculum supports traditional ways of communicating and knowing, such as collaborative learning and cognitive apprenticeship.

Experimental studies using a pretest-posttest control group design found that students in classrooms using MCC make more progress toward the state mathematics standards than students in classrooms not using it (Lipka, Yanez, Andrew-Ihrke & Adam, 2009). In addition to making mathematical concepts comprehensible for Yup'ik children, MCC also improves Yup'ik teachers' practice by drawing on what is culturally familiar to them, giving them confidence and authority over what they are teaching (Lipka, Sharp, Brenner, Yanez & Sharp, 2005). Lipka et al. (2009) conclude that this project "does appear to reverse sociohistoric power relations and assimilative processes and replace them with more collaborative and inclusive ways of producing curriculum and pedagogy" (p. 278).

Chicago Grassroots Curriculum

The Chicago Grassroots Curriculum Task Force is creating a series of curriculum toolkits entitled *A People's History of Chicago: Our Stories of Change and Struggle*. The toolkits' authors delineate four dimensions of the theoretical framework informing the curriculum: critical pedagogy (Duncan-Andrade & Morrell, 2008); youth participatory action research that "positions students to become subjects of their own research" that "then leads to actions for justice;" cultural relevance and critical multiculturalism based on non-essentialized and coalition-building ethnic studies; and grassroots curriculum "that is deeply embedded in the lives of students and their particular communities" (www.grassrootscurriculum.org/index.php/curriculum/our-pedagogy-). As its title suggests, the series draws inspiration from Howard Zinn's *A People's History of the United States* (2005), a U.S. history re-narrated from a grassroots perspective that makes visible structures of race and class oppression, and struggles of marginalized groups. It sits within the traditions of Paulo Freire and Myles Horton, both of whom spent their lives engaged with popular movements for participation, freedom, and justice (Bell, Gaventa & Peters, 1990). It also draws on the work of *Rethinking Schools* (2012), which is grounded in the conviction that "schools are integral not only to preparing all children to be full participants in society, but also to be full participants in this country's ever-tenuous experiment in democracy. That this vision has yet to be fully realized does not mean it should be abandoned."

Urban renewal or urban removal? (Chicago Grassroots Curriculum Task Force, 2012) is the first curriculum toolkit in the series. Its primary purpose is to empower Chicago's young people of color and/or from poor communities—academically, personally, and politically—by engaging them in developing a politically sophisticated analysis of Chicago from grassroots perspectives, and by learning to use academic skills to speak up for and work on behalf of their communities specifically, and social justice more broadly. The toolkit weaves together three main goals for students: gaining critical awareness of historical and contemporary forces shaping the city; learning to investigate one's own community, envision what its residents want and need, and act on behalf of that vision; and developing college-ready academic skills. Students cannot simply be marched lock-step through the materials; to foster democratic processes in the classroom, the authors (most of whom are teachers and students) intend that teachers co-construct use of the materials with their students. The set of materials includes a text, a student learning and action journal, two CDs, and a website.

The text, written for students eighth grade and up, provides a history of the movements, locations, relocations, and struggles of peoples of Chicago, from First Nations peoples beginning 10,000 years ago, through the foreclosure crisis of the present (Miglietta, Lopez, Stovall & Williams, 2012). Using a "bottom-up" perspective, readings offer students a historic as well as contemporary analysis of why various communities live where they do, how current patterns came to be, systems of exploitation Whites in power used to displace and control communities of color, and strategies communities of color and poor people used to fight back. The text is vividly illustrated with original artwork by Terrence T.z Eye Haymer and the arts team. Six core questions are used throughout: Why? How did people respond? Where? What's up with that? What's the root of that? and Who was that? For example, Part V examines "Building a New Chicago: 1980s to Today." Students learn terms such as Reganomics, privatization, and globalization while studying competing visions for Chicago: the Global Capital City, the Social Justice City, and the default position or Real World City. Students study what it means to be a "growth machine" for global capital, how real estate speculation works, and what it means to invest, disinvest, and reinvest in neighborhoods—in other words, how neoliberalism is shaping Chicago. They also study how Black and Latino activists organized to promote a vision of an affordable and just city, examining several specific activist groups and "ordinary people" who became leaders. Students then examine specific current problems, such as too little affordable housing, along with solutions that have been proposed.

The Student Learning and Action Journal provides a set of learning tools, mostly organized by academic discipline. After giving an overview of the text, the Journal invites teachers and students to map their intended learning against the Common Core standards, Illinois Learning Goals, ACT College Readiness, and UCLA Historical Thinking Standards. The authors emphasize that academic learning should be culturally relevant to students and oriented toward social justice; teachers and students should plan how to integrate the text and activities into their curriculum in the most meaningful and impactful way. The journal is packed with strategies, templates, guides, activities and projects that can readily be connected with the text. For example, students are given steps for writing a letter to a local politician and rubrics to evaluate the letter before sending it; math problems on subprime lending that both practice math reasoning as well as illustrate why subprime lending is a problem; and guidance on creating a Chicago big book out of posters of students' analyses of suggested topics in Chicago history. The Toolkit CD includes PDFs and Word documents that teachers can use as planning tools, and it also includes examples of work produced by other teachers and students. The Mixtape CD includes music and other audio resources that can be used with units. The website (http://www.grassrootscurriculum.org/) is structured to become a growing resource library and networking tool.

So far this curriculum is too new for its impact on students to have been studied. However, the fact that it is being written by Chicago teachers in collaboration with students, parents, and community members suggests that its tools and resources are highly engaging and relevant to urban students. In addition, the fact that teachers can map the curriculum against the academic standards they are using increases the likelihood that it will enhance student achievement as measured by traditional means.

Confronting the Education Reform Paradigm

I have argued that the dominant paradigm driving education reform over the past two decades has been rooted in neoliberalism, which itself is a project that is succeeding in restoring the power and wealth of a small elite. Although it has been sold to the public as a paradigm for improving student achievement and closing racial achievement gaps, data do not support that claim. One of the major problems with the dominant paradigm is that it avoids interrogating how race, class, and culture work in communities, schools and classrooms, and how these impact on students' experiences in and engagement with schooling. The three examples of curriculum presented in this chapter offer distinct contrasts with that institutionalized in most schools. All three illustrate the potential of an alternative paradigm for education reform that links community knowledge, ethnic studies, and student participation with high levels of academic work. It is time that the dominant paradigm is confronted for the elitism and racism that it supports, and that we learn from alternatives such as those discussed here.

References

Alridge, D. P. (2006). The limits of master narratives in history textbooks. *Teachers College Record, 108*(4), 662–686.

Altschul, I., Oyserman, D., & Bybee, D. (2008). Racial-ethnic self-schemas and segmented assimilation: Identity and the academic achievement of Hispanic youth. *Social Psychology Quarterly, 71*(3), 302–320.

Apple, M. W. (1993). The politics of official knowledge: Does a national curriculum make sense? *Teachers College Record, 95*(2), 221–241.

Bell, B., Gaventa, J., & Peters, J. (1990). *We make the road by walking*. Philadelphia: Temple University Press.

Berliner, D. C. (2006). Our impoverished view of educational reform. *Teachers College Record, 108*(6), 949–995.

Bracey, G. W. (2005). *No Child Left Behind: Where does the money go?* Arizona State University: Educational Policy Studies Unit. Retrieved from http://epsl.asu.edu/epru/documents/EPSL-0506-114-EPRU.pdf

Brown, K. D., & Brown, A. L. (2010). Silenced memories: An examination of the sociocultural knowledge on race and racial violence in official school curriculum. *Equity & Excellence in Education, 43*(2), 139–154.

Business Roundtable (1999). *Transforming education policy: Assessing ten years of progress in the states*. Washington, DC: The Business Roundtable.

Cabrera, N. L., Milem, J. F., & Marx, R. D. (2012). *An empirical analysis of the effects of Mexican American Studies participation on student achievement within Tucson Unified School District*. Report submitted June 20, 2012, to Willis D. Hawley, Special Master for the Tucson Unified School District Desegregation Case. Retrieved from http://works.bepresscom/nolan_1_cabrera/17

Cambium Learning & National Academic Educational Partners. (2011). *Curriculum audit of the Mexican American Studies Department, Tucson Unified School District*. Retrieved from http:// http://saveethnicstudies.org/assets/docs/state_audit/Cambium_Audit.pdf.

Cammarota, J. (2007). A social justice approach to achievement. *Equity & Excellence in Education, 40*, 87–96.

Cammarota, J., & Romero, A. (2009). The Social Justice Education Project: A critically compassionate intellectualism for Chicana/o students. In W. Ayers, T. Quinn, & D. Stovall (Eds.), *Handbook for social justice education* (pp. 465–476). New York: Lawrence Erlbaum.

Cammarota, J., & Romero, A. (2011). Participatory action research for high school students. *Educational Policy, 25*(3), 488–506.

Carter, D. (2008). Achievement as resistance: Development of a critical race achievement ideology among Black achievers. *Harvard Educational Review, 78*(3), 466–497.

Chicago Grassroots Curriculum Task Force. (2012). *Urban renewal or urban removal?* Chicago: Author.

Davis, D. H., & Raymond, M. E. (2012). Choices for studying choice: Assessing charter school effectiveness using two quasi-experimental methods. *Economics of Education Review, 31*, 225–236

Duncan-Andrade, J., & Morrell, E. (2008). *The art of critical pedagogy*. New York: Peter Lang.

Durdin, T. R. (2007). African centered schooling: Facilitating holistic excellence for Black children. *The Negro Educational Review, 58*(1–2), 23–34.

Epstein, T. (2009). *Interpreting national history*. New York: Routledge.

Hacker, J. S., & Pierson, P. (2010). *Winner-take-all politics*. New York: Simon & Schuster.

Hargreaves, A., & Shirley, D. (2009). *The fourth way: The inspiring future for educational change*. Thousand Oaks, CA: Corwin Press.

Harvey, D. (2005). *A brief history of neoliberalism*. New York: Oxford University Press.

Heilig, J. V., Brown, K. D., & Brown, A. L. (2012). The illusion of inclusion: A critical race theory textual analysis of race and standards. *Harvard Educational Review, 82*(3), 403–424.

Herold, B. (2011). Why aren't African-centered charters running turnarounds? *Philadelphia Public School Notebook, 18*(4). Retrieved from http://thenotebook.org/february-2011/113303/school-closings

Hickman, H. (2012). Handling heteronormativity in high school literature texts. In H. Hickman & B. J. Porfolio (Eds.), *The new politics of the textbook* (pp. 71–86). Boston: Sense.

Hickman, H., & Porfolio, B. J. (Eds.). (2012). *The new politics of the textbook*. Boston: Sense.

Jaeger, E. (2012). The *Open Court* reality: Stories of success for unsuccessful readers. In H. Hickman & B. J. Porfolio (Eds.), *The new politics of the textbook* (pp. 87–106). Boston: Sense.

Jobrack, B. (2012). *Tyranny of the textbook*. Lanham, MD: Rowman & Littlefield.

Kelly, A. P., & Lovelace, T. (2012). Comparing new school effects in charter and traditional public schools. *American Journal of Education, 118*(4), 427–453.

Klein, N. (2008). *The shock doctrine: The rise of disaster capitalism*. New York: Henry Holt.

Kumashiro, K. (2012). *Bad teacher!* New York: Teachers College Press.

Lipka, J., Andrew-Ihrke, D., & Yanez, E. E. (2011). Yup'ik cosmology to school mathematics: The power of symmetry and proportional measuring. *Interchange, 42*(2), 157–183

Lipka, J., Sharp, N., Brenner, B., Yanez, E., & Sharp, F. (2005). The relevance of culturally based curriculum and instruction: The case of Nancy Sharp. *Journal of American Indian Education, 44*(3), 31–54.

Lipka, J., Yanez, E., Andrew-Ihrke, D., & Adam, S. (2009). A two-way process for developing effective culturally based math. In B. Greer, S. Mukhopadhyay, A. B. Powell, & S. Nelson-Barber (Eds.), *Culturally Responsive mathematics education* (pp. 257–280). New York: Routledge.

Loewen, J. W. (1995*). Lies my teacher told me*. New York: The New Press.

Logan, D. (2011, Oct. 24). *Summary of latest federal individual income tax data*. Tax Foundation. Retrieved from: http://taxfoundation.org/article/summary-latest-federal-individual-income-tax-data-0.

Miglietta, A., Lopez, A., Stovall, D., & Williams, E. Eds. (2012). *Urban renewal or urban removal?* Chicago: Chicago Grassroots Curriculum Taskforce.

Miller, D., & Macintosh, R. (1999). Promoting resilience in urban African American adolescents. *Social Work Research, 3*, 159–169.

Montaño, T., & Quintanar-Sarellana, R. (2012). Finding my serpent tongue: Do ESL textbooks tap the linguistic and cultural capital of our long-term English language learners? In H. Hickman & B. J. Porfolio (Eds.), *The new politics of the textbook* (pp. 17–30). Boston: Sense.

National Center for Education Statistics. (2011). *The nation's report card: Reading 2011* (NCES 2012–457). Washington, DC: Institute of Education Sciences, U.S. Department of Education.

O'Connor, C. (1997). Dispositions toward (collective) struggle and educational resilience in the inner city: A case analysis of six African-American high school students. *American Educational Research Journal, 34*(4), 593–629.

Oliff, P., Mai, C., & Leachman, M. (2012). *New school year brings more cuts in state funding for schools.* Center on Budget and Policy Priorities. Retrieved from http://www.cbpp.org/cms/index.cfm?fa=view&id=3825

Palos, A., McGinnis, E., Fifer, S. J., Bricca, J., & Amor, N. (2011). *Precious knowledge* [DVD]. Tucson, AZ: Dos Vatos Productions.

Pienta, R. S., & Smith, A. M. (2012). Women on the margins: The politics of gender in the language and content of science textbooks. In H. Hickman & B. J. Porfolio (Eds.), *The new politics of the textbook* (pp. 33–48). Boston: Sense.

Rethinking Schools (2012). About Rethinking Schools. Retrieved from: http://www.rethinkingschools.org/about/index.shtml.

Romero, A., Arce, S., & Cammarota, J. (2007). A barrio pedagogy: Identity, intellectualism, activism, and academic achievement through the evolution of critically compassionate intellectualism. *Race Ethnicity and Education, 12*(2), 217–233.

Saez, E. (2010). *Striking it richer: The evolution of top incomes in the United States.* Berkeley: University of California Berkeley. Retrieved from: http://elsa.berkeley.edu/~saez/saez-UStopincomes-2010.pdf

Saltman, K. J. (2007). *Capitalizing on disaster.* Boulder, CO: Paradigm.

Sellers, R. M., Chavous, T. M., & Cooke, D. Y. (1998). Racial ideology and racial centrality as predictors of African American college students' academic performance. *Journal of Black Psychology, 24*(1), 8–27.

Sleeter, C. E. (2002). State curriculum standards and student consciousness. *Social Justice, 29*(4), 8–25.

Sleeter, C. E. (2011). *The academic and social value of ethnic studies: A research review.* Washington, DC: National Education Association.

Sleeter, C. E., & Grant, C. A. (1991). Textbooks and race, class, gender and disability. In M. W. Apple & L. Christian-Smith (Eds.), *The Politics of the textbook* (pp. 78–110). New York: Routledge.

Stanton, C. R. (2012). Context and community: Resisting curricular colonization in American history courses. In H. Hickman & B. J. Porfolio (Eds.), *The new politics of the textbook* (pp. 173–194). Boston: Sense.

Vecchio, D. (2004). Immigrant and ethnic history in the United States survey. *The History Teacher, 37*(4), 494–500.

Zinn, H. (2005). *A people's history of the United States.* New York: Harper Perennial Modern Classics.

CHAPTER ELEVEN

Rethinking School Reform and Neighborhood Schools

DONYELL L. ROSEBORO

School desegregation efforts in the United States represent a complex interrogation of the nation's history of racism and a persistent hope that our founding ideals might become reality. Such collective desegregation efforts illustrate a dynamic interplay between philosophical principles of equity and freedom and the everyday practices that reflect, reject, and/or ignore such ideals. The relevance of public education in a democratic country whose governing documents express a commitment to equity and freedom remains a fundamental question today. Given the long and varied arguments surrounding the purposes of education in the U.S. (Cooper, 1988; Cremin, 1980; Du Bois, 1903; Jefferson, 1778, cited in Berkes, 2009; Mann, 1848; Spring, 2011), today's policy makers must consider how public education might serve to support our nation's competing interests. These interests, broadly defined, include education for the public good, education to globally compete, and education to undo past injustices. With these competing interests, questions of equity, access, and persistence remain: How can public schools serve the best interests of a public that is diverse in identity, thought, and action?

Considering recent efforts to return to neighborhood schools (understanding that, in many areas, school desegregation efforts never resulted in truly integrated schools), this chapter will explore neighborhood schools within a larger historical context, paying particular attention to school desegregation as a problematic reform movement. A particular focus will be on two neighborhood schools located in Wilmington, North Carolina—Williston Senior High School, an all-Black school that closed in 1968, and D.C. Virgo Preparatory Academy, a middle school that re-opened in 2010 with 96% of the student population identified as African American.

Arguments in support of neighborhood schools often suggest that such schools can enhance parental involvement which, in turn, will lead to more positive connections between schools, families, and the communities they serve (Edelberg & Kurland, 2009). In contrast, opponents of neighborhood schools cite the ways in which they become racially and socio-economically segregated spaces with young people who live in poverty often trapped with the least qualified teachers (Nixon, 1972; Peterson, 1998; Wegmann, 1975). In recent years, scholars have framed this debate in a post-*Brown* structure, emphasizing the disconnect between expected gains and unexpected losses of school desegregation. So while neighborhood schools post-*Brown* disproportionally represent racial and socio-economic spaces that often lack authentic learning (Anyon, 2005; Darling-Hammond, 2010; Delpit, 2012), segregated schools with all Black students have been hailed as caring spaces marked by real-world learning activities (Baker, 2006; Hughes, 2006; Norrell, 2011; Washington, 1900). They have been characterized as schools that nurtured the identities of Black students as they challenged them intellectually (Kelly, 2010).

The History of Neighborhood Schools

In a post-*Brown* era, the discourse(s) surrounding neighborhood schools typically dichotomizes segregation and desegregation in ways that characterize desegregation as a fundamental reform in U.S. society. This reform has held particular relevance for public schools in that schools became working spaces for the Civil Rights Movement and for subsequent efforts to ensure equitable learning opportunities for all students. As working spaces for societal reform, schools facilitated change at the same time that their structures, processes, and resources perpetuated the disparities that plagued segregated U.S. society. Exploring neighborhood schools as part of a larger reform movement thus requires us to take a brief historical look into such at schools, the policies that framed them, and the discourses that currently posit them as integral community centers.

Neighborhood schools are schools that serve a local community. Though geography is important in this definition, most important are the children and their families who are served by the schools (Litwak & Meyer, 1974). While the literal boundaries of the neighborhood shape the school's context, the families who are directly connected with the school actually interject meaning into the school through the interactions and relationships in which they engage. As these interactions and relationships form, a sense of community can develop within and around the school. It is this sense of community that has come to epitomize neighborhood schools despite the obvious reality that not all of them will engender a strong sense of community. By 1972, 18 years after the *Brown* decision, some were bemoaning the "demise of the community" exacerbated by an "overemphasis placed on individual and societal needs as two polar extremes, with little or no attention given to the vitality of the groups that bridge the individual and society" (Sarri, 1972, p. 20). This demise of community resulted also from an "overemphasis on specialization, fragmentation, and bureaucratic conformity" that put individuals at odds with one another while clinging to separate and competing interests.

Litwak and Meyer (1972) connected the demise of community to the rise of neighborhood schools even though these schools symbolized a resurrection of an integrated sense of community. They argued: "Other problems have arisen because of the concept of neighborhood school, which also had a laudable objective at one time but now results in total separation of the slum and suburban child from one another" (p. 21). In this context, neighborhood schools illustrate the growing socio-economic divide in U.S. society; yet they also fundamentally represent residual expectations of marginalized groups since the Civil Rights and anti-poverty movements to exert some measure of control over public schools, in ways that would help to undo the social injustices they experienced in their daily lives (Kahn, 1972). For such groups, schools might be seen as "the only place in many parts of the country to which local community people can turn when they are deprived" (p. 50). In this context, a neighborhood school evokes two parallel sets of expectations that come from two different frames. The first expectation stems from a hope that the school can be a space of redress, reconciliation, and healing. This belief comes from a social and political frame grounded in the movement work that led to *Brown* and related legislation post-*Brown*. It is more typically connected to broader arguments of schooling as a social good and a collective responsibility. The second expectation comes from a belief that community control will protect and advance the interests and values of the families it serves. It is often loosely grounded in freedom of choice as a democratic principle and success as a universal right (de los Reyes & Gozemba, 2002). This expectation has fueled efforts to create neighborhood schools even when those schools seemingly damage a larger collective good of racial integration.

Debates to define public schools as a collective good narrowed in the aftermath of the *Brown* decision. Race mattered. It became a central argument as school communities struggled to desegregate. But, in an era when desegregated communities did not exist, configuring a way to desegregate schools would inevitably entail transporting groups of young people from one neighborhood to another (Cecelski, 1994). Desegregation would, therefore, later be criticized for the ways in which it disrupted African American communities, de-legitimized the expertise of African American educators, and disconnected African American students from extended kinship networks of support (Anderson, 2010; Baker, 2006; Siddle-Walker, 1996). In the years following the *Brown* decision, the nation grappled with distinguishing between desegregation and integration, a distinction that represented larger philosophical perspectives on equal education and white supremacy (Bell, 1980; Carter, 1980). Perhaps most telling, Robert Carter (1980), one of the attorneys for the *Brown* case, said in retrospect:

> Up to that point, we had neither sought nor received any guidance from professional educators as to what equal education might connote to them in terms of their educational responsibilities. We felt no need for such guidance because of our conviction that equal education meant integrated education, and those educators who supported us never challenged that view. (p. 23)

For the NAACP attorneys that argued the case, there were no practical discussions about how equal education might translate in desegregated schools. There were no visions of what teachers and administrative leaders might do and no clear articulations about what student learning would emerge. Carter would go on to say that they recognized the problem of residential segregation but they expected that once discriminatory housing practices ended, neighborhoods would desegregate.

Decades of practice in desegregation has led to several clear outcomes for the majority of African American students in urban districts. Urban districts have been largely abandoned by middle-class whites (and some African Americans) since the late 1960s and beyond (Boustan, 2010), leaving students of color attending school with majority minority populations, most of whom live in poverty. These schools are disproportionately staffed with the least experienced teachers (Anyon, 2005; Darling-Hammond, 2010; Delpit, 2012). Given these outcomes, many question the success of school desegregation. Bell (1980) argued that "many Black parents are disenchanted and have lost faith in integration ideology" (p. xi). Indeed, Baker (2006) claimed that with "privatization, standardized testing, and the improvement of separate educational facilities—political and educational authorities refined a new racial order in education" (p. 158). African Americans were being denied access to desegregated schools by the 1960s. Given these conditions, some African Americans began to advocate against desegregation. In so doing, they re-captured an argument that Du Bois (1935) made when he asked "Does the Negro Need Separate Schools?" If desegregated schools meant uncaring teachers who lowered expectations for African American students, Du Bois declared that African American students should remain in racially segregated schools.

Decades after *Brown*, the discourse of community control continued even as the rationale for the claim held different meaning for varied constituent groups. Even with a move toward community control post-*Brown*, Kahn (1972) cautioned that complete community control was impractical given that some resources and policies would inevitably come from outside of the local community. This tension between local, state, and national control has become a central point of disagreement in debates about neighborhood schools, with each side challenging who should set the policies and determine the practices that govern public schools. For African Americans, this tension has come to represent a larger one grounded in a need for collective voice, a desire to shift the public memory of segregated African American schools, and an expectation that public schools will prepare African American students to fill leadership roles in the African American community and beyond (Jackson, 2007). Given the monumental jurisprudential shift that the *Brown* decision represented, many African Americans were initially hesitant to criticize the decision; yet it was clear from the outset that the loss of community influence in segregated schools was devastating to many African American communities.

This loss of community influence, particularly for a community that has historically been oppressed, symbolized more than a loss of control. Instead, it represented a broader disenfranchisement—a loss of place, possibility, and self-affirmation. What African Americans and others came to realize post-*Brown* was that segregated schools supported and shaped African American students in certain intangible yet important ways: Teachers expected excellence and nurtured students to be leaders; the school served as a community center, one which mediated a collective political and social voice; and African American leaders modeled for students middle-class rules and behaviors such that students learned the language and behaviors that would allow them access to middle-class society (Jackson, 2007). More specifically, *Brown* changed the politics of community control in schools:

> Not only has it influenced who is in the classroom (both teachers and students) and who leads the school (principals and other administrative staff), but also in many fields, it definitely has influenced curriculum and instruction. That is, what we study, how we study it, and how we teach it. (Larke, Larke, & Castle, 2007, p. 104)

In retrospect, the loss of schools in African American communities has not yet been offset by the gains of desegregation—in part because there was always a tension between who taught, who led, and how content was taught in public schools, particularly when schools de-segregated and Black teachers were forced to move to White schools. Equally important, the expected gains from desegregation never fully materialized (Baker, 2006; Jackson, 2007; Larke et al., 2007; Siddle-Walker, 1996).

Finally, the *Brown* decision profoundly altered the landscape of educational reform because it centered education as a space of societal reform. In this centering, public education came to represent much more than a place where young people learned facts and skills. Instead, *Brown* illustrated the importance of public schools to the extension of our country's democratic principles, to the development of curricula that would support those principles, and to the nurturing of pedagogies that could translate equality and justice into everyday practices. *Brown* also taught us that educational reform could not occur divorced from other societal reforms, in particular, housing and neighborhood reform (Carter, 1980; Smrekar, 2009). Absent any genuine efforts to eliminate discrimination in housing (lending and location practices) and without efforts to re-structure public housing, neighborhoods would remain segregated and would not represent the ideal that *Brown* promised.

Methodology

Research Context

Wilmington, North Carolina, is a coastal city with a troubled history of race relations. After settlement, it operated with a distinct hierarchy of citizens, led by a traditional planter class and merchants who made their wealth in trade (Wilmington Race Riot Commission, 2006). There was a free Black population comprised mainly of skilled laborers who primarily worked in carpentry and masonry (p. 5). There were 672 free Blacks living in New Hanover County just prior to the start of the Civil War and 573 of those lived in the city. After the Civil War, Black Wilmingtonians formed a Union League, owned businesses, and delved into politics. Black men held a Freedmen's Convention in Raleigh just after the official end of the war. By 1898, however, the Democratic Party had succeeded in capitalizing on Whites' fears that collaboration between Republicans and Populists would lead to Blacks gaining more political offices. Immediately after the 1898 election, Whites formed the Committee of 25 and presented a list of demands to the Committee of Colored Citizens. By November 10, 1898, Whites had burned the offices of Alex Manly's *Daily Record*, had attacked and/or killed at least 25 African Americans, and had banished others.[1]

The collective memory of these events endures in Wilmington. In 2000, the city established the 1898 Commission to examine and report the history of these events to document how they have shaped the county's development in the decades since. These events, coupled with the Civil Rights movement and the desegregation of public schools, have marked Wilmington's race relations narrative as a deeply divided one with injustices clearly documented, publicly debated, and distinctly remembered. When school desegregation efforts began in the city, this historical context tempered the idealism of the legislation that prompted the change. After the School Board decided to close Williston Senior High School, the county's Black high school, another loss was recorded in the annals of Black history in Wilmington.

Williston High School started under a different name in 1866 just after the end of the Civil War. In 1873 the Wilmington Board of Education purchased the school, which had been located at the intersection of Seventh and Nun Streets, for $3,000 and renamed it Williston Graded School. A new school, Williston Primary and Industrial School, was built in 1914 at the intersection of Tenth and Church Streets. The first principal was David Clarke Virgo. The school expanded in 1923 and 1925 and a new school, named Williston Industrial School, was opened in 1933. After fire destroyed this building in 1936, another building opened in 1937. After a lawsuit was filed by parents who complained of the inadequate facilities, the school board authorized the building of a new school, Williston Senior High School, which welcomed students in 1954. Despite the fact that Williston's newest building had been constructed in the 1950s and New Hanover High School's (the nearby White high school) had been built in the 1920s, the school board closed Williston in 1968 (Steelman, 2010).

Opened in 1964 and named after Dr. David Clarke Virgo, Virgo Middle School is located in downtown Wilmington. The school became increasingly important as a neighborhood school after the closing of Williston Senior High School. It operated as a middle school until June of 2011, when the local school board (with the support of the superintendent) elected to close the school, citing declining enrollment and test scores. After holding several community meetings, the superintendent decided to try to re-open the school as a charter school with the hope that, as a charter, the school would be able to implement more innovative approaches to teaching and to school governance. When the charter application was denied, the superintendent moved forward with re-opening the school as a middle school with a different governance structure. In partnership with the Blue Ribbon Commission, a commission modeled after the Harlem (NY) Children's Zone, the district re-opened the school in the fall of 2012.

Virgo Preparatory Academy[2] serves children who live in poverty, whose parents do not hold high school diplomas, and who, with these factors, have been identified as at risk for school failure. With per capita income hovering at $12, 295, 48% of families living in poverty, and 55% of individuals 18–24 not having a high school diploma, the school serves a community that struggles to survive. In addition, 94% of the families are African American and 70% of households are run by single parents (according to Virgo's 2011 Charter School Application, http://www.ncpublicschools.org/docs/charterschools/resources/application/2011fasttrack/virgo.pdf). In 2011, only 51% of students scored at or above grade level on End of Grade tests (EOG), the state-mandated reading assessment. Seventh graders were lowest, with only 42% on or at grade level in reading. Mathematics scores were better, with 75% of students scoring at or above grade level.

Methods

This study is a conceptual content analysis (Krippendorf, 2004) using two sets of documents. Set one includes 11 oral history interviews with 21 African Americans who attended Williston, a segregated high school in Wilmington, North Carolina.[3] Set two includes 45 newspaper articles related to the closure and re-opening of D.C. Virgo Preparatory Academy.[4] My initial research questions were 1) How does the language of the documents characterize teaching and learning for African American students? 2) How does this language define the neighborhood school? and 3) How does this language define community involvement? To select the documents, I used a purposive sampling of texts. In set one, I used only interviews of individuals who attended and/or taught at Williston High School while it was a segregated school. In set two, I selected documents published in the *Star News* and *Wilmington Journal* from January 2007 through April 2012, which covered pre-closure to the re-opening of D.C. Virgo Preparatory Academy. To analyze the documents, I engaged in open coding and categorizing to identify patterns in the language of the documents. Once I grouped codes by categories, I created a thematic framework to engage in dialogue about segregated neighborhood schools for African Americans pre- and post-*Brown*.

The Greatest School under the Sun: Defining a Neighborhood School for African Americans at Williston Senior High School

The interviews of Williston High School graduates spoke to the pride and connection students had to the school, the sense of belonging that it engendered, and the identities that it nurtured. They described daily life at Williston, the expectations to excel, and the accomplishments reached because of their experiences at Williston. The school was described in four interviews as "the greatest school under the sun" and remembered mostly for its teachers. In many ways, graduation from Williston was a rite of passage. It involved a series of ritualized behaviors that sustained a collective identity associated with the school. From their language, it was clear that Williston served as more than just a school. Indeed, in two interviews it was characterized as an "institution," a characterization that illustrated its enduring legacy to the neighborhoods and families it served.

The Epistemology of Teaching: What Teachers at Williston Knew

Teachers knew families and communities as well as they knew young people's abilities and the discrimination they would face when they left Williston. In each interview, teachers are revered, honored, and remembered by name. They were role models to be emulated (Lethia Hankins, p. 4) and, in this role, inspired many of the interviewees to enter the teaching profession. They were described as caring, dedicated, committed, loved, and cherished at the same time they were described as intimidating, with high expectations. Rosa Chadwick Handley had this to say: "But it seems like the school was much more a part of the culture than it is today... the teachers stalked you and 'I know your mother' and that's so true" (p. 10). Cornelia Campbell added: "It was just a...it was like a family. Everybody knew everybody and you couldn't do anything that it didn't get back to your parents" (p. 8). Interviewees characterized that knowledge of family as important as content knowledge. It was an epistemology that framed expectations and allowed for a seamless transition between home and school.

Teachers knew their content. They studied in the summers, traveled to other institutions and countries to learn, and brought that knowledge back to the school and community. This transfer of knowledge epitomized the teaching and learning process for them; once they learned, they taught students that content and they expected students to learn it. Campbell recalled:

> ...my music teacher told me one time, she said: "What is music? It is combining tones to please the ear." She said, "I don't care where I see you, if I ask you, I want you to be able to tell me." So one day I went visiting her church and she said, "What is music?" I said, "Using combining tones to please the ear." And I know that today. (p. 8)

Students recalled being expected to excel in all subjects by all teachers. Lethia Hankins captures this philosophy when she states, "We were taught at Williston, you must excel, you have no choice" (p. 4). Repeatedly, each interviewee recounted these high expectations, how they carried over from school to home, to public performances, and post-graduation. And many, like David Nixon, remarked on how they felt prepared after graduation, calling specific attention to when their academic preparation proved better than their White counterparts.

Teachers' connections to families and their knowledge of content led them to be perceived as role models for the students at Williston. Indeed, they inspired many to pursue teaching as a career. Seven out of the 21 interviewed in this collection went on to become teachers. Rosa Chadwick Handley related: "Well, I've already mentioned several times Miss Anna Burnett; and she was actually a role model for me. She was the business education teacher, so in my mind that's what I wanted to be when I grew up…" (p. 3). Kathryn Ennett added: "That's why we have that display at the museum that tells you, it has pictures of when they were students and what their professions became. A lot of them went into teaching. They loved it because their teachers were so good" (p. 10). As role models, teachers inspired Williston students to enter the professional world post-graduation. Though Williston graduates went on to work in a variety of capacities, their pursuit of teaching sustained the teaching and learning continuum that they had enjoyed—in going back into the classroom, they would use what they had learned from committed Black teachers to inspire a new generation.

Rites of Passage: Ritualized Transitions and Identity Building

Williston graduates emphasized the importance of rites of passage. Though they did not refer to these transitions as such, their repeated mention of them and the ways in which each interviewee emphasized their importance led me to characterize them as rites of passage. They were more than simple transitions or singular events. They represented ritualized acts that worked to create a collective identity with the school. Perhaps more important, they were transitions that symbolized students' move from one space to another, from being an underclassman to being a senior, from being a Williston student to being an alumnus.

The first rite of passage that graduates described was "the walk." They recounted stories of the walk to school to illustrate how this walk was a communal one that represented the transition from home to school. It was a walk during which one stopped to pick up one's extended kinship network along the way, speak to other-mothers and other-fathers,[5] and prepare to enter the halls of Williston. Kathryn Ennett talked about the significance of "getting to Williston" and the meaning this held. It was a milestone in a student's life, a symbol of her/his growing up, nearing adulthood (p. 9). Cornelia Campbell also says: "Well, we lived about two blocks from the school and we always walked…they'd say, 'Oh Miss Inell is up.' She'd have the porch light on waiting for us" (p. 7). Their characterization of the walk to and from school illustrates its ritualized nature. It was more than just a walk to school. It was a pivotal point in one's life journey to finally get to Williston Senior High. And this point symbolized a collective transition, one supported by the elders in the community, who kept the porch light on while watching the students as they walked.

The sense of community fostered by the walk also supported students' transition to senior high school. Carl Byrd described how the community came to be, how kinship networks were established along the walk:

> You had your friends that you picked up along the way in walking back home. They dropped off along the way. It could be two, three, four of us, whatever and we share that honey bun and water or soda, whatever we were able to get. It was the friendships, and I'll say lifelong friendships that were established in that walk (p. 6).

It was a community that kept students' safe, yet also pushed them to take risks and to excel. Linda Pearce described this community as a "cocoon" (p. 5) that prepared her to face the discriminatory real world. But, it was also a network that would extend beyond high school and would continue to sustain students as they took risks, embarked on new professional adventures, and, ultimately, used what they had learned at Williston.

The community came to represent a more extended network that would take students beyond their neighborhoods and into a much wider professional community. It was a network grounded in the relationships established along the walk to Williston, such that Byrd said: "When you left Wilmington, be it military and college, I can speak to that, if you were from home, home in Wilmington, you know, everything was immediately ok" (p. 6). Being grounded in home thus made it possible for one to leave, to explore, and to work in the world, whether that world was segregated or desegregated.

Finally, alumni talked about the rituals associated with becoming a senior, graduating, and returning home. They spoke of special privileges that seniors were allowed, the importance of homecoming celebrations and class reunions, and of returning after venturing out to explore the world. Beatrice Sharpless Moore recalled:

> One thing I remember especially—when you were seniors, you could use the front steps. You could come to school and use the front steps. During lunchtime, you could sit with your friends, that was really a treat, you had arrived when you can go up the front steps. (p. 4)

Herman Johnson, Eva Mae Smith, and Lela Pierce also talked about becoming seniors and being able to go through the front door and being able to sit on the front steps. As they described the privilege of being able to enter through the front door, they also remarked that after their time the front door was closed and a new entrance created. In the context of the conversation, sitting on the steps and entering through the front door was more than a privilege. It was a rite of passage from childhood to adulthood, one that was given its place and time in the high school process. It represented a growing sense of independence and responsibility and, in that space on the steps, allowed for conversations to support this transition. Seniors could share their hopes, dreams, and fears on the steps—still within the cocoon that Linda Pearce described, but in preparation to take flight.

Graduation then served as the beginning of a final transition from home to world and back again. Edna Ray captured it best when she said: "As most of us did during that time, for opportunities, we left home right after high school and I'm real excited right now because I just now the past couple of years returned to home after living away for 40 years." Of the 21 alumni interviewed, 15 left home at some point soon after graduation. They left to attend college, to work, or to marry. Though no one cast those who remained in Wilmington as inferior, there was a clear sense from the narratives that leaving was a common expectation and, in some ways, necessary, especially given the economic and political contexts of the South. They left to find more promising work, to travel, and to experience the world. Beatrice Sharpless Moore explained:

> Somewhere along the way, we lose a lot of good people and I think Wilmington is an example. I know a lot of southern cities who have lost good minds because the opportunity at that time was not there. If the opportunities had been here, I always wanted to take typing. They didn't offer typing at Williston, but at New Hanover High School they offered typing and everything…so I think the South has lost a lot of good talent. (p. 5)

Though Ms. Moore did not return to live in Wilmington, she did discuss ways that she maintains a connection to her fellow Willstonians through alumni celebrations. Maintaining this connection, even when individuals did not physically return home, came through as a central component of their narratives.

These transitions to Williston, in graduation, and in the return to home, came to represent a life-learning cycle that allowed students to identify with Williston. The rituals fostered collective identity; they helped students develop as independent individuals in community. And though alumni talked about the physical space of the front steps, these steps also metaphorically symbolized progress, entrance into a world of opportunity and challenge. What one learned at Williston made this transition conceivable, expected, and possible.

The School as an Institution: Enduring Values and Dispositions

As alumni repeatedly referred to Williston as "the greatest school under the sun," it became clear that they remembered Williston as more than a building. It was more than a neutral physical space with little influence on the interactions that took place in its halls and classrooms. The building fostered solidarity-building, such that the community defined its challenges, advocated for its needs, and operated with a collective voice. Given its place as a segregated school with teachers who expected their students to push boundaries, this solidarity-building represented more than what it might have meant at an all-White high school. Because it was a space that nurtured relationships, self-sufficiency, and academic risk-taking, its physical structure contributed to its intangible definitions. Ethel Gerald perhaps best captured this connection between physical space and community when she said, "Yes, and they had this feeling that they belonged to Williston and Williston belonged to me" (p. 15). Kathryn Ennett said, "I loved going to school" and David Nixon added, "I look back and all of it started with the foundation that I got out of Williston" (p. 12). The building generated a sense of belonging, a connection that inspired students to want to learn, and, in retrospect, served as a physical repository of that inspiration.

The closing of the school in 1968 was clearly a painful memory for the alumni interviewed. In looking back, all of them expressed frustration at the way it was closed, and with the lack of communication from the district and school board. They wondered why it could not have been desegregated as well. Carl Byrd connected the closing of the building to the challenges facing African American students in desegregated schools (to which they were bused):

> Again, I feel that the generations to follow us, had they been able to walk some of those halls, be taught by some of those teachers in that setting that their parents, aunts, uncles, grandparents, maybe again that type of feeling of extended family could have motivated more of them to have the desire for education. (p. 5)

The building space thus served as a place of intergenerational support, a place brought to life by the teachers who taught students how to act in that space (and beyond). He added that he would remember Mrs. Hankins and "flash back to those days when she was standing in the halls with her arms folded and would just give you that look, you know, 'Boy you better get to your room or where you're supposed to be'" (p. 3). Although the alumni talked about the tangible reality as the authoritative approach teachers used at the school, they framed this approach within a larger context of preparing them to take risks in an integrated society, to overcome discriminatory attitudes and practices, to be able to support themselves (emotionally and financially), and to return to give back to the community.

Finally, the language used by the alumni characterized Williston as an institution, a term that denotes its legacy, even after the school closed. As an institution, its memory lives on, the effects of teaching and learning remain, and its loss has become part of the permanent narrative. James MacRae called it a "noble institution," one that Linda Pearce described as "like a member of the family" (p. 4), a building that Georgia Bowden said brought some comfort (p. 19). Without the space, alumni find it difficult to remember and this remembering is important to them. Herman Johnson said:

> For those of us who graduated from the school it's like we don't have nothing to connect with now, yeah. Now it's a junior high school and the homes are still there but many of the memories are not like they used to be because they've done a lot of things to convert it into…. (p. 20)

The loss of the physical building as a high school became an issue of control, support, and collective memory. In that closure, the community lost a space of solidarity-building through education, a space of learning used as activism. Teachers taught students middle-class norms, behaviors, and dispositions such that students would have access to middle-class society and, in consequence, access to positions of leadership. Lethia Hankins elaborated, "So you went there with the sense of wanting to achieve. For some reason, that just radiated all over the build ing…that's all we heard from our teachers from day one" (p. 3). She added her perspective as a teacher at Williston: "I believed in oral expression. I still do. I'll let you say it your way for a while, but after a while, you're going to say it my way" (p. 7). In this way, the space of Williston became a space of resistance and transcendence—resistance to the oppressive structures that shaped segregated society and transcendence of those structures through academic achievement by learning the norms and behaviors of those in power.

To Virgo or Not to Virgo: Defining a Neighborhood School for African Americans at D.C. Virgo Preparatory Academy

In the newspaper articles analyzed for this study, the language framing D.C. Virgo as a neighborhood school generally represented two distinct perspectives. Virgo was a beloved space that linked communities to the school (and to the history that shaped both) in remarkable ways. But, it also carried a stigmatized identity (Goffman, 1963), solidified by the school's low test scores and dwindling student population. Some community members expressed serious concerns about the school's ability to transcend that stigma, to move beyond its identity as an inferior learning space. The stigmatizing language used to characterize the school personified the school and, in so doing, illustrated ways that the it would have to engage in stigma management techniques—concealing, disclosing, or rejecting the stigma. Some doubted that fresh paint, new teachers, and a redesigned curriculum would be enough to erase decades of negative public discourse about the school. This dual identity of Virgo, as beloved and stigmatized, captures current debates about the possibilities and drawbacks of neighborhood schools. In many ways they connect communities; yet in others, they represent how inequitable public schooling can be.

The Neighborhood School as Beloved

Like Williston, Virgo was described in the familial, with a clear expectation that the building represented far more than space; it was a space that engendered emotional connections.

In this way, it was a familiar and familial place, connected to and by the families who live in the surrounding neighborhoods. In the documents I analyzed for this study, it was personi- fied as a family member, with human characteristics and expectations. The school maintained memories and nurtured hope. In a May 29, 2011, article in the *Star News*, reporter Amanda Greene noted that, just prior to closing, the school's office contained a sign that read "D.C. Virgo: Serving the community for 47 years. Good luck!" In this sense, Virgo acted as a servant, beholden to its community, with a responsibility to fulfill the expectations of that community. Yet, it was also, as someone stated in a September 26, 2011, article in the *Star News*, a school that needed reviving. In the August 26, 2012, edition of the *Star News*, just after the re- opening, a headline read, "Resuscitated Virgo Middle School ready to open its doors." Revival and resuscitation connote a calling forth of life, a demand that someone or something come back to serve a purpose. Metaphorically, the article captured the belief in Virgo as central to the community, a life-force that held deep possibility for the students and families it served.

When describing Virgo, community members identified the ways the school fostered love, encouraged students to dream, and operated with an extended kinship network. The school existed as the soul of the community, a place in which the community placed its trust. Despite the criticism leveled at the school, it was a place that served a downtown Black community. When considering the possible closing of Virgo, Karen Beatty, in a letter to the editor pub- lished in the February 24, 2011, edition of the *Wilmington Journal*, stated:

> Once again, a fix or solution to a problem comes at the expense of the Black community. The decision to "fix" the budget deficit within New Hanover Count Schools is slated to fall on backs of the Black com- munity. The recent decision to close D.C. Virgo Middle School is not good for the Black community. I believe it will have a long-term negative effect on the City, is a travesty, and has a subsequent effect of eradicating the history of Blacks in Wilmington. (p. 4A)

For Beatty and others, the decision to close Virgo illustrates the deep distrust between the White and Black communities in Wilmington. It is a distrust stemming from citizens' learned experiences with the closure of Williston High School. In describing the closure as a purpose- ful eradication, she implies that the school board seeks to devalue the Black community in Wilmington. In another *Wilmington Journal* article, dated September 29–October 5, 2011, District Attorney Ben David says, "a school of such historical significance can't close, at least not permanently….this is a defining moment for the City and County. What we do tonight will shape our history" (p. 1). In presenting the decision to close or keep open Virgo as a de- fining moment, David suggests that this moment will emerge as yet another one in the city's troubled history with race relations.

The School as an Identifying Space
The texts also presented Virgo as a space of active identity work. This identity work represented a public performance of identity that came with the repetition of specific acts and rituals. Stu- dents were expected to perform and to compete. In this performing and competing, they did more than demonstrate academic competence; they expressed a confidence in themselves—one that families hoped would translate into their work in high school. The quotes from the docu- ments referenced making a difference, understanding their culture and speaking their language, promoting and serving the community, and "I can do this, I can try." Despite these perceptions of families, the school was still characterized in the texts as a failing school (based primarily on

low test scores). Even so, reporter Amanda Greene noted in a February 16, 2011, article in the *Star News* that "some call it [Virgo] downtown's best kept secret" (and, notably, "the home of Michael Jordan's first slam dunk"). Greene later quoted Avone Treadwell, a former student at Virgo, who said, "Being here provided me with an identity before high school." As downtown's best kept secret, the home of Michael Jordan's first slam dunk, and a provider of identity, the discourse of Virgo subtly switched to Virgo as place, Virgo as center, Virgo as home.

This representation of Virgo as place, center, and home came through in 27 codes that emphasized the importance of space and/or movement. They characterized Virgo as space replete with memories—a space capable of nurturing excellence, and a space that brought the community to the school and vice versa. In a February 23, 2011, editorial from the *Star News*, the editor comments, "Virgo, in the Brooklyn community on Wilmington's Northside, is one of the county's few true 'neighborhood' schools that the district is so fond of promoting." The editor goes on to say, "To the superintendent and the school board, the impending decision may be about money and efficiency, but to a neighborhood, it is about identity." Called a disenfranchised, "downtrodden" community in one article, other articles referred to Virgo as a space of promise. In a May 29, 2011, *Star News* article, reporter Amanda Greene quoted Lee Bellamy, the custodian who maintained Virgo: "What is lost with the closing of Virgo's building is a sense of family…when I work and clean up, these kids talk to me, and I can mentor them." He suggested that Virgo was a parental space, one that demanded a tending to, and looking out for, of the young people who attended the school.

Certainly, Virgo was not characterized in the documents as an entirely perfect space. In several documents, it was described as a "pit,"—beyond revival or resuscitation, a space that could never be converted into a positive for learning. It was a school in which poor kids of color would be trapped, unable to escape, and prone to acts of violence. In a February 3, 2010, *Star News* article, Williston Middle School principal Mary Paul Beal said, "Our kids are good, but they're also kids—they're going to do messy things." In her response, she tried to debunk the characterization of poor kids of color as inherently violent. Noble Middle School principal Wade Smith added, "Crime can happen anywhere…anything's possible anywhere…you can try to control everything you can control and have eyes and ears in as many places as you possibly can." To challenge the presumption that a neighborhood school in a predominantly African American community would inevitably promote and/or harbor violent criminals, district personnel stressed the safety measures they would take at each school, including a requirement that all school visitors check in at the school office and wear a visitor's badge. Despite these efforts, the *Star News* reported in February 3, 2010 that, despite being the smallest of the middle schools, Virgo had 30% of the "reports of insubordination and inappropriate language and/or disrespect in the district middle schools." Some opponents of re-opening Virgo used these statistics in their argument, while others claimed that "a school full of poor students starts from a place of inequality" (Greene, *Star News*, February 22, 2010).

Ultimately, Virgo was debated either as a beloved member of the community or as a pit from which there was no possibility of escape. It was a debate grounded in the historical trauma of the 1898 race riots and, more recently, the closing of Williston Senior High School. It was a debate about teaching and learning, space, and loss. And, perhaps more important, it extended the narrative of race relations in New Hanover County. Together, the memories of Williston and the public debates about Virgo inform our understanding of neighborhood school as having distinctly different relevance for African American (or other historically oppressed) communities. Such schools are not just about community control. They are also about resisting discrimination and overcoming oppression through education—with teachers who love and are loved, in spaces that radiate an expectation of excellence.

Conclusion

The closure of Williston Senior High School and the movement to re-open D.C. Virgo as a neighborhood school shed light on how such schools might be the soul of a community. As that soul, they inspire wonder, awe, and imagination (Steinberg, 2010), such that the school becomes a focal point for academic, political, and social literacy. The school can thus write a counter-narrative, one that defies white privilege and excavates a space for anti-oppressive education (Kumashiro, 2009). At best, Virgo stands as a soul of circumstance. It is the only middle school in the Youth Enrichment Zone. [6]

But if a school can represent the soul of a community, it would thus serve as a space that would move us to educate in ways that allow us to bear witness (Dillard, Abdur-Rashid, & Tyson, 2000), unravel oppressive structures, and inspire transformative interactions. It would be a space of intimate connection to personal suffering, collective memory, and political possibility. It would be a sanctuary (Antrop-González, 2006)—a protected and cherished learning space, a place of solidarity-building (Waites, 2009), a place of intergenerational support, a place of flight (Scott, 2006), a place to innovate, take ethical risks, and a place to learn independence. Yet, in many ways, the question remains: Should Williston have closed and should Virgo have been re-opened? If we have learned any lessons from the past, we should understand what can make a neighborhood school great—teachers who expect excellence, rituals to support that excellence, and extended kinship networks between the school and the community. How we translate these lessons into current contexts is a continuing debate—one that requires an acknowledgment of the injustices that persist in education.

Notes

1. This number has been reported as 25 but is speculated to be much higher. http://www.learnnc.org/lp/editions/nchist-newsouth/4360
2. Virgo Preparatory Academy was formerly named D.C. Virgo Middle School. All prior school report cards use the D.C. Virgo Middle School name.
3. These interviews were obtained from the Digital Archives collection at the University of North Carolina Wilmington, located at http://randall3.uncw.edu/ascod/?p=collections/findingaid&id=251&q=&rootcontentid=176#id176, Series 2, Southeast North Carolina, sub-series 2. Due to page limitations I could not include a summary table of the interviews.
4. The *Star News* articles were from April 30, 2007, through September 12, 2012. The *Wilmington Journal* articles spanned February 24, 2011, to March 29, 2012. Due to page limitations, I could not include a summary table of the articles used.
5. Stack (1994) describes these as other adults who acted as parental figures for young people in African American communities.
6. The Youth Enrichment Zone in Wilmington, NC is modeled after the Harlem Children's Zone in New York. For more information on the YEZ, visit http://www.brcyez.org/

References

Anderson, K. (2010). *Little Rock: Race and resistance at Central High School*. Princeton, NJ: Princeton University Press.

Antrop-González, R. (2006). Toward the school as sanctuary concept in multicultural education: Implications for small high school reform. *Curriculum Inquiry, 36*(3), 273–301.

Anyon, J. (2005). *Radical possibilities: Public policy, urban education, and a new social movement.* New York: Routledge.

Baker, R. S. (2006). *Paradoxes of desegregation: African American struggles for educational equity in Charleston, South Carolina, 1926–1972.* Columbia: University of South Carolina Press.

Bell, D. (Ed.) (1980). *Shades of Brown: New perspectives on school desegregation.* New York: Teachers College Press.

Berkes, A. (2009). A Bill for the more general diffusion of knowledge. Retrieved from http://www.monticello.org/site/research-and-collections/bill-more-general-diffusion-knowledge

Boustan, L. P. (2010). Was post-war suburbanization "White flight" evidence from the Black migration? *The Quarterly Journal of Economics, 125*(1), 417–443.

Carter, R. L. (1980). A reassessment of Brown. In D. Bell (Ed.), *Shades of Brown: New perspectives on school desegregation* (pp. 20–29). New York: Teachers College Press.

Cecelski, D. (1994). *Along Freedom Road: Hyde County, North Carolina and the fate of Black schools in the South.* Chapel Hill: University of Chapel Hill Press.

Cooper, A. (1988). *A voice from the south.* New York: Oxford University Press. (Original work published 1892)

Cremin, L. (1980). *American education: The national experience.* New York: Harper & Row.

Darling-Hammond, L. (2010). *The flat world and education: How America's commitment to equity will determine our future.* New York: Teachers College Press.

De los Reyes, E., & Gozemba, P. A. (2002). *Pockets of hope: How students and teachers change the world.* Westport, CT.: Bergin and Garvey.

Delpit, L. (2012). *Multiplication is for White people: Raising expectations for other people's children.* New York: The New Press.

Dillard, C., Abdur-Rashid, D., & Tyson, C. (2000). My soul is a witness: Affirming pedagogies of the spirit. *International Journal of Qualitative Studies in Education, 13*(5), 447–462.

Du Bois, W. E. B. (1903). *The souls of black folk.* In E. J. Sundquist (Ed.), *The Oxford W. E. B. Dubois Du Bois reader* (pp. 97–240). Oxford: Oxford University Press.

Du Bois, W. E. B. (1935). Does the Negro need separate schools? *The Journal of Negro Education, 4,* 328–335.

Edelberg, J., & Kurland, S. (2009). *How to walk to school: Blueprint for a neighborhood school renaissance.* Lanham, MD: Rowman & Littlefield Education.

Goffman, E. (1963). *Stigma: Notes on the management of spoiled identity.* New York: J. Aronson.

Hughes, S. A. (2006). *Black hands in the biscuits not in the classrooms: Unveiling hope in a struggle for Brown's promise.* New York: Peter Lang.

Jackson , C. (2007). The Brown decision in retrospect: Commemoration or Celebration. *The Western Journal of Black Studies, 31*(2), 28–33.

Kahn, A. J. (1972). The schools: Social change and social welfare. In R. Sarri & F. F. Maple (Eds.). *The school in the community* (pp. 44–51). Washington, DC: National Association of Social Workers.

Kelly, H. (2010). *Race, remembering, and Jim Crow's teachers.* New York: Routledge.

Krippendorf, K. (2004). *Content analysis: An introduction to its methodology* (2nd edition). Beverly Hills, CA: Sage.

Kumashiro, K. (2009). *Against common sense: Teaching and learning towards social justice (Reconstructing the public sphere in curriculum studies).* New York: Routledge.

Larke, P. J., Larke, A. Jr., & Castle, E. M. (2007). The Brown decision and its impact on African Americans: Examining teacher education, the sociology of education, and agricultural education. In M. C. Brown II (Ed.), *Still not equal: Expanding educational opportunity in society* (pp. 103–110). New York: Peter Lang.

Litwak, E., & Meyer, H. J. (1974). *School, family, and neighborhood: The theory and practice of school-community relations.* New York: Columbia University Press.

Mann, H. (1848). *Twelfth annual report of the secretary of the board of education for Massachusetts.* Retrieved from https://learn.usf.edu/bbcswebdav/users/ljohnso2/3604/Readings/Mann%252012th.htm

Nixon, R. M. (1972). Education and busing: Neighborhood schools. *Vital Speeches of the Day, 38*(12), 354–355.

Norrell, R. J. (2011). *Up from history: The Life of Booker T. Washington.* Cambridge, MA: Harvard University Press.

Peterson, B. (1998). Neighborhood schools, busing, and the struggle for equality. *Rethinking Schools 12*(3). Retrieved from http://www.rethinkingschools.org/archive/12_03/bus123.shtml

Purpel, D. (1999). The politics of character education. In D. Purpel (Ed.) *Moral outrage in education*, (83–87). New York: Peter Lang.

Sarri, R. C. (1972). Education in transition. In R. Sarri & F. F. Maple (Eds.). *The school in the community* (pp. 15–29). Washington, DC: National Association of Social Workers.

Scott, D. G. (2006). Wrestling with the spirit(ual): Grappling with theory, practice, and pedagogy. *International Journal of Children's Spirituality, 11*(1), 87–97. doi:10.1080/13644360500503431

Siddle-Walker, V. (1996). *Their highest potential: An African American school community in the segregated south*. Chapel Hill: University of North Carolina Press.

Smrekar, C. (2009). Public housing reform and neighborhood schools: How local contexts must matter. *Yearbook of the National Society for the Study of Education, 108*(1), 41–62.

Spring, J. (2009). *Deculturalization and the struggle for equality: A brief history of dominated cultures in the U.S.* (6th ed.). New York: McGrawHill.

Spring, J. (2011). *American education* (15th ed.). New York: McGraw-Hill.

Stack, C. (1994). *Call to home: African Americans reclaim the rural south*. New York: Basic Books.

Steelman, B. (2010). What is the history of Williston high school? Retrieved from http://www.myreporter.com/?p=6513

Steinberg, S. (2010). The philosophical soul: Where did it come from? Where did it go? In Kincheloe, J. & Hewitt, R. (Eds.). *Regenerating the philosophy of education: What happened to soul?* (pp. 3-10). New York: Peter Lang.

Waites, C. (2009). Building on strengths: Intergenerational practices with African American families. *Social Work, 54*(3), 278–287.

Washington, B. T. (1900). *Up from slavery*. Retrieved from; http://docsouth.unc.edu/fpn/washington/washing.html

Wegmann, R. G. (1975). Neighborhoods and schools in racial transition. *Growth & Change, 6*(3), 4–8.

Wilmington Race Riot Commission. (2006). *1898 Wilmington race riot report*. Retrieved from http://www.history.ncdcr.gov/1898-wrrc/default.htm

CHAPTER TWELVE

Obama and Antiracist Education

Lessons for Teachers

TIAN YU

Since Barack Obama was elected as America's first racial-minority president in 2008, an important question has remained: What does his election mean for antiracist education? On a practical level, and as indicated in the nation's numerous classrooms, it seems that such a question has been addressed only on the surface. We have witnessed the celebration of the historical significance of that election and its positive impact on children. However, the complexity of the Obama effect has been simplified and the real influence of his elections on antiracist education largely remains unexamined. As the Obama presidency continues in the initial years of his second term, we are now in a better position to raise and ponder the following questions: What have we missed in the celebration of the Obama victories? How can we make sense of the rising post-racialism resulting from the elections? What role has Obama himself played in the national conversation on race? And what actions should we take as antiracist educators to continue our collective struggle for social justice and equity? In this chapter I will attempt to explore these questions.

"A Radical Thing": The Symbolic Importance of Obama's Election

Millions of Americans welcomed the election of Barack Obama as America's 44th president in 2008 with exuberance and jubilation. One reason was certainly enough for such celebration: Obama is the first-ever racial minority president of the United States. As the President himself remarked shortly after the election: "There is an entire generation that will grow up taking for granted that the highest office in the land is filled by an African American.… I mean, that's a radical thing. It changes how black children look at themselves. It also changes how white children look at black children. And I wouldn't underestimate the force of that" (in Burkholder, 2009). Though decidedly less enthusiastic than him about the "changes" he envisioned—I will argue why throughout this chapter—I do not want to downplay, or underestimate, the positive impact of Obama's election, especially on minority children.

Its positive impact is largely symbolic; but that effect *is* significant educationally. It seems hard to reject Obama's victory as conspicuous evidence that America really is a place where anyone with talent and drive can succeed. Minority kids themselves voiced this uplifting message everywhere in the aftermath of the election. In the *Harvard Educational Review*'s 2009 special issue on "Education and the Obama Presidency," we heard upbeat testimonies from a great number of children, among whom many are black and Latino. A 2nd-grade black boy in New Jersey said: "Barack Obama being the first black president gives me hope that I can be the president of the United States or anything else I want to be" (Johnson, 2009, p. 179). Another 8th grader wrote: "Mr. President, you have inspired me to work harder to reach my goal of becoming the first Hispanic woman president" (Silvas, 2009, p. 195). Another 9th grader in Houston, Texas, told us: "Obama has instilled hope in me. I feel like I am a Nigerian American who can do anything and be anything from a fashion designer to a doctor" (Subulade, 2009, p. 197).

Make no mistake: hearing minority children's words about the hope that Obama inspired is heartening. I am in agreement with Wayne Au (2009), who fully acknowledges the positive impact of Obama's election on the self-esteem of youth of color in America and the potential gains in our children's sense of possibility. Yet, we should not simply survey this rosy image of hope without also attending to the other side of the story. If we listen to children and youth more carefully, a truer view of our current situation comes into focus. According to Justin Ewers (2009) of the *U.S. News and World Report*, among young black voters, there is a growing sense that, on matters of race, the country has taken two steps forward but may be poised to take a step back. Ewers cites Cathy Cohen, a professor of political science at the University of Chicago, who spent the first few months of the Obama administration talking to focus groups of African Americans under 35 about their conflicted reactions to the new president. After the election, three times as many young blacks as whites said they thought the election could bring about real change. But as time has passed, day-to-day life has begun to cloud that enthusiasm. "If you ask them, 'How do you feel about Obama?' they're effusive, very proud," says Cohen. "But you ask them if they think Obama's election will impact their interactions with the police, and to a person, they say, 'Absolutely not.' They understand it doesn't trickle down to their lives" (in Ewers, 2009).

"It doesn't trickle down to their lives." A similar observation is offered by renowned African American scholar Cornel West, who said: "Obama's victory shatters the glass ceiling at the top but folks are still in the basement" (in Adams, 2010). These messages don't sound uplifting, but we must attend to them. Indeed, it is important to do a reality check amidst all the self-congratulatory rhetoric following the elections. At a time when we are increasingly trapped in a cultural and political discourse that glorifies anti-intellectual "common sense," denigrates reasoning and self-critique, and equates public debates with partisan ideological bickering, a more sober look is needed. The reality about race in America is hidden in plain view as the symbolic importance of Obama continues to be hyped, especially in the rhetoric of a "post-racial" society.

"Post-Racial" Society and White Denial of Racism

The election of Barack Obama as the nation's first racial-minority president signaled, for many, the end of an era. Charges of racism, even talks of race in general, suddenly reached a new level of unpopularity. In fact, many white Americans were ready to declare the struggle against racism over and discussion on race no longer important. On election eve in 2008, former New York City mayor Rudy Giuliani, a prominent figure on America's political scene, noted: "We've achieved history tonight and we've moved beyond…the whole idea of race and racial separation and unfairness" ("Decision 2008," 2008). The day after Obama's victory, a *Wall Street Journal* editorial ("President-elect Obama," 2008) commented: "One promise of his victory is that perhaps we put to rest the myth of racism as a barrier to achievement in this splendid country." In another *Washington Post* article, columnist Richard Cohen (2008) said: "It is not just that he [Obama] is post-racial; so is the nation he is generationally primed to lead.… We have overcome" (p. A17). Lydia Lum (2009) summarizes the claim of "post-racialism" in this way:

> With Barack Obama ensconced as the nation's first black president, plenty of voices in the national conversation are trumpeting America as a post-racial society—that race matters much less than it used to, that the boundaries of race have been overcome, that racism is no longer a big problem. "It's smack down to think America is still all about racism," says Dr. John McWhorter, a senior fellow at The Manhattan Institute, a prominent Republican think tank. "Racism is not Black people's main problem anymore. To say that is like saying the earth is flat." (in Lum, 2009)

Antiracist educator Tim Wise (2009) equates the above conclusion—that the accomplishment of one person of color signifies a complete victory over racism—as sheer lunacy. As he points out, what white America has apparently missed, despite all the Black History Month celebrations, is that there have always been individually successful persons of color and that the triumph of individuals of color cannot, in itself, serve as proof of widespread systemic change (see p. 29). The post-racialism claim is more a mirage rather than a seal of merit because far too many significant disparities remain between whites and minorities in educational attainment, income and net worth, career advancement and health care outcomes; and these disparities are inextricably linked to white racism, both individual and institutionalized (Tatum, 2003; Wise, 2009, 2010). As Cornel West (2013) recently pointed out:

> Certainly the election of Barack Obama means that we are less racist than we were 30 years ago when it comes to electoral politics; there is no doubt about that. But unfortunately, sadly the legacy of white supremacy is still quite vicious; it is still very overt at times. It's overt in terms of stop and frisk policy. It's overt in the differential treatment of black and brown poor people in regard to the war on drugs. So that you end up with two very contradictory realities: less racist in terms of electoral politics but deeply racist in terms of practices and policies as it relates especially to people of color who are poor. (in Botz, 2013)

Post-racialism is clearly a goal not yet reached. The President himself must know better than anyone else whether America has truly overcome racial barriers. Racist opposition never ceased to greet him during his campaign and right into his presidency. Fueled by widespread and deeply entrenched white anxiety and resentment over a black man occupying the highest office in the nation, racially charged attacks on the President during his first term were overt and rampant. Recall those ugly Tea Party protests and Donald Trump's "birther" investigation? Remember the outrageous cry of "Take our country back [to a white, Protestant, and straight America]!"? A black man's liberal-leaning presidency has provided white racism a perfect opportunity to flourish.

In addition to the disingenuousness and untruth of its claim, what else does post-racialism hide? Let's make this point as clear as possible: The outrageous claim of the death of racism due to one black man's election as president reflects the historically entrenched white denial of racism and institutionalized racial inequities. *Wall Street Journal's* charge of racism as myth certainly reflects public opinion. A summer 2008 Gallup/*USA Today* poll indicates that a) 77 percent of whites say that blacks have just as good a chance as whites to get any job for which they are qualified; b) 80 percent of whites say blacks have just as good a chance as whites to get a good education; and c) 85 percent of whites claim blacks have just as good a chance to get any housing they can afford (Page & Risser, 2008). According to another survey conducted around the same time by CNN and *Essence* magazine, only 11 percent of whites believe racial discrimination against blacks in this country is still a very serious problem at all (CNN/*Essence*, 2008).

This present-day white denial of racism is just a continuation of an historical pattern. Similar white attitudes were documented in surveys conducted in the 1960s, 1930s, and 1890s (see Wise, 2009, pp. 31–34). It is pretty clear that "at no point in American history have whites, by and large, believed that folks of color were getting a raw deal" (Wise, 2009, p. 34). It is not surprising that we continue to experience white rejection of racism as whining, as "playing the race card." Such rejection is well reflected in my classes in teacher education, indicated by such comments from my white students as "Haven't we heard enough [about racism and minority struggles]?" "We will never move forward unless we stop these race talks"; and "We already have a black president. If he could make it, everyone can!"

Conservative Backlash and the Retreat from Racial Equity: Obama's Complicity

Obama's election and the resulting emergence of post-racialism have given a green light to a troublesome conservative backlash. As Justin Ewers (2009) observes, it is conservatives, not civil rights groups, who are seizing the political moment of Obama election, using the promise of "post-racialism" to launch an all-around attack on racial equity. They especially try to scale back protections for minorities in the legal system. There has been a growing chorus on the right demanding the repeal of everything from affirmative action to the Voting Rights Act (Ewers, 2009). They, once again, call for a color-blind government and believe Obama's victory helps their case. If America can elect a black president, so goes their logic, then racism must be less of an obstacle to black progress than previously thought. The time for racial preferences, they argue, must surely be past. A number of states, such as Nebraska, have passed legislation to ban so-called "official discrimination" in favor of "under-represented" minorities in hiring, contracting, and public education. And now the U.S. Supreme Court is taking on the issue, and the prospect is dim for people fighting for racial justice. Obama's re-election in 2012 has certainly not reversed this conservative trend.

Unfortunately, Obama himself, as candidate and president, has done little so far to curb such conservative backlash; instead, he has done much to assist the retreat from racial equity. An early sign of his racial views is found in his two best-selling books, *Dreams from My Father* and *The Audacity of Hope*. Especially in the latter, Obama evinced a clear desire to downplay racism as an issue by repeatedly reminding readers that things were getting better, that black folks were often their own worst enemies, and that we were really all in the same boat (Wise,

2010, p. 37). During his campaign and right into his first term in office, his general approach to race was either total avoidance of it or speaking of "a rhetoric of racial transcendence" (Wise, 2010).

As a candidate, Obama consciously and carefully catered to the white public's desire not to talk about race. This was true during both his original and re-election campaigns. When he had to talk about it, he chose to gloss over the historical and ongoing racial inequities and instead over-emphasized progress America had made on racial fronts. This is best demonstrated in his forced response to white America's collective denouncement of inflammatory remarks made by his former pastor, Jeremiah Wright—especially in his widely praised (predominantly by whites) March 18, 2008, race speech in Philadelphia. To be fair, it might have been the most thoughtful and significant speech on the subject by any American president; and it indeed involved some bold and sensitive acknowledgment of complexity and nuance surrounding race matters. However, what really stands out in the speech is his curious treatment of some critical issues. For example, Obama talked about how the historic legacy of racism had shaped the contours of racial inequity and had fed the black anger expressed by Wright. "By speaking in terms of past injuries and the lingering grievances generated by the same, Obama deftly managed to speak about racism without forcing white folks to confront just how real and how present-day the problem is" (Wise, 2009, p. 36).

Not only did he discuss racism and black suffering in the past tense (so as to relieve present-day whites of any responsibilities for racial justice); he also balanced out his commentary on the understandable nature of black anger with some talk on "a similar anger [that] exists within segments of the white community." Suggesting that there is equivalent historical justification between black and white anger, Obama "fudged the difference between institutional racism and white bitterness" (Mansbach, in Wise, 2010, p. 50).

> In doing so, Obama managed to obscure the nature of structural injustice and to place black and white anger on the level playing field of mere "feelings," perhaps legitimate, perhaps not, but always merely personal, and never indicative of a deeply ingrained system of oppression deployed against some and in favor of others. (Wise, 2010, pp. 50–51)

In emphasizing possible solutions to the nation's racial divide (in income, housing, health care, education, and so on), Obama echoes a classic post-racial liberal stance that denigrates structural reform and glorifies personal responsibility. He promotes a narrative of color-blind meritocracy—a narrative he knows is much preferred by white folks. Let's consider another example. On Father's Day, 2008, in a black church in Chicago, candidate Obama delivered some harsh criticism of black families, and especially black fathers. Embracing a long-established tradition of social thought that advances an analysis of a "culture of poverty" or a "culture of pathology," which characterizes black families as largely responsible for their own troubles, Obama urged his own people to seek self-salvation through strong values and hard work.

Obama has the right to promote values he personally adheres to; but in that particular circumstance, his criticism of blacks for lacking those values adds to the prevailing stereotypes about negligent black fathers—stereotypes that have little basis in reality. Research by Boston College scholar Rebekah Levine Coley has revealed a complex view of the causes of absenteeism among black fathers: Far from being irresponsible, it is the failure to live up to expectations to provide for their families (due to a severe lack of economic and educational opportunities) that drives poor black men into despair and away from their families. In addition, as shocking as it may be, Coley found that black fathers not living at home are actually more likely to keep in contact with their children than fathers of any other ethnic or racial group (in Dyson, 2008, p. 38).

Obama's rebuff of black fathers and his firm insistence on personal responsibility might have been calculated to win over socially conservative whites who were turned off by criticisms of persistent white racism, such as those voiced by Rev. Wright. His rebuke may have scored points politically for him; but it certainly did not and would not help solve the real problems plaguing the black community—such as high unemployment rates, racist mortgage practices, weakened childcare support, and lack of training programs for blue-collar workers, all of which require systemic and substantial investment and reform (Dyson, 2008, p. 38).

Throughout his first term as president, Obama's position on race did not change much. He made great efforts to build a race-neutral administration. Even some Republicans acknowledged his efforts. Bill McInturff, a Republican pollster, said, "I don't think you can find a guy who's done more to try to put this issue [of race] off the table" (in Walsh, 2011). And despite facing criticism for his weak stance on race issues near the end of his first term, the President still defended his position. In an interview with Kenneth Walsh in March 2011, he said: "Americans, since the victories of the civil rights movement, I think, have broadly come to accept the notion that everybody has to be treated equally; everybody has to be treated fairly. And I think that the whole debate about how do you make up for past history creates a complicated wrinkle in that principle of equality" (in Walsh, 2011).

Such a statement is problematic on multiple levels. As he did during his first campaign, Obama prefers to talk about race in the past tense, totally overlooking or ignoring ongoing, present-day racism and racial inequity. In addition, following the liberal tradition that falsely views everyone living under capitalism as "free and equal," he puts meritocracy and color-blindness upfront when he addresses race matters. In doing so, he promotes an ahistorical and apolitical understanding of "equality" and "fairness." Such "equality" and "fairness" narratives are indeed mundane; they are frequently echoed by white folks in the nation's classrooms and those on the political right who adamantly oppose race-conscious policies such as affirmative action.

Obama's position on race is clearly linked to his understanding of what kind of president he should be. He repeatedly makes clear that he is President of all Americans, not just of African Americans, and doesn't want to be thought of only as a black president. This again may be viewed as a political calculation because he knows that white voters heralded his election as a sign that long-standing racial gaps were closing; and they expected him to play a post-racial role, i.e., as the president for everyone—one who just happened to be black. Some might see Obama's adoption of this role as completely justified. Still, what is problematic is that he has used this position as an excuse for not advancing racial justice. He has failed to recognize and fully attempt to solve racial inequalities as president. The point is, any president, black or otherwise, has a responsibility to tackle racism and racial inequity and advance the cause of racial and social justice in America. Disappointingly, this president has been extremely inactive in that regard. The irony is that now we cannot openly talk about racism at the presidential level precisely because we have elected and re-elected a racial-minority president!

Both critics and supporters of the President agree that he has failed to adequately address the issue of poverty, especially poverty among the nation's minority populations. Cornel West graded Obama's first-year presidency as a C-. West said, "When it comes to policy, when it comes to priority, when it comes to focusing on poor people and working people—which has to do with the vast majority of black people—that he has really not come through in any substantial and significant way" (in Wells, 2010). Similarly, in 2011, Representative Maxine Waters chided the President for failing to craft policies that would explicitly target black unemployment and for otherwise neglecting to evince a proper acknowledgment of the baleful and disproportionate pain being experienced in black communities during the economic downturn (in Kennedy, 2011). And in the aftermath of Obama's re-election in November 2012, Toure (2012) noted: "Obama as president has failed to combat poverty and now we are in a world where 28% of black Americans are poor, compared to 10% of whites, over 13% of blacks are unemployed, and black household wealth is at its lowest point in decades."

When pressed by Walsh (2011) about whether he felt a special obligation or responsibility as the first African American president to advance racial justice and make up for some of the past disparities between blacks and whites, Obama did suggest his view of the issue was entangled with some "personal experiences." He admitted that he does feel strongly about it; however, he quickly turned to his usual rhetoric: "…if those populations don't feel fully assimilated into the culture, aren't performing at high levels educationally, are caught in cycles of poverty—that is not good for America's future." He may have correctly identified some of the key problems faced by African Americans, but he failed to go further with that identification. Lack of social and cultural integration, low education performance, poverty, and so on are not African Americans' personal life choices; rather, these are the consequences and burdens of larger structural failures that many individual blacks are forced to address on an everyday basis.

It is simply not sufficient for a president to merely recognize those problems, and it is utterly unacceptable for the President to identify those problems as individual deficiencies and blame the victims. It is ludicrous for Obama to continue to sing the lead in a chorus that blames poor black people for what the system does to them. As Carl Dix (2013) rightfully asks, how often has he faulted poverty and the miserable conditions faced by black children on absent black fathers without mentioning how the criminal "injustice" system targets black men disproportionately and warehouses hundreds of thousands of them in prison? And how could he repeatedly assault black parents for the high drop-out rates of their children while giving a pass to the education system that is geared to fail those children?

As in other cases, Obama's unyielding emphasis on meritocracy and personal salvation was once again made clear in the Walsh interview. Was that still out of a political calculation or a genuine and deeply held personal belief? Either way, it was truly problematic and troublesome.

And now, in early 2013, a re-election emboldened president seems confident, and we understandably expect him to advance a more progressive agenda, including taking a stronger stance on race issues. However, we need to remain cautious about what he is willing and able to do in his second term. There is no excuse this time around for us to be as delusional as we were after his first victory. It is especially doubtful that he will tackle racism in America head-on or take substantial actions to advance racial justice. His second inaugural address shed some light in this regard. Though both right and left generally viewed it as a powerfully liberal speech that touched on many important bases, it stopped short of a direct mention of race or racism. Without emphasizing racial justice, his general talk on civil rights is essentially empty. Eric Alterman (2013) of *The Nation*, despite being moved by "the poetry of inclusion" reflected in Obama's strong emphasis on the liberal social and cultural agendas, criticizes the speech's serious omission of economic inequality. As we know, poverty in America is racialized;

economic inequality is essentially racial inequality. Obama's unwillingness to confront that issue is disheartening.

Confronting the Dilemma: What Can Teachers Do?

We are facing a disturbing dilemma, politically and educationally, in light of Obama's election and re-election. Obama's political ascent may represent the rising power of minorities; however, it reflects much more the power of whiteness. Given the fact that systemic racial discrimination and profound inequity of opportunity continue to mark the lives of persons of color, his success certainly does not signify the death of white racism as a personal or institutional phenomenon. Rather, it may well signal the intensifying of a more subtle form of racism, "racism 2.0," as Tim Wise (2009) terms it, which "allows for and even celebrates the achievements of individual persons of color, but only because those individuals generally are seen as different from a less appealing, even pathological black or brown rule" (p. 9). From that perspective, we may conclude that 43% of whites voted for Obama in 2008 not because they genuinely accepted his blackness or looked beyond race altogether but because he successfully eased white fears and transcended his still-problematic blackness. Remember how regularly "transcending race" and "moving beyond race" from various political sides were used to describe Obama during the campaign? Those expressions basically implied that he is different from most black folks. He certainly looks not as black as most blacks; he speaks standard white English with even more eloquence than most whites; he holds degrees from the finest mostly white institutions; and, most importantly, he avoids discussing race and racism as often as whites. And when he has to discuss those issues, he takes a typically white view, seeing racism in historical terms and calling for personal responsibility to address the ongoing institutionalized racial problems. His presence and his ideas do not represent a threat to white America's way of life. He makes white America quite comfortable. Accordingly, white America has largely accepted him, on its own established terms.

Indeed, it was candidate Obama's general avoidance of race matters and his active use of racial transcendence rhetoric that twice made his victories possible. He eased white fear of a black president who would focus on racial injustice and reinforced the dominant white narrative of color blindness and meritocracy. However, his avoidance and racial transcendence rhetoric has made it more difficult than ever to address racial problems, even to fight back against the most blatant racist oppositions to his presidency. Recall, again, his timid reaction and inaction in response to Donald Trump's overly racially charged "birther" investigation? Indeed, Obama's appeal to post-racialism has been an unmitigated disaster. "By refusing to address the tidal wave of racist rhetoric engulfing the Republic, Obama has multiplied its power" (Bean, 2010). Furthermore, along with his pronouncement of racial transcendence, he has maintained a race-neutral policy agenda as president and has forsaken any direct, and much needed, focus on narrowing racial gaps in education, income, wealth, housing and health care. As educators, we know how the President has been slow to reform Bush's No Child Left Behind Act and instead quite swiftly created such policy mandates as Race to the Top that continue to promote a neoliberal, market-driven approach to education—one that denigrates the role of race and other critical social issues in teaching and learning. Unfortunately, such race-neutral policies have not fared well with his opponents either. "For all his heroic attempts to remain race-neutral, he is widely perceived as a radical agent of racial redistribution" (Bean, 2010).

Obama's positioning poses a serious challenge to classroom teachers. Remember those up-lifting messages voiced by the children he had inspired? While celebrating Obama as the first minority president who has personally overcome many racial barriers and given us hope and inspiration, we are likely retelling a time-honored classic American lie that everyone can make it in the "land of opportunity." We present Obama to our children as a role model; however, in doing so, we may also be irresponsibly promoting a message of color-blind meritocracy and downplaying racial justice and social change.

Obama represents a real conundrum to antiracist educators. Recognizing this conflicted reality and thinking about ways to deal with it is the first step we must take in our struggle for educational equity and social justice. I now offer several recommendations for concerned educators to consider in their practice. I do this without being overly positive or prescriptive, knowing that my ideas may simply be unworkable in complex, real, and specific situations and that there might well be other and better practical strategies:

1. Break the silence and openly, honestly, and regularly talk about race and racism with students. Contrary to what Obama has done, and against the conventional wisdom in our national discourse, educators must be provocative in addressing race issues. We don't have to wait until something happens and be forced to deal with it. We don't have to seek a "teachable moment." Lessons on race and racism should be integral parts of our regular curriculum and we must make them a felt reality. Antiracist education is an ongoing, everyday struggle; and that is the message we must share with students. We need to communicate with students as clearly as we can that race matters today as much as yesterday and that the fight against racism is far from over—even though we have elected and re-elected a black president. One way of doing this is to use real-life examples (they are indeed abundant) to illustrate the salience of race in contemporary America and how it continues to influence the lives of minorities and whites alike.

2. Examine the trajectory and evolution of racism in the age of Obama. The point is to show how racism functions today, often in new ways unseen before. We can certainly investigate how racism has played out prior to and after Obama's election. We won't miss seeing nasty and blatant racist assaults on Obama; and we will also have a chance to dig deeper, uncovering subtler forms of racism. As Tim Wise points out for us, the Obama victory doesn't signal the death or retreat of racism; rather it shows racism has taken on new faces. Amid the celebratory atmosphere surrounding Obama, this sober note is necessary to allow students an opportunity to think and reason.

3. Teach students about the nature, history, and current state of institutional racism. A common challenge in antiracist education is how to help students look beyond racism at personal levels and see racism as institutionalized and culturalized. We have to help students see the limitations of viewing racism as merely personal bias or prejudice. The message should be that racism may take personal or individualized forms, but it is not part of human nature; rather it has a history that serves particular political and economic functions. The best way to help students see and understand institutional and cultural racism is to present "hard data." The readily available statistics about racial disparities in America can serve to deconstruct the deeply entrenched myth of

"equal opportunity in a free land," a myth most of our students hold dear and one that Obama, thus far, has widely reinforced.

4.   Help students build a balanced and nuanced understanding of the complex dynamic of the individual and the social. We do not have to stop sending an uplifting message to children that they can reach for a star if they want to; but meanwhile we must teach young people about the reality that profound structural barriers, including institutional racism, still prevail in our society. Those real restraints work to prevent many aspiring individuals from achieving their personal dreams. We want to tell Obama-style success stories to motivate children to do their best; but we must also present numerous other unsuccessful, even tragic, stories (of equally dedicated and talented but less fortunate individuals) to make youth more cognizant of harsher realities. This is responsible teaching. It is multi-dimensional and dialectic.

5.   Finally and most importantly, we want to encourage students to continue our collective struggle for social change—a message Obama has certainly inspired, but a promise he has failed to deliver on in his first term. We must show young people that it is still a worthy and noble cause to fight against racism, personal or institutionalized, and to strive for a more just and equitable society. Obama's election is not the end of this story; it is only a beginning.

References

Adams, B. (2010, January 21). Dr. Cornel West evaluates president Obama's 1st year in office. *Hip Hop Wired*. Retrieved January 6, 2012 from http://hiphopwired.com/2010/01/21/hhwired-exclusive-dr-cornel-west-evaluates-president-obamas-1st-year-in-office/

Alterman, E. (2013, February 25). The missing link in Obama's liberalism. *The Nation*, p. 9.

Au, W. (2009) Obama, where art thou? Hoping for change in U.S. education policy. *Harvard Education Review, 79*(2), 309–320.

Bean, A. (2010). Tim Wise: Obama's post-racial road to nowhere. Retrieved March 10, 2013 from www.friendsofjustice.wordpress.com/2010/10/29

Botz, D. L (2013). President Obama and the crisis of black America: Interview with Cornel West. *New Politics, XIV*(2). Retrieved March 10, 13 from http://newpol.org.

Burkholder, Z. (2009, February 9). "A radical thing": Educational perspectives on race in the age of Obama. *Teachers College Record*. Retrieved December 28, 2010 from http://www.tcrecord.org

Cohen, R. (2008, November 4). The election that LBJ won. *Washington Post*, p. A17.

CNN/Essence. (2008). CNN/Essence Magazine/Opinion Research Corporation Poll, March 26–April 2 2008. Retrieved January 7, 2012 from http://www.pollingreport.com/race2.htm

Decision 2008. (2008, November 4). New York: NBC News. Retrieved January 6, 2012 from http://www6.lexisnexis.com

Dix, C. (2013). Cornel West slammed by Obama supporters for telling the truth about Obama. Retrieved March 3, 2013 from http://www.worldcantwait.net

Dyson, M. E. (2008, June 30). The blame game. *Time*, p. 38.

Ewers, J. (2009, April 30). Obama and race relations: Civil rights leaders aren't satisfied. *U.S. News and World Report*. Retrieved January 6, 2012 from http://www.usnews.com/news/obama/articles/2009/04/30/obama-and-race-relations-civil-rights-leaders-arent-satisfied?PageNr=3

Johnson, V. (2009). President Obama. *Harvard Educational Review, 79*(2), 179

Kennedy, R. (2011, September 19). Why Obama's black critics are wrong. *CNN*. Retrieved January 6, 2012 from www.cnn.com/2011/09/19/opinion/...obama/index.html

Lum, L. (2009, February 5). The Obama era: A post-racial society? *Diverse Issues in Higher Education Magazine*. Retrieved January 6, 2012 from http://diverseeducation.com/article/12238/

Page, S., & Risser, W. (2008, July 23). Poll: racial divide narrowing but persists. *USA Today*. Retrieved January 7, 2012 from http://www.usatoday.com/news/politics/election2008/2008-07-23-Race-poll_N.htm

President-elect Obama [Editorial]. (2008, November 5). *Wall Street Journal*. Retrieved January 6, 2012 from http://online.wsj.com

Silvas, C. (2009). Letter to Barack Obama. *Harvard Educational Review, 79*(2), 195.

Subulade, O. (2009). The wanted hope. *Harvard Educational Review, 79*(2), 197.

Tatum, B. D. (2003). *"Why are all the black kids sitting together in the cafeteria?" And other conversations about race.* New York: Basic Books.

Toure. (2012, November 15). What's behind Cornel West's attacks on Obama? *Time*. Retrieved March 5, 2013 from www.ideas.time.com/2012/11/15

Walsh, K. (2011, March 2). Obama says race a key component in Tea Party protests. *U.S. News and World Report*. Retrieved January 6, 2012 from http://www.usnews.com/news/articles/2011/03/02/

Wells, K. (2010, February 23). A conversation with Dr. Cornel West. *Race-Talk*. Retrieved January 6, 2012 from http://www.race-talk.org/?p=2981&all=1

Wise, T. (2009) *Between Barack and a hard place: Racism and white denial in the age of Obama.* San Francisco: City Lights Books.

Wise, T. (2010). *Color-blind: The rise of post-racial politics and the retreat from racial equity.* San Francisco: City Lights Books.

PART FIVE

Voices from the Field

"I sometimes think that every education writer, every would-be education expert, and every politician who pontificates, as many do so condescendingly, about the 'failings' of the teachers in the front lines of our nation's public schools ought to be obliged to come into a classroom once a year and teach the class, not just for an hour with the TV cameras watching but for an entire day, and find out what it's like. It might at least impart some moderation to the disrespectful tone with which so many politicians speak of teachers."
    —Jonathan Kozol

"It has always seemed strange to me…. The things we admire in men, kindness and generosity, openness, honesty, understanding and feeling, are the concomitants of failure in our system. And those traits we detest, sharpness, greed, acquisitiveness, meanness, egotism and self-interest, are the traits of success. And while men admire the quality of the first they love the produce of the second."
    —John Steinbeck

"To be changed by ideas was pure pleasure. But to learn ideas that ran counter to values and beliefs learned at home was to place oneself at risk, to enter the danger zone. Home was the place where I was forced to conform to someone else's image of who and what I should be. School was the place where I could forget that self and, through ideas, reinvent myself."
    —bell hooks

CHAPTER THIRTEEN

No Voices Left Behind

MARTIN J. WASSERBERG

Elementary schools that do not make Adequate Yearly Progress (AYP) by federal standards often shift their instruction to focus on standardized test preparation (Meier & Wood, 2004). These changes are overwhelmingly implemented in schools serving African American and Latino children from communities in poverty (Kozol, 2005). Teachers have made it clear that testing pressures in such schools result in more stress and less job satisfaction (Moon, Brighton, Jarvis, & Hall, 2007), as they focus on practice testing, and largely teach students using low-level instructional methods (Ahlquist, 2003). Students' perceptions of education are undoubtedly affected by such curricular and pedagogical shifts, yet student voices are largely missing from the conversation. T. C. Howard (2001) argues that for K-12 schools "the scant attention paid to students' voice is inexcusable given their role as the primary clientele" (p. 132).

I have been listening to those voices for years. I have worked in elementary schools like those described throughout my professional career—first as a teacher, then as a curriculum leader, and most recently as a researcher and teacher-educator. The dialogue included in this chapter compiles quotes from conversations with African American and Latino elementary students from two such schools. Dialogues with students at Sunny Lake Elementary (pseudonyms are used for all schools and students) took place in 2009. Sunny Lake is located in a large urban district in South Florida. Over 99% of the students at Sunny Lake are African American or Latino, and over 95% qualify for free or reduced lunch. I was a third- and fourth-grade teacher at Sunny Lake for the majority of my career and maintained a presence in the school as a mentor and researcher through 2010. Dialogues at Coastal Elementary took place in 2011 and 2012. Coastal is located in a medium-sized district in Eastern North Carolina. At Coastal, 88% of the students are African American or Latino and 85% qualify for free or reduced lunch. My presence at Coastal elementary was in the role of a supervisor of pre-service teachers and as a researcher. Neither Sunny Lake nor Coastal had ever made AYP and had implemented a series of test-preparation protocols as a response. This chapter presents student perceptions of and experiences with the curricula and pedagogies at these two schools and student recommendations for change. From Sunny Lake, I include quotes from four African American fourth graders (Asia, Floyd, Latavia, and Johnny), who were focus group participants for a research project investigating student perceptions of standardized testing environments. From Coastal, I include quotes from 4 fourth graders (three African Americans: Eric, Tyrell, and Chris; and one Latina: Julissa) and 4 fifth graders (three African Americans: Aaliyah, Tanya, and Jeremy; and one Latina: Ariel), who were participant-researchers in a participatory action research project aimed at creating a safe space for student voice and enhancing student academic engagement.

Specific themes that have emerged from the conversations that will be focused on in this chapter include (a) student perceptions of education as test preparation, (b) student perceptions that they are viewed stereotypically, and (c) student definitions of quality teachers and meaningful learning experiences. These "voices left behind" demonstrate how opportunities for the implementation of engaging pedagogies and the freedom to forge meaningful student-teacher relationships are sacrificed under the demands of test-practice protocols. An argument will be made that present reform should begin with a re-evaluation of classroom pedagogies in marginalized schools.

Education as Test Preparation

I was a third-grade teacher at Sunny Lake Elementary when Florida initiated a policy of grading schools based on student performance on the state's standardized reading and math tests, known as the Florida Comprehensive Assessment Test (FCAT). At the time, teachers at Sunny Lake, and other schools designated as "low-performing," were sent in droves to district workshops where we were instructed in "FCAT strategies" and "data-driven instruction," with a goal of improving our students' test scores. To complement these workshops, the administration at Sunny Lake, and at other similar schools nationwide (Meier & Wood, 2004), adopted a series of instructional programs that largely involved scripted lessons in practice test booklets. One requirement of these programs was for teachers (particularly those teaching students in grades subjected to state testing) to explicitly link each reading and math lesson to an "FCAT Benchmark." FCAT Benchmarks were a list of topics, generated by the state, representing the different types of questions that might be asked on the state test. For reading class, the FCAT Benchmarks included Vocabulary, Author's Purpose, Main Idea, Cause and Effect, Compare and Contrast, Plot Resolution, and References and Research. To the district officials who conducted our workshops, it was imperative that FCAT Benchmarks be posted on the wall each week, and that students be able to recite the name of the week's benchmark focus. This was presented as an indicator of quality teaching. An administrator would occasionally walk into my class and ask students, "What benchmark are you working on?" When the students answered correctly, I would receive a complimentary nod of encouragement. An announcement was made each morning on the loudspeaker to the effect of, "This week the FCAT benchmark for fourth graders in reading is compare and contrast. Fourth graders are focusing on compare and contrast questions in their reading class." This was as much a reminder for teachers as it was for students. Teachers were encouraged to guide students in identifying the types of questions that would be most prevalent on the state test. After evaluation of my students' pre-test scores, I was told things like "It would be a good idea to review more compare and contrast multiple choice questions than plot resolution ones. This will result in the biggest gains for your students." My assessment questions would then be examined by a reading coach, or assigned from a test-practice booklet, to verify that they mirrored the types of questions asked on the state test.

Effects of the new mandate on teachers were immediately apparent. As a vivid example, a colleague of mine scrapped her annual poetry unit (a favorite of hers and her students). In the past she had taken three weeks of reading class to focus on the works of one or two authors (for example, Langston Hughes and Shel Silverstein). The main goal of her poetry unit was largely to inspire interest and provoke enjoyment; however, now she felt she could only utilize a poem to meet an FCAT Benchmark. Observing a lesson in her class years later, I noticed that instead of taking time to appreciate the imagery and learn about the historical context of Langston Hughes' "Dreams," students were asked to read it and highlight the word "barren" to be added to their vocabulary list for the week. Of course, this is not to say that the requirement of linking lessons to objectives is not a normal practice throughout the country. However, the requirement that teachers in low-performing schools must apply this practice to every min-iscule segment of instruction seemed to render student enjoyment an irrelevant distraction.

In mathematics, the FCAT benchmarks were Number Sense, Measurement, Geometry, Algebraic Thinking and Data Analysis (benchmarks have changed slightly since the new 2011 incarnation of the state test, FCAT 2.0). Data from practice tests were disaggregated by these benchmarks, and teachers were expected to group their students based on this data. I was once told by a district observer, assigned to observe teachers only at the low-performing schools in the area, that "It is clear that Carlos has an understanding of Geometry since he got 7 out of the 8 of those questions correct on the practice test, but he is weak on Number Sense since he got only 5 out of 10 of those types of questions correct." She then recommended that Carlos spend time on multiplication word problems (Number Sense benchmark items) instead of those I was currently exploring on area (Geometry benchmark item). I can only assume that her focus on test-based protocols had caused her to overlook the inextricable link between the two topics. Nonetheless, any semblance of an integrated approach fell out of favor, as every few weeks teachers were required to spend time compiling lists of scores and charts, matching test-score gains on specific skills to benchmarks and standard numbers, and reorganizing their groups based on perceived student weaknesses in this manner.

Teacher evaluations were based largely on our following of such protocols, and for me this led to an absurd situation where I felt I was doing my worst teaching to receive stellar evaluations from administrators. I would transition into test-based instruction as my observation began, and back to a more integrated, inquiry-based, model as the observer left. Most teachers, however, followed protocol throughout the day (and I do not blame them, as we were made to feel our jobs depended on it!).

Unfortunately, not much changed at Sunny Lake in terms of these expectations as I transitioned from a teacher to a curriculum leader to a researcher. In fact, FCAT benchmarks became more prominent, as they were posted near each teacher's door (with corresponding pages in the test-practice booklet). Of course, there were individual teachers who created exciting, engaging classrooms when their doors were closed (as I hope I did), but the test-preparation mandate from the district remained clear. The students painted a clear picture of their experience. Asia talked to me about how her class prepared for the exam during their math and reading times.

"We have to do this book, 'FCAT Advantage,' in math and reading, and it helps us to understand more about the FCAT, almost every day for the whole year." This experience was far from unique to Sunny Lake. Miles away in North Carolina, the students at Coastal shared a similar experience—all that was different was the name of the test (The North Carolina state standardized test is known as the End of Grade Test [EOG]). In fact, Eric's description of his math and reading classes at Coastal was almost identical to Asia's at Sunny Lake. He said that these classes consisted of "the EOG review book, like every day." Students at both schools spoke predominantly of standardized test preparation in descriptions of their reading and math classes; these were the subjects that were tested by the state. At Sunny Lake, Floyd described vividly what his reading class was like for the three months leading up to the state test, "The teachers will never let you get up, not even to get your paper or pencil. It takes mostly all of the day." LaTavia added, "Sometimes you can't even get up to use the bathroom;" and Asia, "You can't even get water. I was so thirsty for an hour." This experience, which the principal at Sunny Lake called "Test Lockdown," again was not unique. At Coastal Elementary, Chris's description of test-based instruction was again almost identical, despite its hyperbole, "You can't go to the bathroom, because if you make one noise in the hall the whole school will have to start over." Aaliyah talked about longing to get out of her seat, and when asked her favorite part of reading class, she responded, "I like it when you get to stand up for a two to three-minute break to stretch out." Students who are subject to consistent test-practice protocols often become disengaged from the learning process (Moon, et al., 2007; Readiness Project, 2008). Julissa exemplified this in a description of her math lessons. "I like to learn," she said before changing course, "but sometimes I don't like to learn, sometimes you're sitting there for a long time just waiting for the break." Ariel put it even more vividly: "We just sit there and my butt gets numb!"

Perhaps predictably, the elementary students I spoke to from Sunny Lake described their work in terms of the FCAT Benchmarks; explanations that are meaningless to any learning outside of the context of the Florida state test. For example, Asia explained, "The questions are asking about the pictures, so you have to do Records and Research, or it might be asking about Plot Development." LaTonya chimed in, "I am ready to answer all the different benchmarks, Cause and Effect, and mostly Author's Purpose." Throughout the day, students are asked to phrase both written and oral answers in "FCAT terms," and to use "FCAT strategies" like labeling paragraphs by FCAT benchmarks. "We don't have to read it, just scanning and underlining," LaTonya explained. At Coastal the names of particular benchmarks were less salient, but the strategies were similar. Tanya described the test-based strategies they had been taught to use: "We have to highlight stuff, and we have to like label, not really read;" and Kristi said that "with the longer stories we're just scanning through to find the answers, not reading." In all of my conversations with students at both schools about their reading classes there was no talk of enjoying reading, and rare mention of a story they loved.

Nonetheless, the students staunchly defended the importance of state tests. The message transmitted to teachers and administrators had clearly been passed on to them. The students expressed a belief that without the state test, no real education would take place. At Sunny Lake, LaTonya said, "The school, without FCAT, would be—I don't know how the kids would go on to the next grade if they don't know anything. They'll be kind of slow, and they won't know the stuff." Asia predicted, "School would be just messing around all the time;" and Johnny added that there would "be kids bouncing off the walls." At Coastal, Jeremy agreed that students "would go crazy because they would be like 'No EOG!' and then everybody would not pay attention in class." The students clearly viewed the test as the driving force for the curriculum, learning, and even classroom management. LaTonya explained that if she were a teacher she would assign her students "stuff that related to the FCAT, so they could be more focused." When asked what kind of "stuff," LaTonya replied, "I don't know—whatever's on the FCAT." Similarly, Tyrell explained that if he were a teacher he would have only to be "skilled in math and reading, because that is all you have to teach for a math and reading EOG."

Perceived Stereotyping

For students in these communities, the specter of state testing stretched well beyond the school walls. The local newspapers published stories regarding schools' test scores every year, and specific information was easily found online. This practice is still commonplace across the country. The students I spoke to were acutely aware of how easily accessible their schools' test scores were. In Florida, for example, schools are assigned a letter grade; following one of our conversations on testing, the students at Sunny Lake showed me how to pull up their school's grade (a D) online in a manner of seconds. They mentioned this grade in almost every discussion on testing. "Have you seen the grade on this school? They have the grade right on top of the school. What if they put a 'D' right on top of the roof of the school, and helicopters could see it!" Floyd said metaphorically. The students clearly struggled with the feeling that the test performance of their school was being broadcasted to the greater community. Notably, the schools in Florida that were labeled D or F predominantly served African American and Latino children, and race was a salient part of the conversations about test scores with students at Sunny Lake. To be clear, the students likely would not have engaged in such conversations with all researchers. At the time of these conversations I had long been a part of the Sunny Lake community. I had been a classroom teacher for hundreds of students, including many siblings, before transitioning to a curriculum leader (a role that provided me with a presence in all classrooms). Over a period of ten years I established positive relationships with Sunny Lake students, families and community members that persist to this day. When I left my teaching position and returned to the school as a researcher, I was still perceived by most students as a trusted member of the Sunny Lake community. As a White male, the students' willingness to discuss issues of race with me was, at least in part, a product of this insider status. In contrast, no mention of race emerged from similar conversations at Coastal, where I had a much more limited presence over a shorter time period. The students at Sunny Lake were clear, however, in expressing a belief that their school's test scores led to stereotypes by outsiders, particularly White people, and a desire to prove these stereotypes wrong. The feeling derived from being in a situation where one feels one is being viewed stereotypically, and the subsequent fear of doing something that would inadvertently confirm the stereotype, is known as *stereotype threat* (Steele, 1997; Steele & Aronson, 1995). Steele (1997) explains that when individuals from stigmatized groups are placed in a situation where stereotypes about them become salient, efforts to disprove the stereotype can be debilitating. This pressure has been shown to increase anxiety (Blascovich, Spencer, Quinn, & Steele, 2001; Osborne, 2001), and have negative effects on the performance of African American and Latino students as early as elementary school (McKown & Strambler, 2009; McKown & Weinstein, 2003).

There are a limited number of studies that have specifically examined stereotype threat with elementary school children, but the existing evidence suggests that children's academic performance can be influenced by the subtle activation of stereotypes as early as the lower elementary grades (Ambady, Shih, Kim, & Pittinsky, 2001). A majority of all children are aware of common societal stereotypes by the age of upper elementary school, and African American and Latino children are more likely to be aware of academic stereotypes than White children (McKown & Weinstein, 2003). This awareness has been shown to negatively influence performance of African American and Latino children in environments where a stereotype is applicable (i.e., standardized testing scenarios; McKown & Strambler, 2009; McKown & Weinstein, 2003, Wasserberg, 2013). Additionally, Steele (1997) explains that stereotype threat effects are tied to the perceived importance of the task at hand. That is, the prospect of being negatively stereotyped is most threatening when performance in the domain is of high importance to the individual (Lawrence, Marks, & Jackson, 2010), and the students I spoke to made it clear that they perceived their state tests as very important; in fact, as the reason for education.

With the prospect that it may have a negative effect on performance, the perceived stereotyping that was a salient part of student comments at Sunny Lake was all the more troubling. "White people gonna be thinking that it's just an F," Asia said, "White people gonna be thinking, maybe to themselves, forever [Sunny Lake] is gonna get an F." Johnny explained, "White people, they might think that since we're a D school, we might be writing on the walls. We might be writing cuss words on the walls!" LaTonya agreed, "They might think we have a lot of fights and stuff. They think that you're dumb, and you fight a lot." The students also expressed a clear desire to repudiate these stereotypes. Asia explained, "I think it's bad because they're talking about my school…that offends me." LaTonya offered, "It makes me feel kind of sad because—well it kind of makes me a little *mad* because just because I go to a D school, that does not mean that I'm a D student, or a D average student." The students felt a responsibility to change the perceptions of outsiders by trying harder on the test. "I'm trying to bring the scores of my school up, man!" Floyd said adamantly. Asia said, "We are going to put maximum effort because we don't want the school to be torn down." A nearby elementary school was recently shut down by the state for consecutive years of poor test scores. Johnny was succinct: "I don't want them to see these grades and think bad about us." The argument can certainly be made that the omnipresence of test and test-centered curriculum has made these debilitating thoughts a salient part of the students' school experience. Unsettlingly, a response to continued school-based stereotype threat experiences may be eventual disidentification from the academic domain (Major, Spencer, Schmader, Wolfe, & Crocker, 1998; Steele, 1997; Wong, Eccles, & Sameroff, 2003).

In addition to the normal stress associated with state testing, it is clear that African American and Latino students in classroom environments like those explored at Sunny Lake and Coastal Elementary may feel an extra burden of disproving stereotypes. As early as kindergarten, children experience a significant increase in anxiety in testing situations (Fleege, Charlesworth, Burts, & Hart, 1992), and an additional layer of anxiety has been shown for children in stereotype threat situations (K. E. Howard, 2005). Correspondingly, descriptions of test day at Sunny Lake and Coastal were characterized by talk of queasiness, nail-biting, butterflies, and "feeling like I have to go to the bathroom." Floyd told me: "The FCAT is the most important thing in the world. You can't even drop the thing! If you drop it, how you gonna breathe, man, how you gonna breathe!?" Here he vividly captured his peers' feelings towards the test. As a helpful suggestion, Asia said that if she were a teacher, on practice-test days she "would tell the kids that it's not a practice FCAT, that it's just a regular test that we do. It would make things feel, like, less nervous." Her suggestion is consistent with stereotype threat theory, and research (e.g. McKown & Strambler, 2009; McKown & Weinstein, 2003; Wasserberg, 2013) suggesting that the performance of African American and Latino students is affected only when stereotypes are made salient. The students at Sunny Lake made it clear that a standardized testing situation is one of those times of stereotype salience. As mandated test-practice protocols are further operationalized in low-performing schools, the pressure on children is increased, and test anxiety can be expected to worsen. This is significant in an era where students are pressured to do well on state tests not only as determinants of school funding, but as determinants of teacher salaries. These phenomena clearly have a disproportionate effect on children of color. Alarmingly, the conversations with students here support research (e.g., Townsend, 2002) indicating that, particularly for African American students, feelings of anxiety can be tied to their perceived failure. At Sunny Lake, Floyd predicted he would fail, "That's why it's called the FCAT. It's spelled with letters—and the first letter is an 'F.'" At Coastal, Tanya said, "We try hard but the school is still low,"

Student-Generated Solutions

The conversations delineated above should be alarming for most educators. Yet, nationally, definitions of teacher quality continue to be tied largely to the standardized test performance of their students. In 2011, the Florida legislature passed a merit pay law for teachers linked to FCAT test scores. In 2012, North Carolina revised its teacher evaluation process, adding a standard related to the "academic success" of students, which will largely be measured by standardized test scores. Although standardized test scores are one piece of information that should be used to evaluate teachers, scores alone are not reliable or valid indicators of teacher quality (Baker et al., 2010). Elementary school student voices tell us that, despite increased test scores, overemphasis leads to boredom, disengagement, and anxiety, particularly for students of color.

In late 2010, I left the classroom and moved to North Carolina, accepting a position as a university professor. Frustrated with a top-down educational policy focused on testing and saddened by my conversations with elementary students during the previous few years, I initiated a participatory action research project at Coastal Elementary committed to fostering positive environments for elementary students in low-performing schools by exploring creative ways of boosting engagement. Goals of the initiative included establishing a model for student academic engagement in contrast to the test-centered model prevalent in the school, while creating a safe space for student voice where children could share their opinions on school issues. Particularly for students who have become disengaged recipients of test-practice curricula, such a space provides for growth of agency, belonging, and competence, which are all central to youth development (Mitra, 2004; Mitra & Serriere, 2012). In fact, interviews revealed that being positioned as the "experts," and the validation of their voice, was a motivating factor for their scholarly engagement throughout the project. My initial meetings with elementary students involved conversations centered on questions such as, "What makes a great teacher?" and "How do we learn best?" An early conversation with Eric went as follows:

Describe your favorite teacher.
Eric: My favorite teacher?
Yes. Have you had a favorite teacher so far?
Eric: No.
Ok, have you had a really good teacher so far?
Eric: No.
Have you liked any of your teachers?
Eric: No.

Nonetheless, Eric had shown significant growth on his test scores throughout the semester and was described as a "star student" at Coastal; and his teacher, like those of the Florida students, was rated as a "high-quality teacher." To be clear, this is not an indictment of these teachers, who are largely doing exactly what is expected of them based on the evaluation criteria. It is the evaluation criteria that I am challenging, by advocating for an expanded definition of teacher quality that takes into account the "left behind" perspectives of students.

Based on questions derived from the dialogues on teacher quality, the students at Coastal conducted and analyzed a number of interviews with a purposefully selected sample of their peers and created presentations with their definitions of great teachers and great teaching. They agreed on common characteristics of great teachers, which included: (a) they are helpful, (b) they do not yell, (c) they can be funny, and (d) they create exciting lessons. Students also agreed on the characteristics of exciting and memorable lessons. Some of these characteristics included: (a) working in groups, (b) hands-on projects, and (c) a lot of movement.

I challenge the reader to think back and describe their favorite elementary school teacher. Is your description more in line with these students, or with the state? I would imagine that your descriptions would be similar to those of Kristi and Julissa, who couldn't stop talking about their favorite teacher from the previous year. "She makes learning fun!" Julissa yelled right away when asked about her. "She sprayed water on us sometimes, or we would have to do jumping jacks. We had to do jumping jacks based on the food period. Six, five, four, three, two, one! Six jumping jacks, and hop on one leg, and spin around!" She could not contain her excitement. Then she went on to talk about her teacher's personal connection with her students: "Sometimes, if we had vocabulary words, she would give an example of something that her husband does. He is in the army. Then we would ask different questions that were sometimes off topic about what he does, but we loved talking about it." Kristi, a student that a teacher described as "disengaged," touched on two things that clearly engaged her in the learning process: a personal connection with her teacher, and being able to get up and move while learning—two things manifestly sacrificed under test-practice curricular models.

Many of the students at Coastal longed for a comfortable learning environment (Jeremy said school would be great if his classroom was "a happy place where everyone would feel comfortable") and better relationships with teachers. Ariel said teachers should "talk to students like one of their family… Make them feel comfortable because, if they knew how to do that, the students would like school and not feel negative towards it." Tanya said, "Teachers don't always have to yell at kids if they do something bad, like running down the hall. Just talk to them and tell them to calm down, don't be mean." The students are correct in their desire because personalized relationships like those they describe have been shown to promote student engagement, effort and academic achievement in the school setting (Bryk & Schneider, 2002; Delpit, 2006; Rodríguez, 2008). For African American elementary school students in particular, these positive student-teacher relationships are a central facet of a positive school climate (Slaughter-Defoe & Carlson, 1996) and are the factor most frequently mentioned when discussing what creates an optimal learning environment (T. C. Howard, 2001)—just as they were for the students I spoke to. Trusting relationships were also a prerequisite for any successful stereotype threat-based intervention (Steele, 2003).

Aaliyah and Ariel told me that a great teacher is one who "helps students with their work" and "gives students a chance to earn rewards"—but also one who "lets students dance," and "talks in funny voices." It is these unmeasured things that often disappear from the school day when schools are focused only on test scores. Aaliyah and Ariel presented the benefits of having a great teacher, by their definition, to university students and faculty. "When the students go home," they said, "they will have a positive attitude towards school. And that is what's important!"

Conclusion

Test scores at both Sunny Lake and Coastal have improved, but at what cost? While students' scores rise when taught with test-preparation protocols, this is not necessarily representative of their learning (Smith & Fey, 2000). Kozol (1992) puts it well when he says that "the result of this regime is that the children who survive do slightly better on their tests, because that's all they study… What have they learned, however? They have learned that education is a brittle, abstract ritual to ready them for an examination" (pp. 144–145).

The overemphasis on test preparation in the lowest-performing schools across the country has in many ways stifled student engagement. It is clear from the students in this project that a curricular focus on test preparation can inherently limit opportunities for more engaging pedagogical practices and for positive relationship development between teachers and students.

Much of the popular discourse utilizes a cultural deficit framework to characterize student engagement issues in the thousands of schools like Sunny Lake and Coastal across the nation (Nasir & Hand, 2006). Such negative judgments are often framed within the context of standardized test scores (Lewis, James, Hancock, & Hill-Jackson, 2008) and amplify negative stigmatization of African American and Latino students, while restricting their access to the most engaging educational programs. As Ladson-Billings (1999) suggests, in this sense the standardized testing movement has been "a movement to legitimize [the notion of] African American students' deficiency under the guise of scientific rationalism" (p. 23). Such a framework downplays the effects of test-preparation pedagogies, underdeveloped teacher-student relationships, and other contextual issues present in low-performing schools, while having negative implications for racial identity development (Ford, Harris, & Schuerger, 1993) and academic achievement (Ford & Harris, 1997; McKown & Strambler, 2009; McKown & Weinstein, 2003).

Present reform should begin with a re-evaluation of classroom pedagogy in schools like Sunny Lake and Coastal. Schools serving low-income African American and Latino youth are increasingly subject to top-down policy mandates that have, in many ways, determined curriculum and pedagogy. Pedagogical reform should therefore focus on ways to reduce test-related stressors, as opposed to increasing them. Pedagogies driven by stereotypes and test practice need to change if educators are interested in changing the perceptions of students documented here. It is important to note that, with rare exceptions, the students here spoke not of memorable interactions with their teacher in descriptions of their day, but instead of monotonous interactions with test-practice protocols. Is this what the nation wants for its children?

References

Ahlquist, R. (2003). Challenges to academic freedom: California teacher educators mobilize to resist state-mandated control of the curriculum. *Teacher Education Quarterly, 30*(1), 57–64.

Ambady, N., Shih, M., Kim, A., & Pittinsky, T. L. (2001). Stereotype susceptibility in children: Effects of identity activation on quantitative performance. *Psychological Science, 12*, 385–390.

Baker, E. L., Barton, P. E., Darling-Hammond, L., Haertel, E., Ladd, H. F., Linn, R. L., et al. (2010). *Problems with the use of student test scores to evaluate teachers.* Washington, DC: Economic Policy Institute.

Blascovich, J., Spencer, S. J., Quinn, D., & Steele, C. (2001). African Americans and high blood pressure: the role of stereotype threat. *Psychological Science, 12*, 225–229.

Bryk, A. S., & Schneider, B. L. (2002). *Trust in schools: A core resource for improvement.* New York: Russell Sage Foundation.

Delpit, L. (2006). Lessons from teachers. *Journal of Teacher Education, 57*(3), 220–231.

Fleege, P. O., Charlesworth, R., Burts, D. C., & Hart, C. H. (1992). Stress begins in kindergarten: A look at behavior during standardized testing. *Journal of Research in Childhood Education, 7*(1), 20–26.

Ford, D. Y., & Harris, J. J. (1997). A study of the racial identity and achievement of Black males and females. *Roeper Review, 20*(2), 105–110.

Ford, D. Y., Harris, J. J., & Schuerger, J. M. (1993). Racial identity development among gifted Black students: Counseling issues and concerns. *Journal of Counseling & Development, 71*(4), 409–417.

Howard, K. E. (2005). *Stereotype threat and anxiety: Examining their connection to working memory capacity in middle school children*
(Doctoral dissertation). University of Southern California, Los Angeles, CA. Retrieved from ProQuest Dissertations and Theses database. (AAT 3196818)

Howard, T. C. (2001). Telling their side of the story: African-American students' perceptions of culturally relevant teaching. *The Urban Review, 33*(2), 131–149.

Kozol, J. (1992). *Savage inequalities: Children in America's schools.* New York: HarperCollins.

Kozol, J. (2005). *The shame of the nation: The restoration of apartheid schooling in America.* New York: Crown.

Ladson-Billings, G. (1999). Just what is critical race theory and what's it doing in a *nice* field like education? In L. Parker, D. Deyhle & S. Villenas (Eds.), *Race is...race isn't: Critical race theory and qualitative studies in education* (pp. 7–30). Boulder, CO: Westview Press.

Lawrence, J., Marks, B., & Jackson, J. (2010). Domain identification predicts black students' underperformance on moderately-difficult tests. *Motivation and Emotion, 34*(2), 105–109. doi:10.1007/s11031-010-9159-8

Lewis, C. W., James, M., Hancock, S., & Hill-Jackson, V. (2008). Framing African American students' success and failure in urban settings. *Urban Education, 43*(2), 127–153.

Major, B., Spencer, S. J., Schmader, T., Wolfe, C., & Crocker, J. (1998). Coping with negative stereotypes about intellectual performance: The role of psychological disengagement. *Personality and Social Psychology Bulletin, 24*(1), 34–50.

McKown, C., & Strambler, M. J. (2009). Developmental antecedents and social and academic consequences of stereotype-consciousness in middle childhood. *Child Development, 80*(6), 1643–1659. doi:10.1111/j.1467-8624.2009.01359.x

McKown, C., & Weinstein, R. S. (2003). The development and consequences of stereotype consciousness in middle childhood. *Child Development, 74*(2), 498–515.

Meier, D., & Wood, G. (Eds.). (2004). *Many children left behind: How the No Child Left Behind Act is damaging our children and our schools.* Boston: Beacon Press.

Mitra, D. L. (2004). The significance of students: Can increasing" student voice" in schools lead to gains in youth development? *The Teachers College Record, 106*(4), 651–688.

Mitra, D. L., & Serriere, S. C. (2012). Student voice in elementary school reform: Examining youth development in fifth graders. *American Educational Research Journal, 49*(4), 743–774.

Moon, T. R., Brighton, C. M., Jarvis, J. M., & Hall, C. J. (2007). *State standardized testing programs: Their effects on teachers and students.* Storrs, CT: The National Research Center on the Gifted and Talented, University of Connecticut.

Nasir, N. S., & Hand, V. M. (2006). Exploring sociocultural perspectives on race, culture, and learning. *Review of Educational Research, 76*(4), 449–475.

Osborne, J. W. (2001). Testing stereotype threat: Does anxiety explain race and sex differences in achievement? *Contemporary Educational Psychology, 26*(3), 291–310.

Readiness Project and MA MCAS Subcommittee. (2008). Readiness Final Report. Retrieved from http://www.mass.gov/edu/readiness-final-report.html

Rodríguez, L. F. (2008). Struggling to recognize their existence: Examining student–adult relationships in the urban high school context. *The Urban Review, 40*(5), 436–453.

Slaughter-Defoe, D. T., & Carlson, K. G. (1996). Young African American and Latino children in high-poverty urban schools: How they perceive school climate. *Journal of Negro Education, 65*(1), 60–70.

Smith, M. L., & Fey, P. (2000). Validity and accountability in high-stakes testing. *Journal of Teacher Education, 51*(5), 334–344.

Steele, C. M. (1997). A threat in the air: How stereotypes shape intellectual identity and performance. *American Psychologist, 52*(6), 613–629.

Steele, C. M. (2003). Stereotype threat and African-American student achievement. In T. Perry, C. M. Steele & A. G. Hilliard (Eds.), *Young, gifted, and Black: Promoting high achievement among African-American students* (pp. 109–130). Boston: Beacon Press.

Steele, C. M., & Aronson, J. (1995). Stereotype threat and the intellectual test performance of African Americans. *Journal of Personality and Social Psychology, 69*(5), 797–811.

Townsend, B. L. (2002). "Testing while Black": Standards-based school reform and African American learners. *Remedial and Special Education, 23*(4), 222.

Wasserberg, M. J. (2013). Stereotype threat effects on African American children in an urban elementary school. Manuscript submitted for publication.

Wong, C. A., Eccles, J. S., & Sameroff, A. (2003). The influence of ethnic discrimination and ethnic identification on African American adolescents' school and socioemotional adjustment. *Journal of Personality, 71*(6), 1197–1232.

CHAPTER FOURTEEN

Teaching Under the Weight of Race to the Top in New York State

CHRISTOPHER LEAHEY

In the spring of 2010, New York Governor David Patterson signed into law Chapter 103 of the laws of 2010. Introduced in the Assembly on May 25 and passed in the Senate just three days later without public deliberation, Section 3012-C of the law prescribed sweeping, radical changes in the evaluation of New York's public school teachers and principals. Written to meet the requirements of the Race to the Top program and procure roughly $700 million in federal funds, this law requires all teachers and administrators to be evaluated annually, assigned a composite score ranging from 0 to 100, and be assigned to one of four categories: Ineffective (0–64), Developing (65–74), Effective (75–90), and Highly Effective (91–100). Under New York's Annual Professional Performance Review Plan (APPR), teachers labeled "ineffective" for two consecutive years may be charged with incompetence and consequently terminated through an expedited hearing process (Laws of New York, 2010).

Doing School Reform in Real Time

To meet the demands of Race to the Top, New York State rushed to develop several bureaucratic structures and mandates that would go into effect for classroom teachers and building principals during the 2012–2013 school year. Rather than working with district officials to create policies and structures acknowledging local resources, school improvement initiatives, and existing labor agreements, the New York State Education Department (NYSED), along with New York State United Teachers (NYSUT) leaders, developed an evaluation system that effectively replaced all existing teacher evaluation systems. Centered in Albany, NYSED and NYSUT invited local officials to intense workshops to share the new policy initiatives and supported implementation by creating a website (EngageNY) featuring resources and directives reinforced by a series of e-mail "blasts" used to continuously update school officials on the creation of new policies and mandates. Responding to requests for more information and clarification, state and union officials explained to classroom teachers and school administrators (who had little voice in the reform process) to be patient, trust the process, and that "we are building the plane as we fly it." Teachers who asked how we could build a single evaluation system for teachers working in such disparate student populations, with unequal resources and in so many disciplines, were met with a similar response: "Good teaching is good teaching."

The speed and efficiency with which Race to the Top measures have been implemented throughout New York State is staggering. K-12 school officials are completely dependent upon EngageNY for continuous updates on implementing the core curriculum, data-driven instruction, and the teacher evaluation system. This one-way system of communicating reform initiatives is placing administrators and teachers in a perpetual state of dependence as they work feverishly to keep apace and determine how to implement these policies while teaching students and running their local schools. This chapter examines New York's APPR system, the problems associated with quantifying teaching and learning, and the harmful impact of RTTT reforms.

Measuring Teaching Quality with Standardized Tests

New York State's APPR rests on the assumption that teaching and learning can be reduced to standardized test scores and a series of quantifiable behaviors that can be objectively captured in classroom observations, aligned with a standardized rubric, and converted into a numerical score. At the heart of this assumption is the bureaucratic imperative that values only that which can be measured, quantified, and reported. Rather than engaging the complexity of life in schools, New York State has designed a series of devices and tools that simultaneously obscure the complexity of teaching and learning and promote a false sense of objectivity. These devices come in the form of standardized tests, instructional rubrics, learning bands, and growth scales. Each device promises to offer a true and accurate rendering of some aspect of teacher quality. Once applied, each device is designed to produce an objective number that can be plugged into a larger equation used to determine a teacher's composite score and ultimately assign New York's teachers to one of four arbitrary categories (i.e., Highly Effective, Effective, Developing, and Ineffective).

Local Measures of Student Achievement (the First 20%)

To meet RTTT requirements, New York State's APPR system requires each teacher to have a composite score of 100 points broken into three categories: 20% is derived from locally determined measures of student success, 20% is calculated from student growth on standardized tests, and the final 60% is derived from classroom observation and other evidence of instructional quality. For the first 20% of a teacher's composite score, NYSED provides school districts a limited choice in the way standardized state exams or locally developed assessments can be used to measure teacher effectiveness. Once an assessment is selected, districts are permitted to use target scores or proficiency levels or choose to use NYSED or locally developed growth formulas for determining the first 20% of a teacher's composite score (NYSED, 2012a).

Using test scores to determine instructional quality is problematic in that standardized tests represent one of many ways to measure learning. Tests are constructed to evaluate the degree to which students have learned the content, skills, and concepts in a given subject area, or domain of learning. Koretz (2008) cautions against using tests as the only indicator of student learning.

He explains, "A test score is just one indicator of what a student has learned—an exceptionally useful one in many ways, but one that is incomplete and error prone" (Koretz, 2008, p. 10). As he suggests, tests measure only a fraction of what is featured in the curriculum and, therefore, offer an incomplete assessment of student learning and ability to apply important concepts and skills. To use a single test score to determine how much a students has learned discounts the multiple forms of learning that may take place in a given classroom. Authentic forms of assessments (which have their own limitations) that might include performing complex tasks, sustained inquiry, solving real-world problems, or presenting research findings are de-valued and are not recognized under New York's evaluation system as evidence of student learning.

Rather than using authentic assessments, NYSED has elected to repurpose standardized exams originally designed to measure student learning in a content area to instead measure instructional quality. Popham (1999) suggests that using standardized test scores in this fashion is like "measuring temperature with a tablespoon" (p. 10). In order to meet the limited time frame in which tests are given, most standardized tests measure only a fraction of the curriculum content. He explains that standardized tests designed to make distinctions between students who take the test produce a spread of test scores, or variance. To make such distinctions in student performance, sample test items answered correctly by a high percentage of students are omitted and replaced with items that approximately half of students correctly answer. This means that material that may be central to a course and emphasized by teachers is unlikely to appear on the test that is being repurposed to measure teacher quality. Using a measurement device that evaluates a fraction of the curriculum, and does not feature items that measure central curriculum content, is clearly not a valid way of measuring instructional quality. Or, as Popham puts it, "To evaluate teachers' instructional effectiveness by using assessment tools that deliberately avoid important content is fundamentally foolish" (Popham, 1999, p. 10).

If using standardized tests is problematic for measuring teacher effectiveness, what may be more problematic is that teachers who work in areas where there is no state exam will have this part of their composite score derived from factors beyond their control. With the priority being to place every teacher under the APPR regulations and assign them a composite score, many districts strapped for time and resources have decided against developing, administering, and evaluating yet another set of exams. Instead, New York State allows districts to choose measures of school-wide growth (e.g., graduation rates) or state exam scores administered in a teacher's building (but not necessarily their content area) to calculate composite scores (NYSED, 2012a). The result is that teachers who do not work in core subject areas will find that the first 20% of their composite score will be calculated by factors they cannot control, test scores from students whom they may have never taught, or possibly from student test scores gleaned from disciplines in which they do not teach. Knowing that 20% of a teacher's score will be determined largely by external factors beyond their control, teachers are forced to accept that what they do with their students, their curriculum, and in their classrooms may have little influence over the first 20% of their evaluation. Nonetheless, these evaluations and composite scores will be shared with the public and used to make major decisions about teacher retention, tenure, and termination.

Student Growth on State Assessments (the Second 20%)
The second 20% of a teacher's composite score is derived from student growth on standardized tests as compared to similar students across New York State. To be "highly effective," teachers

must exceed the state average for growth of similar students. "Effective" teachers meet the state average for growth for similar students; "developing" teachers are "below the state average;" and "ineffective" is a category reserved for teachers who have students who score "well below" the state average for growth on standardized exams (NYSED, n.d., p. 5).

In 2011–2012, ELA and Math teachers' effectiveness was measured by student performance on state exams. Working with American Institutes for Research, NYSED has developed a statistical model to measure and predict student growth (and ultimately teacher quality). Drawing upon three years of test scores and acknowledging diversity with a limited set of student characteristics (i.e., poverty, status as an English Language Learner, and disability status), NYSED's growth model was used in 2011–2012 to measure and predict appropriate levels of student "growth" on test scores, award composite points, and classify teachers in one of the four categories (American Institutes for Research, 2012).

This system also operates under the assumption that variation does not exist within these identified student characteristics and that such characteristics are static. In reality, classroom teachers know that students with disabilities often exhibit a range of behaviors, dispositions, skills, and cognitive levels. Likewise, students can be designated as having a disability at any point as they make their way through the public school system: some students are designated in the early grades while some students are not designated until middle school. Some students are misdiagnosed and their designations are modified, and some students are declassified as they make their way through the public school system. To assume that students carry classifications that do not change in the thirteen years they spend in public schools is problematic. Assigning point values to students with designations simplifies and distorts the complexity of the students the system claims to serve. Rather than acknowledge the dynamic nature of classifications, New York State's APPR system acknowledges these three types of designations and simply lowers the expectations for these students' performance on standardized exams.

Using growth scores is also problematic in that it is predicated on the notion that schools are static environments. For this system to be valid, it would be necessary for the three-year period to be nearly identical and all factors influencing teaching and learning (e.g., class size, curricular resources, teacher experience, number of students with special needs, number of teaching assistants, or team teachers) to be constant over that period. In a time when schools are slashing budgets, eliminating positions, and reassigning teachers, significant changes can take place in a single year, confounding efforts to set student growth rates on three years of test results.

This dynamic nature of schools also poses significant problems for using student growth models to determine teacher effectiveness. Acknowledging the complex nature of schools and the interactive nature of the classroom, Schafer et. al. (2012) found that five of six different student growth models did not provide reliable data to make high-stakes decisions about teacher quality. It appears that, despite the application of complex statistical growth models, there are simply too many variables (e.g., student-teacher interactions, course goals and purposes, school demographics, teaching assignments that may include assistants or a team teacher) to measure, draw comparisons, and calculate a number accurately representing teacher effectiveness.

Similarly, in his study of value-added models, Papay (2011) found fairly minor details such as the time a test is administered (e.g., March versus May) could significantly influence student performance and consequently a teacher's value-added growth score. Citing another variable influencing student performance, in his study of a Rhode Island school district, Papay also found that the choice of reading assessment used to measure student performance significantly influenced a teacher's value-added score. This becomes a serious problem when using scores to make high-stakes employment decisions. He explains:

> In fact, if this [Rhode Island] district implemented a high-stakes pay-for-performance program similar to the one currently operating in Houston, Texas, simply switching the outcome measure would affect the performance bonuses for nearly half of all teachers and the average teacher's salary would change by more than $2,000. (Papay, 2011, p. 165)

Taken together, this research suggests that much work needs to be accomplished before we can be confident about using data gleaned from student growth models to measure teacher effectiveness and make major employment decisions.

Student Learning Objectives

For subjects without state exams, New York State mandates teachers to develop Student Learning Objectives (SLOs) to determine student growth. This requires administering pre-assessments at the start of instruction, setting student target scores, and administering a summative assessment at the end of the school year. Students who perform poorly on the pre-assessment are expected to produce modest test score increases (i.e., 20 points) and students who score high on the pre-assessments are assigned more ambitious target scores (i.e., 30 points) (NYSED, 2012b). A teacher's growth (and, therefore, degree of effectiveness) is determined by the percentage of students who meet a targeted growth score on a standardized exam. A teacher who has 80% of his students meet their target scores receives a rating of 16 out of 20 points and is placed at the high end of the effective range. A teacher who has 40% of their students meet the target is awarded 8 points, placed in the developing category and, depending upon other parts of her composite score, could find her employment status in jeopardy (NYSED, 2012b).

Creating SLOs diverts time and resources away from teaching students. The time teachers spend developing baseline exams, setting target scores, and writing SLOs is time that could be better used preparing high-quality instruction for students. Further, requiring students to sit for baseline exams is an unproductive use of instructional time that essentially places them in the service of the teacher evaluation system. To satisfy the requirements of APPR, New York's students are required to sit for exams and be tested on content that they have yet to receive instruction for and that will have no bearing on their learning. In the very first year of this new system, several students saw this as intrusive and ridiculous while many tipped their hats to their teachers, acknowledging they didn't even try to answer questions correctly, thus leaving room for "growth." Requiring students to sit for baseline tests also communicates that raising test scores, regardless of the quality of the exam or its intended purpose, is a priority of New York State's school reform agenda and the mark of a highly effective teacher.

This system of using test scores to measure teacher quality obscures the complexity of teaching and learning. It is based on a false assumption that teachers have complete control of the learning environments in which they work and that, somehow, the right mixture of planning, instructional strategies, and motivation will produce higher test scores for all students. In reality, there are several significant factors influencing test scores that teachers cannot control. For instance, few teachers can positively state the following about all of their students:

1. Students come to class daily.

2.   Students complete all assignments.

3.   Students enter the year with the skills to be successful in the curriculum.

4.   Schools have adequate resources to support struggling students.

5.   Class sizes are stable and manageable.

If we take the first point and examine trends in student attendance, we see that the APPR system fails to acknowledge a significant problem associated with public schools. Teachers cannot compel students to come to class; and if students do not attend class, they will miss instructional time, which will likely result in low test scores and little growth. A recent Johns Hopkins study indicates 10–15% of U.S. students are chronically absent (i.e., missing more than a month of school per year) from school (Balfanz & Byrnes, 2012). This means that 5 to 7.5 million students do not come to school on a regular basis. Looking closely at Maryland (a state considered to be a national leader in providing quality public education), this study highlights the severity of the problem:

> In Maryland…there are 58 elementary schools that have 50 or more chronically absent students; that is, two classrooms of students who miss more than a month of school a year. In high school, where chronic absenteeism is higher, there are 61 schools where 250 or more students are missing a month or more of school. (Balfanz & Byrnes, 2012, p. 3)

If chronic absenteeism is a significant problem for public schools throughout the nation, and if there is a link between attendance and student performance, one might wonder if it is appropriate to use test scores to measure teacher quality. Furthermore, external factors such as chronic absenteeism also raise questions about whether it is appropriate to spend precious instructional time and limited district resources to measure growth on test scores when we have yet to address the larger problem of getting a significant percentage of our students to come to school on a regular basis.

In addition to concerns over external factors and the limitations of state tests, the APPR system also posits that mass-produced standardized tests are appropriate tools to measure student growth in areas such as music, art, social studies, or English Language Arts. Not all courses and curriculum content can be presented in a linear format. Many of the most important aspects of learning cannot be measured with simple test items or canned essay prompts. These disciplines feature curricula requiring students to develop complex skills, understand and apply abstract concepts, think critically, navigate different mediums, and ultimately create authentic work. Corcoran (2010) questions whether we should be forcing skills associated with the humanities and social sciences to conform to the limited structure of standardized tests solely for the purpose of measuring student growth and assigning a teacher a composite score. My world history students, for example, are presently creating digital documentaries. This multimodal inquiry project starts with students identifying topics of interest and progresses into a series of other tasks that include writing focus questions, conducting library research using digital and traditional resources, interpreting documents, writing and recording narratives, collecting open source images, and using iMovie to create a digital documentary. In completing this project, students will use a variety of crosscutting skills (e.g., creating questions, reading critically, organizing information, writing for an audience, speaking publicly, and employing multiple computer programs) that simply cannot be reduced to the limited format of a mass-produced paper and pencil test. Nonetheless, New York State's APPR codifies the use of test scores as the most reliable, truest measure of student growth.

Teaching to the Rubric (the Other 60%)

In an effort to evaluate the quality of teachers, NYSED has also developed a system to quantify the instructional process. Sixty percent of New York's teachers' composite score is derived from the degree to which classroom teachers can demonstrate and provide evidence that their instruction is aligned with the New York State Teaching Standards. The standards are divided into seven areas: (I) Knowledge of Students and Student Learning, (II) Knowledge of Content and Instructional Planning, (III) Instructional Practice, (IV) Learning Environment, (V) Assessment for Student Learning, (VI) Professional Responsibilities and Collaboration, and (VII) Professional Growth. To capture the degree to which teachers have met these standards, school districts are required to adopt one of 12 state-approved rubrics (NYSED, 2013). These rubrics effectively break teaching down into a series of observable behaviors and pieces of evidence converted into points contributing to a teacher's composite score. The NYSUT rubric (the one my district is using) breaks the seven teaching standards into 36 instructional elements, divided into 78 classroom indicators, with each classroom indicator further divided into one of four levels of effectiveness: Highly Effective, Effective, Developing, and Ineffective (NYSUT, 2012).

Quantifying Classroom Instruction

At first glance the development of a rubric to measure teaching standards seems like a practical and reasonable approach. The rubric articulates the types of instructional strategies (e.g., formative assessment, differentiated instruction) that are valued and allows teachers to reflect and improve upon their practice. These types of instructional strategies are valued, however, because they support a form of instruction that proposes to reach all students, placing them on the road to retaining content and learning skills that can be measured with standardized tests. The NYSUT rubric does not include any reference to inquiry, innovation, creativity, or critical thinking. These concepts, long considered to be the foundation of American education, have no role in an evaluation system in which all activities can be evaluated with a rubric and converted to a numerical value.

Aside from the notion that the NYSUT rubric inherently values a form of standardized instruction, it may not actually deliver the purely objective evaluation it claims to produce. At some point, what happens in the classroom has to be reduced to a numerical value, and this is where problems begin to emerge. For instance, "Standard V: Assessment for Student Learning, Element V.1" evaluates the degree to which "teachers design, select, and use a range of assessment tools and processes to measure and document student learning and growth" (NYSUT, 2012, p. 26). The indicators for meeting this standard are broken into the following categories:

Ineffective
Teacher does not design or select appropriate, accessible diagnostic or ongoing formative assessment to establish learning goals or to inform instruction.

Developing
Teacher occasionally designs or selects appropriate, accessible diagnostic and ongoing formative assessment to establish learning goals and inform instruction.

Effective
Teacher frequently designs or selects appropriate, accessible diagnostic and ongoing formative assessment to establish learning goals and inform instruction.

Highly Effective
Teacher regularly and skillfully designs and selects appropriate, accessible diagnostic and ongoing formative assessment to establish learning goals and inform instruction. (NYSUT, 2012, p. 26)

While the ineffective descriptor suggests the teacher simply does not design appropriate assessment strategies, making a distinction between a rating of developing, effective, and highly effective requires the evaluator to be able to discern between the words "occasionally," "frequently," and "regularly." One might wonder if such a fine distinction can be made when it comes to evaluating instructional preparation in a single scheduled observation and an unannounced observation. Should a teacher's composite score and possibly her larger classification as highly effective, effective, developing, and ineffective rely on such fine and perhaps subjective distinctions? Going a step further, one might wonder if these distinctions can be made without directly observing more than just a few hours of a teacher's classroom instruction.

To achieve full compliance with the APPR process, principals and district administrators are required to evaluate every teacher within the school district. For each teacher, principals must have a formal pre-conference observation, informal, unannounced post-conference observation, and a culminating conversation. To document that these steps have been taken, principals must write copious notes and collect evidence demonstrating a teacher's ability to meet New York's seven teaching standards. Once this evidence is collected, principals are required to match the evidence with state-approved rubrics. The result is that teachers are compelled to spend hours upon hours designing lessons and collecting evidence demonstrating they are meeting the requirements of the rubric, diverting from instructional planning and working with students. Likewise, principals are spending a disproportionate amount of time completing the required paperwork. Some principals suggest that documenting, coding, and quantifying a one-hour lesson can result in 10 hours of paperwork. Rather than working on building initiatives, supporting teachers, and forging relationships with students and parents, many principals are trapped in their offices working all hours of the day and night, spending hundreds of hours collecting, coding, and quantifying data.

Further, one might also ask how evaluators are trained to make such fine distinctions. School districts working with the NYSUT rubric send principals for an intensive weeklong training session (with some attending a follow-up session) to learn how to use the rubric to evaluate teachers. In New York, one or two weeks of intensive training and an administrative degree qualifies one to evaluate a teacher's classroom instruction and potentially place someone's career in jeopardy. Working under the questionable assumption that this is an objective process, administrators are limited to playing the role of an instrumentality whose function is to dispassionately observe classrooms, collect, code, and rate "data." To achieve some semblance of objectivity, all involved in the process have to imagine that human elements that complicate the process can be factored out of the equation. Teachers and administrators who have worked closely for years, and even decades, are understood to be placed in a controlled setting in which human values, complex relationships, and bias can be carefully placed aside for the purposes of determining a composite score in an "objective" way.

It is difficult to imagine any other profession where the power of evaluation can be granted in such a problematic, reckless manner. Subjecting teachers to such a flawed system of evaluation is somehow acceptable at a time when budgets are being slashed, class sizes are increasing, and public schools and labor unions are under relentless attack and public scrutiny. Accepting these working conditions is now the price of admission to this beleaguered profession. It comes as no surprise that teachers' satisfaction with their jobs has plummeted 23 percentage points since 2008, and has dropped to the lowest point in 25 years (MetLife, 2013).

Conclusion

In its effort to meet RTTT requirements and secure some $700 million in federal funds, it appears that New York State has successfully designed and implemented a teacher evaluation system utilizing multiple measures to calculate composite scores and designate teachers as highly effective, effective, developing, or ineffective. Founded on repurposing exams to measure teacher effectiveness, growth models that fail to capture the complexity of the classroom, and a cumbersome and subjective observation rubric, the APPR system, as it is presently designed, may not be sustainable. School districts throughout the state have been struggling to find the financial resources to build a new comprehensive evaluation system while maintaining program and services amidst state budget cuts. Ken Mitchell, District Superintendent of the South Orangetown School District in Rockland County, has calculated the high costs of implementing APPR throughout a sample of 18 school districts located in the Lower Hudson Valley. He reports that the cost of implementing RTTT initiatives in September 2012 was $6,472,166, while total federal and state funding amounted to $520,415, a difference of $5,951,751that was ultimately passed on to the taxpayers (Mitchell, 2012, p. 2). At the time this is being written, thousands of New York State teachers and principals have signed a petition formally opposing the use of standardized tests in teacher evaluation. The New Paltz School Board has passed a resolution calling for reducing testing requirements and ending the use of tests to evaluate teachers. Courageous superintendents such as Ronald Ross (2013) and principals such as Carole Burris (2011) have openly criticized the failures and high costs associated with Race to the Top. These developments may be part of a larger movement to challenge school reforms taking place throughout the nation. Parents and teachers in Seattle's Garfield High School have successfully boycotted the administration of Measure of Academic Progress (MAP) tests. Students in Portland, Oregon, have started a campaign to opt out of taking the state-mandated Oregon Assessment of Knowledge and Skills exam. Chicago's public schools are home to a "Pencils-Down" initiative to end standardized testing (Sheehy, 2013). Perhaps these individual movements are the seeds of a larger movement that will challenge the prevailing paradigm of student and teacher accountability.

References

American Institutes for Research. (2012). *2010–2011 beta growth model for educator evaluation technical report*. New York State Education Department. Albany: New York State Education Department.

Balfanz, R., & Byrnes, V. (2012). *Chronic absenteeism: Summarizing what we know from nationally available data*. Baltimore: Johns Hopkins University Center for Social Organization of Schools.

Burris, C. (2011, December 29). Forging ahead with the nutty teacher evaluation plan. *Washington Post*. Retrieved from http://www.washingtonpost.com/blogs/answer-sheet/post/forging-ahead-with-nutty-teacher-evaluationplan/2011/12/29/gIQAkMiYQP_blog.html#pagebreak

Corcoran, S. (2010). *Can teachers be evaluated by their students' test scores? Should they be? The use of value-added assessments in policy and practice*. Providence, RI: Annenberg Institute for School Reform at Brown University.

Koretz, D. (2008). *Measuring up: What educational testing really tells us*. Cambridge, MA: Harvard University Press.

Laws of New York. (2010). Education. 3012-c. Retrieved from http://public.leginfo.state.ny.us/LAWSSEAF.cgi?Q UERYTYPE=LAWS+&QUERYDATA=$$EDN3012-C

MetLife. (2013). *The MetLife survey of the American teacher.* Retrieved from https://www.metlife.com/assets/cao/foundation/MetLife-Teacher-Survey-2012.pdf

Mitchell, K. (2012). Federal mandates on local education: Costs and consequences; Yes, it's a race, but is it in the right direction? (Discussion brief #8, Fall 2012). New Paltz, NY: Center for Research, Regional Education and Outreach.

New York State Education Department. (2012a). Locally-selected measures: Teachers and principals. Retrieved from http://usny.nysed.gov/rttt/teachers-leaders/assessments/assess_sd_boces.html

New York State Education Department. (2012b). Student learning objectives: Teacher manual. Retrieved from http://www.lew-port.com/cms/lib/NY19000328/Centricity/Domain/57/slo%20teacher%20manual.pdf

New York State Education Department. (2013). Teacher and principal practice rubrics. Retrieved from http://usny.nysed.gov/rttt/teachers-leaders/practicerubrics/#ATPR

New York State Education Department. (n.d.). *A teacher's guide to interpreting your New York State-provided growth score.* Retrieved from http://engageny.org/sites/default/files/resource/attachments/teachers_guide_to_interpreting_your_growth_score.pdf

New York State Union of Teachers. (2012). New York State teacher practice rubric. Retrieved from http://www.nysut.org/files/2012_SEDapproved_NYSUT_TPR.pdf

Papay, J. P. (2011). Different tests, different answers. *American Education Research Journal, 48*(1), 163–193.

Popham, W. J. (1999). Why standardized tests don't measure educational quality. *Educational Leadership, 56*(6), 8–15. Retrieved from http://www.ascd.org/publications/educational-leadership/mar99/vol56/num06/Why-Standardized-Tests-Don't-Measure-Educational-Quality.aspx

Ross, R. (2013). In the midst of the storm. Retrieved from http://www.greenburgh7.com/pages/Greenburgh7/District/Office_of_the_Superintendent/News/A_Message_from_the_Superintend

Schafer, W. D., Lissitz, R. W., Zhu, X., Zhang, Y., Hou, X., & Li, Y. (2012). Evaluating teachers and schools using student growth models. *Practical Assessment, Research & Evaluation, 17*(17). Retrieved from http://pareonline.net/getvn.asp?v=17&n=17

Sheehy, K. (2013). Testing boycott spreads to Portland high schools and beyond. *U.S News and World Report.* Retrieved from http://www.usnews.com/education/blogs/high-school-notes/2013/02/18/testing-boycott-spreads-to-portland-high-schools-and-beyond

CHAPTER FIFTEEN

Danger Signs

Neglecting the Systemic Complexities of School Reform

JOSHUA P. STARR

When my team and I are discussing a big, complex issue, I always ask, "What's the problem we're trying to solve?" I do this because I fear that too often decisions are made based on one person's perspective, or because a solution has been proffered that seems to address a symptom of a problem. For example, while high-quality after-school programs can help narrow the achievement disparity between different groups of children, the "gap" is not caused by the absence of such programs. Disparities in achievement result from teachers that don't have the beliefs or skills to enable all children to achieve at a high level, and the system they work in doesn't ensure that they have those requisite beliefs and skills. I believe that the fundamental problem with today's so-called "education reformers" is their failure to focus on public education as a system. In this chapter, I use my twenty years of experience working in urban school districts to show the complexity of the systems that support increased student achievement; and I contrast it with the rhetoric of today's so-called reformers.

I got my start in education somewhat serendipitously. Living in San Francisco in 1992, I found that there were few jobs to be had. A good friend of mine who was in college to become a psychologist worked in a residential treatment center; he told me there were positions available for counselors. I'd been a substitute teacher for special education students in New York City, so I qualified for a job at a residential treatment center for teenage boys who were either completing the last part of their prison term or were placed for psychological reasons. It was the beginning of my education and the impetus for my dedication to fixing the systems that fail children.

The residential treatment center was across the Bay Bridge, and I often got a ride from Val. He was about five years older and was a Southern California surfer type who had found his calling working with teenage boys. During our rides in his green Jetta we would talk about our lives and work. One time, Val said to me about our kids: "You know, if they grew up like we did and were White instead of Black and Latino, they wouldn't be where they are. They got involved in the legal system for doing the same stuff I was doing in high school." That's when it hit me that my circumstances were a byproduct of happenstance, i.e., what I looked like and where I grew up. It also raised the lifelong question for me of how decisions by adults who work within public systems influence lives, families, and generations of people. What would it take to change how those decisions are made? Is it possible to influence the system?

Rhetoric v. Reality

So-called reformers are quick to seize on discreet aspects of research that justify their positions and often disregard the mountains of evidence about what actually works to improve public education. I distinctly remember a 2004 conversation I had with a senior staff member when I worked for Joel Klein, the Chancellor of the New York City Department of Education. I had just become the Director of School Performance and Accountability for the NYC DOE. I had been designing accountability systems since the late 1990s, when I was Director of Accountability for Plainfield, New Jersey, Public Schools. Accountability was in its inchoate stages then; and I had the luxury of being able to design a system based on best practices and research, rather than state or federal policy. Hence, when I sat down to talk to this senior staffer, I felt that I had experience and knowledge to support my views on accountability.

The staff member I was speaking with was a former management consultant who had retired in her early 40s and decided to "give back" to society by helping Joel Klein with his reform effort. I found her to be generally thoughtful and smart. Yet, as I laid out my views on using multiple measures to understand school performance, I could sense from her an increased exasperation. There was not a lot of patience at the DOE at the time for a deep understanding of the complex factors that contribute to school performance. There was, in fact, a desire for a simplistic accounting of school performance, including a value-added methodology to assess teachers. Standardized test scores were seen as equivalent to a profit and loss statement.

As I described my perspective on accountability, I referenced researchers such as Erick Hanushek, Michael Fullan, Seymour Sarason, Tom Kane, Richard Elmore, and Linda Darling-Hammond. These were not *Education Week* back-page commentaries that I cited; I based my claims on real empirical research. After laying out my thinking, the staffer said, "You educators just use the research to make excuses for why Black and Latino kids aren't learning." I was dumbfounded. Never having been an apologist for the mediocrity of public education, and being a staunch supporter of accountability, I didn't know how to respond. It was my first major lesson in what I was up against.

This senior staff member refused to see my perspective because of her inability to understand the systemic aspects of public education. She also had what I refer to as a *human capital deployment* theory of change. Many so-called reformers believe that change occurs when individuals take it upon themselves to do what's right. There is some truth to this, as there is evidence that a single principal, teacher or even superintendent, can have a great effect on her school, class, or district through force of will and application of smart policies. And we have to accept the research that shows the difference in student achievement when a child has a great teacher versus a below average one. However, the problem that so-called reformers have identified is the wrong one; it is not a matter of simply finding and deploying human capital to greater effect—it is a matter of building a system that supports the development of people who are able to serve students and school communities at a high level.

In my view, the reform conversation today—and commensurate federal and state policies—is not focused on the appropriate unit of change. Just as I tell my school board that I am their sole employee, the federal government should be focused on the capacity of state departments to support and monitor school districts; and state departments of education should be focused on the capacity of districts to support and monitor schools. Given the complexity of ensuring that all aspects of a system are aligned to support high levels of achievement for all students, it is essential that the regulatory focus be on just that, rather than solely on the performance of individual schools.

In order to properly serve all students, school districts must do the following: 1) establish robust curriculum in all content areas that are aligned to state and best practice standards, 2) regularly assess students in multiple ways relative to the standards, 3) provide extensive professional development for all employees so that their daily practice aligns with the best instructional practices, 4) ensure that school leaders are focused on excellence in instruction, collaboration and teamwork, community engagement, and accountability, 5) maintain a comprehensive accountability system that uses multiple measures to understand school performance and progress, 6) sustain a foundation of operational excellence that provides necessary and stable resources to support instructional reform, 7) offer supports to students and families who are struggling to achieve standards, and 8) engage all aspects of the community to build support for the work and collaborate with other agencies that serve children and families. All of the above must then be supported through collaboration with labor groups so that contracts facilitate and allow for these elements. Perhaps most importantly, the community, the locally elected funding authority, and the board of education must understand the need to align all aspects of the system and then provide stable funding.

In my experience, addressing the above elements is too complex and tedious for many local communities, states, and the federal government to provide the necessary long-term focus. And, they don't align with the overly simplistic corporate-driven reform rhetoric that influences many elected officials and the media. Moreover, most school districts don't have the capacity to do all of them well, since they are typically small and don't have the economy of scale that larger ones do. However, little of this gets talked about in the so-called "reform" conversation. Why do we never hear of accountability for local legislative bodies or funding authorities when they fail to provide adequate funds for instructional improvement? Why do we never hear of accountability for school boards when they focus their energies on issues that have nothing to do with student achievement? When they micromanage, or cycle through, their superintendents every few years? Why do we never hear of accountability for superintendents who fail to align their systems in ways that support instructional improvement, or for labor unions that refuse to collaborate? Instead, it has become all too easy to look at state standardized results and then blame the teacher for not being good enough, rather than looking at all of the systemic aspects that could produce great results at scale.

Great school systems start with clarity about what students need to know and be able to do. Far too often the school reform conversation is about structural solutions, e.g., a longer school day, choice, governance, distribution of quality teachers, recruitment practices or autonomy. I call these "if there were just" conversations. We often hear from people with a narrow view of education that "if there were just no unions, student achievement would improve," or, "if superintendents ran districts like a business, then student achievement would improve," etc. In my experience, these arguments have some merit *within context*. There are business practices that can be applied to school reform: good governance makes a difference and recruitment and assignment of teachers can have a positive impact on student outcomes. However, none of them in isolation will solve problems or create opportunities if they're not in support of what Richard Elmore calls the "Instructional Core": the interaction between the student and the teacher in the presence of great content.

Stamford, Connecticut

When I became Superintendent of Schools in Stamford, Connecticut, in 2005, I faced a systems problem. The district of 15,500 students in 20 schools is very diverse: 40% White, 22% African American, 8% Asian, 30% Latino, 15% English language learners, and 39% free-and-reduced priced meals. There is great wealth in Stamford and significant poverty. The signature element of the school system for forty years has been its voluntary integration policy. Every school is supposed to reflect the district's demographics within ten percentage points. This policy arose from a community engagement process in the late 1960s that sought to get ahead of a lawsuit threatened by the NAACP to force desegregation. A complicated magnet, boundary, and transportation system was born out of these factors that resulted in mostly demographically balanced schools.

The desegregation of schools in Stamford in the early 1970s was offset by the segregation of middle and high school classes. The formal practice had been to desegregate schools so that they reflected the district demographic average, while separating students by so-called ability into distinct tracks. When I arrived in 2005, I found middle and high school students separated into as many as four or five distinct levels of courses. White and Asian students performed extremely well and took the highest level courses while African American, Latino, and poor students were in the bottom tracks and performed very poorly.

I quickly found out that there were no systems for ensuring that all students were being provided a high-quality education. Curriculum largely sat on a shelf, and there was no consistency between schools. A Phi Delta Kappa audit of our literacy work found 153 different approaches to literacy among twelve elementary schools. There was no system for regularly assessing students or collecting data on school performance. Relationships between the district and its partners, whether employee associations or community groups, were mostly non-existent. There was no approach to Board of Education development. Professional development was scattershot; and there was no systemic approach to monitoring, support, and accountability.

In many ways, entering into a school district without systems provides a straightforward challenge and opportunity for a superintendent of schools, i.e., to build an aligned system based on best practices and student needs. Actually embracing and realizing that opportunity, however, is never as straightforward as it seems. The Board of Education that hired me was clear about what it wanted. They had galvanized around the idea that the achievement gap was the number one priority and they realized they needed a new approach. Hiring a superintendent who was thirty-five years old, had an accountability background, and had never been a principal was a bold move for a school board that realized they needed to start doing things differently. By the time I left, six years later, to become Superintendent of Montgomery

County, Maryland, I had had twenty-three Board members, not all of who were supportive of the original agenda.

As I began my superintendency, the largest topic of conversation was the tracking system. Some people told me that I better not eliminate it because of the threat of white flight, while others said I better get rid of it tomorrow. It was obvious to me that tracking had to be eliminated for moral, ethical and educational reasons; yet I also had to offer something better as an alternative or I'd be bogged down in a fight over who sits next to whom rather than what we want students to know and be able to do.

Based on that theory—that we needed to provide a better alternative to the tracking system before we made the necessary structural changes—we started the work of designing a new system to provide access to high-level classes for all students. We also knew that consistency of curriculum and expectations among schools was essential, and that we needed clear measures of student and adult progress and outcomes. The most fundamental aspect, however, was capacity building among staff. Too much of today's so-called reform conversation does not take into account the need for reciprocal accountability—the idea that I can't hold you accountable for something that you do not have the capacity to do; hence, I must first build your capacity before determining your success or failure in meeting the standards. Today's education reform conversation seems to assume that teachers, leaders, and staff know what to do; yet they choose not to because they're not being held accountable, or the unions don't want them to excel, or they're lazy. To the contrary, we assumed that improvement in student learning was largely dependent on improvement in adult learning; adults needed to learn new behaviors and skills in order to teach differently and get different outcomes.

The General Electric (GE) Foundation "Developing Futures" grant program was supporting our approach. This grant was offered to school districts where GE had a large presence, and Stamford is home to many of GE's financial services. Their support could not have come at a better time. Not only were the dollars substantial (by the end of my six-year tenure, they had donated $27 million), they were based on design principles rather than a model program we had to pursue. Unlike other entities that provide funds only if a certain strategy is employed—e.g., small schools—the GE Developing Futures program held us accountable for designing reforms based on the expertise of educators (within and outside of the district) and doing what we said we would do.

We began our work by engaging teachers and leaders throughout the district in collaborative processes to study best practices around consistency, equity, and excellence and design a system-wide approach. This proved to be a critical first step for a number of reasons. One was related to the teacher's union proving to be a difficult partner. While it did not actively obstruct the work, it wasn't moving as fast as I would like and would get bogged down in picayune issues. I had also heard frustration with the union leadership expressed by many educators throughout the district. I decided that I would engage the union and invite it to the table, but that we would also work directly with teachers who were with students every day. The message was clearly sent that teachers' opinions were valuable.

Part of my reasoning behind engaging teachers in the visioning and development work was that, when I had worked in New York City, I found that many so-called reformers disregarded the experiences and knowledge of educators. This created a divide within the system between the new reformers and the veteran educators. I had always felt that both sides had something to offer and that at the very least we had to spend time trying to understand each other. Additionally, I could never understand how to improve a system without the full commitment of everyone, which means that a workforce needs to be inspired by leadership in order to go above and beyond. In every great school or central office division that I've seen, people work collaboratively and beyond the contract because they're motivated by the vision, participate in creating the solution, and are inspired by the leader.

Our best-practice committees and think tanks were a clear signal that we had to mix internal knowledge and expertise with the latest research and outside knowledge. It also provided political cover for me when I took our plan to the schools, the community, and the Board, since it was our own educators that had developed it. Another benefit was that I was able to build relationships with people in the system. Superintendents don't have enough time to get to know everyone, and it's very hard to have comprehensive and timely internal communications with the limited resources of public school systems. By inviting multiple stakeholders into our design processes, I got to know some wonderful educators in the district—some of whom became school and district leaders—and they got to know me in a deeper way than is typical.

One major theme that I had heard from teachers during my entry work was that they wanted more time to collaborate. I knew from the research and my own experience the power of professional collaboration. When I was a special education teacher in Brooklyn in the mid-1990s, I had the advantage of working in a school that had a robust Professional Learning Community (PLC) structure. That experience had an enormous impact on my teaching and formed one of my foundational beliefs about the importance of structured collaboration among professionals as a lever for reform.

A critical aspect to our success in my Brooklyn school was the role of our principal and that of teacher leaders. My first principal was a classic instructional leader. She personally reviewed my lesson plans every two weeks and gave detailed feedback; she was in classrooms every day (I can still hear the click-click of her heels as she walked down the hall); she knew the strengths and needs of every teacher; she organized us in teams, kept us focused, and achieved the right balance between teacher autonomy and school-wide consistency. The principal also created accountability for our PLC. While the designated teacher leader facilitated the meetings, the principal made sure that our conversations were focused on children and instruction. When she left after two years and a new principal came in, that focus and accountability went with her; our PLCs lost their instructional focus, and eventually we stopped having them.

Based on my own teaching experience, the feedback I heard from teachers, and the research on the power of PLCs, I sought to establish them in every school in Stamford. When I discussed this with principals, I heard from many of them that they were already doing it. While I was circumspect about the reality of this claim (given what I had seen regarding inconsistency of instruction, little use of data, and terrible achievement for many children), I responded by saying how pleased I was that they were already doing this important work. I've encountered this dynamic in many ways throughout my career: school leaders claim that they're already doing a "best practice," which we would know if only central office respected them and visited their schools. I've tended to meet these claims with acceptance and appreciation, while building a structure to support, assess, and monitor the reality. In some ways I see my work, and the work of central office, as personal trainers. Many school leaders are like people who go to the gym every day and work out, but perhaps don't get the results that they'd like. Rather than tell them that they're not doing something, or doing it all wrong, the personal trainer has to figure out their needs and goals, and then map out a plan for getting them there. If I had said to the principals in Stamford that their PLCs were in fact simply meetings, they would have had something to argue about with me. Rather, we built structures to increase their capacity, measure their progress, and create accountability for collaborative work within the schools. I'm struck by the rhetoric of people in the so-called reform community who are quick to criticize and demonize, yet fail to understand that the same people who they're criticizing for bad results are the ones who will have to learn something new in order to get better results. Just as children are best able to learn when in a safe nurturing environment, adults are spurred to act differently through inspiration rather than denigration.

Professional Learning Communities were one critical part of our professional development system, but not the only one. I've come to believe that a comprehensive professional development system contains the following elements: 1) exposure, 2) facilitated exploration and learning, 3) just-in-time training, 4) collaboration, and 5) instructional leadership.

Exposure means that teachers need opportunities to see what they're expected to do differently in a low-risk environment with enough lead time to ask questions and really understand what they're expected to do. Ideally, teachers should have a new curriculum six months before they're being asked to implement it.

Facilitated exploration and learning is essentially direct instruction. An expert needs to review the entire curriculum or program with teachers and help them understand the theories behind it as well as the particulars of what they're expected to do.

Just-in-time training is also direct instruction, typically in the form of a workshop that provides teachers with the necessary information they need to implement a unit or a particular aspect of a program. Unfortunately, too much professional development relies on this process almost solely rather than seeing it as one aspect of a comprehensive approach.

Collaboration is an essential ingredient of a comprehensive professional development system. Adults learn best when they're working on a relevant problem of practice with colleagues in a safe environment. They need to be able to ask questions, admit what they don't know, and apply research to a real problem they're facing.

Instructional leadership is quickly becoming a hackneyed phrase in the school improvement conversation. There is no doubt that great school leaders understand content and pedagogy. However, I do not believe that enough time has been spent on articulating how great instructional leaders organize systems within schools to support all students through effective resource allocation. There must be a vision of what great instruction looks like, with commensurate clear and focused goals based on student needs. The leader must know her staff and their strengths and needs and allocate their time accordingly. A great instructional leader distributes leadership in her building by organizing people into teams that lead the school improvement work. Instructional leaders also engender accountability throughout the building through the supervision and evaluation process. Too much of the so-called reform conversation focuses on evaluation and consequence —what happens to a teacher when she doesn't perform to standards and what procedures an administrator uses to determine the progress a teacher has made relative to the standard or outcome. Great instructional leaders, however, spend their time and energy supervising people, which results in a thorough evaluation that may determine consequences for an individual. Supervision means multiple classroom visits, articulation of focused and specific goals for students and standards of practice for adults, establishment of time for adults to learn new skills, and regular formal and informal feedback and supports when the teacher isn't meeting standards. Great instructional leaders create school cultures that engender shared leadership, trust, high standards, engagement of stakeholders, and support and high expectations for all children. Great instructional leaders also learn with their teachers and position themselves as learning leaders and leaders of learning.

The current so-called reform conversation has failed to take into account what Atul Gawande describes as *ineptitude.* In his book *The Checklist Manifesto*, Gawande notes that much of our frustration about inadequate results in any field comes from the gap between what we now know due to the exponential increase in information over the last few decades and our inability to apply it. I would suggest that this *ineptitude gap* between knowledge and effective application is exacerbated by the human capital deployment theory that so-called reformers maintain: tell someone what results you want; if they don't meet the mark, find someone who will. While there is much to be said for holding people accountable for results, the human capital deployment theory doesn't account for the ineptitude gap and what school leaders and teachers face on a daily basis—which is virtually impossible to address alone.

I have never been in a great school where you can isolate one individual as the sole determinant of student success. In a classroom within a school with student achievement needs (which is the focus of the so-called reform movement), one would typically find a host of adults who are working with children. Great schools use a team-based approach to allocate resources according to teacher and student needs. So you might see two teachers in one classroom working with different groups of children. Or a group of students might be pulled out for a period of time to work on reading or math or English language acquisition. Or students might attend an after-school program a few times a week to receive additional support. Whatever the intervention may be, in a school that successfully meets the needs of all its students, multiple adults are working with children. The ineptitude gap is addressed by having many people bring their expertise to bear on a problem, and not relying on one individual to have all the answers. And, in fact, today's business literature is rife with stories about collaborative and empowering cultures that lead to better shareholder value. Why is it, then, that a different model should work for schools?

Once we had built the systems in Stamford for adult learning and improved curriculum, we were ready to begin to dismantle the tracking system. While I knew that there would be resistance, I was struck by the depth of attachment to the old entitlement system by many people throughout the community. This largely manifested in our middle school transformation work, as that was the most formal and entrenched tracking in the system. We had increased heterogeneity in the elementary schools, which was largely going well. In schools where the principal believed that all children should get the best and had the skills of an instructional leader, parents had few problems with increased heterogeneity. But in schools where the principals gave lip-service to our reforms but were unable to lead their teachers and parents to understand and embrace the change, there was great parental outcry about their children not getting what they needed because of the great needs of those other children.

This experience reinforces the primacy of the principal's role in leading school reform, which is consistent with much of the so-called reformer rhetoric. However, the human capital deployment theory would suggest that a system should simply get rid of the principals who can't lead change and find new ones who can. This often manifests itself in efforts that identify and develop new school leaders who will be data-driven, tough-minded, and accept no excuses. The idea that we should only have our best leading schools is obvious and unimpeachable; school systems must take very seriously the supervision and evaluation of principals and not allow for mediocrity. The essential question, however, is whether leadership skills can be developed. The fundamental difference between so-called reformers and true school system change lies in whether one accepts Elmore's notion of reciprocal accountability—the idea that someone can't be held accountable for skills she doesn't have, and it is then incumbent upon the supervisor to build the capacity of the supervisee so that she has the requisite skills to do the job. I've always found that the best way to improve performance and create accountability is by being clear about the standards I hope someone will achieve, ensuring she has the skills to achieve it, and then providing explicit feedback and support along the way.

As we were preparing in Stamford to fundamentally change the middle school tracking structure, we had begun to dismantle homogeneous ability grouping in the elementary schools that practiced it while also increasing access to high-level courses in one of our comprehensive high schools. Westhill High School had successfully applied for the "Project Open Doors" grant, which was part of a national effort to expand access and success in Advanced Placement (AP) courses. One small aspect of the grant became the most controversial nationally and in Stamford. Teachers were provided a monetary bonus of a few thousand dollars based on the number of students who achieved a qualifying score on the AP test. (Students also received a cash reward for passing AP exams.) Teachers received extensive training and monies to provide additional supports to students. The Westhill teachers were raring to go with this effort, as it was consistent with their ethos and supported efforts that they were already taking to eliminate lower-level courses and increase access to AP. The Stamford Education Association (SEA), however, did not support the grant because they did not want teachers paid differently based on results. While I have always rejected the notion of merit pay, simply because it doesn't work, this circumstance was different because the payment to teachers was a small part of the overall effort and because all of the involved teachers I had spoken to told me that the bonus money was nice but wasn't their main motivator. The SEA fought us all the way to arbitration. The arbitrator decided in support of the district, and we were able to go forward with the grant. That decision set the precedent for the State of Connecticut, and many other districts followed suit in implementing the Project Open Doors grant.

Two interesting lessons emerged from this experience. One was that the so-called reformers' estimation of local teachers unions can sometimes be justified. While one always has to approach reform work in a collaborative and constructive manner, one also has to be willing to fight—and fight to win—when necessary. Given how obstructive our local association had been since I had arrived, I had no issue with taking on this fight, as I believed deeply that this grant would accelerate our reforms. And, in fact, because the teachers at the school were so committed to the work and so many were frustrated with the association leadership, they felt supported by my willingness to take on the issue. It also served a symbolic purpose for me as we deepened our reform efforts: the teachers association was now on record as opposing something that their members supported and that was good for kids—and they lost. The bottom line is that while the anti-union rhetoric of so-called reformers is overly generalized, not every decision can be collaborative and not every local association leader wants to work together on reform issues that benefit children.

Another dynamic that emerged simply reinforced what we had been learning from our efforts to increase heterogeneity in the elementary schools. Parents of students who had always taken AP classes started claiming that increased access would lower standards and their children would suffer if they had to learn next to those other kids who had so many problems. Issues of race and class were just under the surface, although my critics took great pains to claim their own enlightenment and color-blind status. The biggest counteraction to this rhetoric was, once again, teacher leaders. The effort at Westhill was driven by teachers and supported by leadership, and the trust they engendered from the community enabled the school to do the difficult work of opening access to higher-level courses.

This experience also taught me one of the most important aspects of school reform: focus on the product. People who raise issues in anticipation of the change can't be the sole focus of a superintendent's communication and engagement efforts. Of course, any change requires massive communication to students, staff, families, and the community. But if we put ninety percent of our energies into the product and the support people in the field need to implement it well, then staff and leaders will be able to support it when asked what's going on with the new program. When a skeptical parent sits down with the teacher at a parent-teacher conference, or sees the principal at the school play, or runs into a staff member on the weekend, it is essential that the district employee can explain what it is we're trying to do and offer her support. I don't expect them to blindly adhere to district messages—in fact, we learn the most from the resistors—but we need them to be able to speak to the support they've been given, the quality of the curriculum, and, most importantly, what it will mean for our children. So-called reformers too often seem to believe that the logic of a new approach or program will countervail any criticism. And when criticism arises they too often use it to justify their anti-union and anti-teacher stance by saying that people don't want to change. The so-called reformers seem to forget that education is an emotional process for many parents—we drop our kids off for the day and trust that the adults we leave them with will do their very best to enable our children to succeed. When districts spend their time working closely with people in the field to implement a new approach, teachers and leaders will trust the central office that is pushing the reform, and then communicate positively to their communities about the reform efforts. It requires substantial investment up front, but pays off in the long run.

Perhaps the greatest benefit of the Westhill Project Open Doors effort was that, when I went to the Board of Education and the community to explain our middle school de-tracking work, I had actual proof that one can increase access and heterogeneity and everyone benefits. Our Black and Latino students were doing well in AP courses, and our White and Asian students were doing as well as they had traditionally done. And there were more AP courses to choose from. This strengthened my arguments in support of de-tracking our middle schools.

After six years at the helm of the Stamford public schools, I was experiencing resistance from some members of the Board of Education and decided to pursue other opportunities. I still had majority Board support, and our student achievement had improved significantly every year that I was superintendent. Following the "get out before they push you out" rule for superintendents, I became the superintendent of Montgomery County, Maryland, public schools. It is a district with very similar demographics to Stamford, yet is ten times the size and has a track record of success.

Two years into this leadership position I find myself reflecting on my experiences in Stamford and New York City, and finding strength in the idea that my job is to create and sustain an architecture that supports social justice and excellence in teaching and learning. It is hard to do so when the rhetoric of so-called reformers is becoming increasingly codified in ill-conceived state and federal laws and when so many other districts pursue the easy money from entities that will benefit from changes in standards, curriculum, data systems, materials, and assessments. I don't believe that all of these reform efforts are ill-intended. However, I also know that the teachers, support professionals, leaders, and parents of Montgomery County want more for their kids than success on standardized tests. And I know that they'll see right through me if I try to blame single individuals without ensuring that there is indeed a comprehensive system to support them.

Contributors

Carlson, Dennis. Dennis Carlson is a professor of curriculum and social foundations of education at Miami University. A past president of the American Educational Studies Association, he is the author of a number of books, including *Gender and Sexualities in Education: A Reader* (Peter Lang, in press); *The Education of Eros: A History of Education and the Problem of Adolescent Sexuality* (Routledge, 2012); *Volunteers of America: The Journey of a Peace Corps Teacher* (Sense, 2012); *The Sexuality Curriculum and Youth Culture*, edited with Donyell L. Roseboro (Peter Lang, 2011); and *Leaving Safe Harbors: Toward a New Progressivism in American Education and Public Life* (Routledge, 2002).

DeVitis, Joseph L. Joseph L. DeVitis has taught at five universities during his 40-year academic career. Recipient of the Distinguished Alumni Award from the University of Illinois at Urbana-Champaign, he is a past president of the American Educational Studies Association (AESA), the Council of Learned Societies in Education, and the Society of Professors of Education. Author or editor of 16 books, his most recent works are a series of notable readers for Peter Lang Publishing: *The College Curriculum* (2013); *Contemporary Colleges and Universities* (2013); *Critical Civic Literacy* (2011); *Character and Moral Education*, with Tianlong Yu (2010); and *Adolescent Education*, with Linda Irwin-DeVitis (2010). The latter three books won Critics Choice Awards from AESA as outstanding books of the year.

Leahey, Christopher. Christopher Leahey is a visiting professor of education at the State University of New York at Oswego. His research focuses on democratic education, critical theory, and civic literacy. He is the author of *Whitewashing War: Historical Myth, Corporate Textbooks, and Possibilities for Democratic Education* (Teachers College Press, 2010). He is a contributor to *Critical Civic Literacy: A Reader* (Peter Lang, 2011) and *Educating for Peace in a Time of Permanent War: Are Schools Part of the Solution or the Problem?* (Routledge, 2012). His articles have appeared in *Social Education* and *The Social Studies*.

Liston, Daniel P. Daniel P. Liston is a professor in the School of Education at the University of Colorado at Boulder. He utilizes philosophy, social theory, and literature to analyze educational issues. His past work includes articles and books in which he examines the social and political context of schooling as well as rationales for programs of teacher preparation and reflective teaching. His current scholarship focuses on the role of reason and emotion in education, features of contemplative teaching, and rationales for teacher education programs.

Noddings, Nel. Nel Noddings is Lee Jacks Professor of Education Emerita, Stanford University. She is a past president of the National Academy of Education, Philosophy of Education Society, and The John Dewey Society. In addition to 19 books, she is the author of more than 200 articles and chapters on various topics, ranging from the ethics of care to mathematical problem solving. Her latest book is *Peace Education: How We Come to Love and Hate War* (Cambridge University Press, 2011).

Ohanian, Susan. Susan Ohanian is a longtime teacher. Her 300 articles have appeared in publications ranging from *The Nation* to *American School Board Journal.* The author of 25 books on education policy and practice, her website received the National Council of Teachers of English (NCTE) George Orwell Award for Distinguished Contribution to Honesty and Clarity in Public Language.

Roseboro, Donyell L. Donyell L. Roseboro is an associate professor in the Department of Instructional Technology, Foundations, and Secondary Education at the University of North Carolina Wilmington. Her research and writing explores the ways in which democratic education might create more equitable learning opportunities for students and better governance processes for teachers. Her most recent articles appear in *Urban Education* and *The Journal of Natural Inquiry and Reflective Practice.* In addition, she has an edited volume with Dennis Carlson, *The Sexuality Curriculum: Youth Culture, Popular Culture, and Democratic Sexuality Education* (Peter Lang, 2011).

Saltman, Kenneth J. Kenneth J. Saltman is a professor of educational policy studies and research at DePaul University. His most recent books are *The Politics of Education: A Critical Introduction* (Paradigm, 2013); *Toward a New Common School Movement*, with Noah DeLissovoy and Alex Means (Paradigm, 2013); *The Failure of Corporate School Reform* (Paradigm, 2012); *The Gift of Education: Venture Philanthropy and Public Education* (Palgrave Macmillan, 2010; American Educational Studies Critics Choice Award for 2011); and *Capitalizing on Disaster: Taking and Breaking Public Schools* (Paradigm, 2007; AESA Critics Choice Award for 2008). His recent edited books include, with David Gabbard, *Education as Enforcement: The Militarization and Corporatization of Schools*, 2nd ed. (Routledge, 2010); *Schooling and the Politics of Disaster* (Routledge, 2007); and, with Enora Brown, *The Critical Middle School Reader* (Routledge, 2005).

Shields, Carolyn M. Carolyn M. Shields is a professor and Dean of the College of Education at Wayne State University. She is past president of the Canadian Association for Studies in Educational Administration (CASEA) and former Canadian representative to the Board of the Commonwealth Council for Educational Administration and Management (CCEAM). Her research focuses on how educational leaders can create learning environments that are deeply democratic, socially just, inclusive of all students' lived experiences, and that prepare students for excellence and citizenship in our global society. She has written over 125 articles and chapters and nine books—most recently, *Transformative Leadership in Education: Equitable Change in an Uncertain and Complex World* (Routledge, 2012). She is the recipient of the Lifetime Achievement Award from CASEA, the Leadership and Social Justice Award from the LSJ Sig of the American Educational Research Association, and has been named a Fellow of the Commonwealth Council.

Sleeter, Christine E. Christine E. Sleeter is a professor emerita in the College of Professional Studies at California State University Monterey Bay, where she was a founding faculty member. She is currently immediate past president of the National Association for Multicultural Education and previously served as vice president of Division K of the American Educational Research Association. Her research focuses on anti-racist multicultural education and teacher education. Her recent books include *Power, Teaching and Teacher Education* (Peter Lang, 2013), *Professional Development for Culturally Responsive and Relationship-Based Pedagogy* (Peter Lang, 2013), and *Creating Solidarity across Diverse Communities*, with Encarnacion Soriano (Teachers College Press, 2012).

Smyth, John. John Smyth is Research Professor of Education, School of Education and Arts, University of Ballarat, Victoria, Australia, and Emeritus Professor, Flinders University of South Australia. He formerly held the Mitte Endowed Chair in School Improvement, Texas State University, San Marcos. He is a Senior Fulbright Research Scholar, recipient of several research awards from the American Educational Research Association, and is a Fellow of the Academy for Social Science in Australia. Among his recent books are *The Socially Just School: Making Space for Youth to Speak Back*, with Barry Down and Peter McInerney (Springer, in press); *Living on the Edge: Rethinking Poverty, Class and Schooling*, with Terry Wrigley (Peter Lang, 2013); *Silent Witnesses to Active Agents: Student Voice in Re-engaging with Learning* (Peter Lang, 2012); *Critical Voices in Teacher Education: Teaching for Social Justice in Conservative Times* (Springer, 2012); and *Hanging in with Kids in Tough Times: Engagement in Contexts of Educational Disadvantage in the Relational School*, with Downey and McInerney (Peter Lang, 2010).

Starr, Joshua P. Joshua P. Starr is the Superintendent of Montgomery County Public Schools in Maryland, the nation's 17th-largest school district. His 20-year career in education has included positions as the accountability director at both urban and suburban districts, including New York City Public Schools. Dr. Starr believes in meaningful accountability systems in K-12 education and has been a vocal critic of school reform efforts that rely too heavily on standardized tests to judge the success of schools and to evaluate teachers. A graduate of the Harvard Graduate School of Education, Dr. Starr has had articles published in several mainstream and professional publications, including the *Washington Post, Education Week*, and *The School Administrator*.

Stedman, Lawrence C. Lawrence C. Stedman is an associate professor in the Graduate School of Education at the State University of New York at Binghamton. He has worked as a school district policy analyst, secondary school teacher, VISTA volunteer, and program evaluator. His research focuses on achievement trends, school reform and federal policy, and the transformation of the high school during the 20th century. He is the co-author of *Literacy in the United States: Readers and Reading Since 1880* (Yale University Press, 1991), with Carl F. Kaestle, Helen Damon-Moore, and Katherine Tinsley, and the author of *The NAEP Long-Term Trend Assessment*, a historical review commissioned by the National Assessment Governing Board. He has also published analyses of *A Nation at Risk*, the international assessments of education, effective schools research, and the Atlanta cheating scandal.

Teitelbaum, Kenneth. Kenneth Teitelbaum is Dean and Professor in the Watson College of Education at the University of North Carolina Wilmington. His research and teaching interests focus on critical reflection in teacher education and teachers' work, school reform as it relates to democracy, social justice and diversity, and school knowledge in current and historical contexts.

Wasserberg, Martin J. Martin J. Wasserberg is an assistant professor of elementary education at the University of North Carolina Wilmington. Guided by ten years of experience as an urban elementary school teacher, his research examines the influence of stereotyping on performance, and he works to build positive relationships between marginalized students and school adults via a participatory action research model. His most recent book is *The Incredible Work of the Elementary School* (Kendall Hunt, 2011).

Yu, Tian. Tian Yu is an associate professor of social foundations of education at Southern Illinois University Edwardsville and a "Taishan Scholar" professor of education at Shandong Normal University in China. His research interests include moral education, multicultural education, and international education. He is co-editor, with Joseph L. DeVitis, of *Character and Moral Education: A Reader* (Peter Lang, 2011), which won a Critics Choice Award from the American Educational Studies Association, and the author of *In the Name of Morality* (Peter Lang, 2004). He has also published articles in such journals as *Equity & Excellence in Education*, *Multiculutral Education*, *Asia Pacific Journal of Education*, and *Discourse: Studies in the Cultural Politics of Education*.

Index

Poverty, 18-21, 53, 60, 64, 78, 110, 114, 119-127, 154, 176, 179, 189-190
Pritzer Foundation, J. B. & M. K., 17
Privatization (in schools), 31-32, 37-38, 49-50, 72-73, 76-77, 80-81, 86, 100, 148-149, 154, 162
Professional Learning Communities (PLC), 216-217
Progressive Policy Institute, 75
Progressivism, 33, 49
Project Open Doors, 219-220

Quinn, D., 193
Quintanar-Sarellana, R., 151

Race to the Top (RITT), 17-18, 21, 50-51, 54, 101-102, 122, 182, 202-210
Racism, 151, 176-183
Ravitch, Diane, 46-49, 51, 63, 102, 117
Raza Studies Project, 152
Raymond, M. E., 147
Reagan, Ronald W., 34, 77, 98, 149, 154
Real World City, 154
Reciprocal Accountability (Elmore, Richard), 219
Reed, J., 47
Reese, William J., 99
Renaissance 2010 (Chicago), 71, 73, 75
Resmovits, J., 120
Rice, John Mayer, 98
Richards, E., 102
Richardson, V., 107
Riedlinger, Brian, 77
Rinne, R., 65
Risser, W., 178
Ritchie, S., 110
RJR Nabisco, 26
Rockland (NY) County, 209
Rodriguez, L. F., 196
Rogers, J., 116, 119, 123
Rogoff, Barbara, 139
Romero, A., 151-152
Roosevelt, Eleanor, 12
Roosevelt, Franklin D., 148
Rose, Mike, 8, 12, 16, 20
Ross, E. Wayne, 48, 50, 54, 99
Rothstein, Richard, 19, 99
Rouse, C. E., 99
Rybczynski A., 151-152

Saez, E., 149
Sahlberg, P., 64-66, 105
Saltman, Kenneth J., 3, 50, 149
Sameroff, A., 194
Sarri, R. C., 160
Sarason, Seymour, 104, 212
Sawchuk, S., 10S
Schafer, W. D., 204
Schmader, T., 194
Schneider, B. L., 196
Schott's Vocab, 18

Schueger, J. M., 197
Scott, D. G., 172
Scott, Rick, 16
Seeger, Pete, 12
Sebelius, Kathleen, 16
Segregation (in schools), 159-162
Sellers, R. M., 151
Serriere, S. C., 195
Servage, L., 49
Shacklock, G., 61-62
Sharp, F., 153
Sharp, N., 153
Sheehy, K., 209
Shih, M., 194
Shields, Carolyn M., 125, 127
Shierholz, Heidi, 20
Shipps, Dorothy, 76
Shirley, Dennis, 149
Shora, Ira, 47
Shubick, T., 121
Siddle-Walker, V., 161-162
Sidwell Friends (DC) School, 21
Silvas, C., 176
Simola, H., 64-66
Siegel-Hawley, G., 118
Sillverstein, Shel, 23, 191
Slaughter-Defoe, D. T., 196-197
Slavery, 150-151
Sleeter, Christine E., 149-150, 153
Smith, A. M., 151
Smith, M. L., 46, 197
Smith, Wade, 171
Smyth, John, 61-64
Snyder, Rick, 116, 121, 123
Social Justice City, 154
Social Justice Education Project, 152
Socially Just School (Smyth, John), 64, 67-69
South Orangetown (NY) School District, 209
Sparks, Nicholas, 23
Spellings, Margaret, 50, 81
Spencer Foundation, 114
Spencer, S. J., 193-194
Spring, Joel H., 159
Sputnik, 98
Stamford (CT)
  Board of Education, 220
  Education Association, 219
  Schools, 214, 217-220
Standards Movement (in schools), 45-57, 202-203, 213
Stanton, C. R., 151
State University of New York, 100
Stedman, Lawrence C., 46-50, 52-54
Steele, Claude, M., 193-194, 196-197
Steiner, David, 26
Stereotype Threat, 193-194
Strambler, M. J., 193-195, 197
Strike, Kenneth, 49